# THE 2005 FORMULA 1 SEASON

Jean-François Galeron

CHRONOSPORTS
EDITEUR

This book is dedicated to his wife Lise and his
children Clément, Pauline and Anne.

© April 2005, CHRONOSPORTS S.A.
ISBN 2-84707-087-7
Rue des Jordils 40,
CH-1025 St-Sulpice,
Switzerland.
Tel.: +41 (0)21-694.24.44
Fax: +41 (0)21-694.24.46
info@chronosports.com
Internet : www.chronosports.com

Jean-François Galeron has written all the texts for this book
and the photos come from his archives. There are also some
from Laurent Charniaux and Jad Sherif his associates at WRI
"World Racing Images".

All the photos in this book can be viewed on the
www.worldracingimages.com site.

The book was produced by Cyril Davillerd, Solange Amara
and Désirée Ianovici.
Circuits illustrations: Emeric de Baré

Fonts:
DIN
TRAJAN

Printed in the European Union by Imprimerie Clerc,
St-Amand Montrond, France.
Bound by SIRC, Marigny-le-Chatel, France.

# THE 2005 FORMULA 1 SEASON

**Jean-François Galeron**
Artistic Director **Cyril Davillerd**
Translated from French **David Waldron**

# Contents

Jean-François Galeron would like to thank Jacques Villeneuve for his preface and all the F1 drivers who helped him create this book, and all the Press Attachés who have made his job easier, Emeric de Baré for his circuit drawings, Luc Domenjoz, Cyril Davillerd and the whole Chronsports team, and last but not least Laurent Charniaux, Jad Sherif, his associates of the WRI agency.

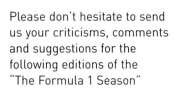

Please don't hesitate to send us your criticisms, comments and suggestions for the following editions of the "The Formula 1 Season"

Thank you.

jfg@galeron.com

## Drivers-Teams

## Magazines

## The 19 GP

## Statistics

# Foreword

In 2004, I was away from the circuits for most of the season apart from three grands prix with the Renault team. This year I'm back again and champing at the bit! My enforced rest did me a power of good and enabled me to shrug off the stresses and pressures caused by several difficult years. I now feel the same way I did in 1996 when I made my debut with Williams. I'm a new man ready to live my passion again with renewed vigour.

To be honest I never doubted my return to the top echelon of motor racing. I continued my physical fitness programme during my lay-off. Despite skiing and ice hockey I kept track of what was happening on the grand prix scene by watching all the races on TV and following the evolution in all areas.

I'm delighted to be back in Formula 1 at a moment when it is facing a crucial turning point concerning its future. The new regulations are a step in the right direction, namely, creating a more gripping spectacle. This is what the spectators want: they want to see us battling wheel to wheel, our cars sliding around as we fight to control them. There is no room for monotony: races have to have thrills and excitement. I also hope that the teams will be much closer to each other.

I'm very happy to join Sauber where I've found a real family atmosphere. I felt at home right away in a warm politics-free environment. These guys have just one thought in mind, racing. I'm really looking forward to the coming year.

I'm delighted to preface the *"The 2005 Formula 1 season"* by Jean-François Galeron. Thanks to this book the reader will be able to follow this year's racing, which looks like being very exciting, in ideal conditions. Reading it you will get to know the all the drivers, teams, circuits and statistics. You'll become an expert on grand prix racing sharing in the same passion that drives us all.

Jacques Villeneuve

# Drivers Teams

**FERRARI**
1 Michael Schumacher
2 Rubens Barrichello

**B.A.R HONDA**
3 Jenson Button
4 Takuma Sato

**RENAULT**
5 Fernando Alonso
6 Giancarlo Fisichella

**WILLIAMS BMW**
7 Mark Webber
8 Nick Heidfeld

**McLAREN MERCEDES**
9 Kimi Räikkönen
10 Juan Pablo Montoya

**SAUBER PETRONAS**
11 Jacques Villeneuve
12 Felipe Massa

**RBR COSWORTH**
14 David Coulthard
15 Christian Klien

**TOYOTA**
16 Jarno Trulli
17 Ralf Schumacher

**JORDAN TOYOTA**
18 Tiago Monteiro
19 Narain Karthikeyan

**MINARDI COSWORTH**
20 Patrick Friesacher
21 Christijan Albers

FOSTER'S
AUSTRALIAN
GRAND PRIX
MELBOURNE 2005

FIA Formula 1
WORLD CHAMPIONSHIP™

Ferrari F2004M / F2005

V10 Ferrari 054 (90°)

Bridgestone

SCUDERIA FERRARI MARLBORO

Address: Gestione Sportiva
Scuderia Ferrari Marlboro
Via Ascari 55-57
41053 Maranello (Mo)
Italy

Tel.: +39 0536 94 91 11
Fax: +39 0536 94 64 88
Internet: www.ferrari.it

Team founded in 1929
Grand Prix debut: Monaco 1950
Number of Grands Prix: 704

First victory: 1951 British Grand Prix (Gonzalez)
Number of victories: 182

First pole position: 1951 British Grand Prix (Gonzalez)
Number of pole positions: 178

First fastest lap: Switzerland 1952 (Taruffi)
Number of fastest laps: 181

First points scored: Monaco 1950 (Ascari, 2nd)
Number of points scored: 3,299.5 (3,346.5)
Points average per race: 4.68 (4.75)

First podium: Monaco 1950 (Ascari, 2nd)
Number of podiums: 553

Constructors' World Titles: 14
(1961, 1964, 1975, 1976, 1977, 1979, 1982,
1983, 1999, 2000, 2001, 2002, 2003 and 2004).
Drivers' World Titles: 14
Ascari: 1952 and 1953,
Fangio: 1956,
Hawthorn: 1958,
P. Hill: 1961,
Surtees: 1964,
Lauda: 1975 and 1977,
Scheckter: 1979 and
M. Schumacher: 2000, 2001, 2002, 2003 and 2004.

## Strengths

- Michael Schumacher's presence.
- Brilliant, complementary drivers.
- The F2004's proven reliability.
- An unchanged, motivated and tightly
  welded team.

## Weaknesses

- Wear and tear of power.
- Season debut with the F2004.
- Scarcity of Bridgestone teams.

## 2004 summary

- Constructors' World Title and
  drivers' World Title

- 15 victories
  (M. Schumacher 13, Barrichello 2)

- 12 pole positions
  (M. Schumacher 8, Barrichello 4)

- 14 fastest laps
  (M. Schumacher 10, Barrichello 4)

- 262 points scored
  (M. Schumacher 148, Barrichello 114)

- 34 finishes out of a possible 36
  (M. Schumacher 17, Barrichello 17)

- 32 points scoring finishes
  (M. Schumacher 16, Barrichello 16)

- 2 drivers used
  (M. Schumacher and Barrichello).

# FERRARI

**Luca di Montezemolo (I)**
President

**Jean Todt (F)**
Team director

**Ross Brawn (GB)**
Technical director

**Luca Badoer (I)**
Test driver

**Marc Gené (E)**
Test driver

**Number of employees**
700

The Scuderia has had a disastrous start to the 2005 season. Even if Barrichello managed to bag second place in Melbourne it all went south for Ferrari in Malaysia where the red cars were scrapping for mid-field positions. Due to falling behind in the design of the new gearbox and engine destined for the F2005, Ferrari decided to begin the season with an up-dated 2004 car complying with the new aero regulations. However, it seems to lack downforce and the Bridgestone tyres don't suit this hybrid. So will the F2005 presented to the world on the eve of the Australian Grand Prix week be the Scuderia's new lethal weapon? It is one of the main points of interest of this 2005 season which looks like being much more open than the previous ones dominated by Schumacher and Ferrari. This produced a certain disaffection among spectators both at the track and in front of the box. The legendary Italian team has become a real 'bête noire' for its rivals who do not appreciate its intransigence concerning private testing limitation. Behind the scenes and on the track everybody is gunning for Ferrari

But with a driver of Michael Schumacher's calibre and Barrichello riding shotgun it is difficult not to see the Scuderia raising its head again like the black horse that symbolises its pride.

# MICHAEL SCHUMACHER

## FERRARI *1

**Date and place of birth**
January 3, 1969 in Hürth-Hermühlheim (Germany)
**Nationality** German
**Place of residence** Vufflens-le-Château (Switzerland)
**Marital status** married to Corina, two children, a daughter Gina Maria, and a son Mick
**Height** 1.74m **Weight** 75kgs
**Internet** www.michael-schumacher.de

## F1 results

Best F1 Championship result:
7 times World Champion in 1994, 95 (Benetton), 2000, 2001, 2002, 2003 and 2004 (Ferrari)
Best F1 result: 1st (83 victories)
Best F1 qualification: 1st (63 pole positions)

1991: Jordan-Ford, Benetton-Ford • (1+5) 6 GP, 4 pts, 12th
1992: Benetton-Ford • 16 GP, 53 points, 3rd
1993: Benetton-Ford • 16 GP, 52 points, 4th
1994: Benetton-Ford • 14 GP, 92 pts, World Champion
1995: Benetton-Renault • 17 GP, 102 pts, World Champion
1996: Ferrari • 16 GP, 59 points, 3rd
1997: Ferrari • 17 GP, 78 pts, (2nd, excluded from the championship)
1998: Ferrari • 16 GP, 86 points, 2nd
1999: Ferrari • 10 GP, 44 points, 5th
2000: Ferrari • 17 GP, 108 pts, World Champion
2001: Ferrari • 17 GP, 123 pts, World Champion
2002: Ferrari • 17 GP, 144 pts, World Champion
2003: Ferrari • 16 GP, 93 pts, World Champion
2004: Ferrari • 18 GP, 148 pts, World Champion

Describing the German's career one very soon runs out of superlatives. He has been the front-runner in Formula 1 for nigh on fifteen years. He just seems to get better and better as the years wear on: he is a real phenomenon. "*I love what I do and I still get a huge kick out of driving. Physically I don't feel the passage of time. Even when I'm playing football I don't have the impression that I'm older than those on the pitch with me. I think that's the key to success. As long as you love what you're doing there's no reason to slide backwards.*"
He has won the F1 World Championship seven times and the only record that still eludes him is that of the number of pole positions held by Ayrton Senna by the tiny margin of two (65 to 63).
His former boss, Flavio Briatore, always has the right quip: "*last year Michael drove with his elbow on the door!*"
This is an apt description of Michael's superiority. Aged thirty-six the oldest member of the pack is as motivated as a newcomer. He has clearly stated his aim: an eighth title with Ferrari, a team that is still as ambitious as ever.
Nonetheless, his task will be a lot harder in 2005 as his rivals are out to get him. Alonso, Fisichella, Räikkönen and Montoya among others want to knock him off his pedestal.
Briatore says, "*this year, he's going to find it a lot tougher.*" The German likes a good scrap and he knows that the general public is fed up with Ferrari processions. He is ready to take up this new challenge. He has been penalised at the start of the season by his out-dated car but once he gets his hands on the F 2005 he will be right there in the thick of it battling for victory.

## Titles

- 1984 and 1985: German Karting Champion.
- 1988: German Formula Koënig Champion.
- 1990: German Formula 3 Champion.
- 1994, 1995, 2000, 2001, 2002, 2003 and 2004: Formula 1 World Champion.

## Career summary

Competition debut: 1973 (karting)
Grand Prix debut: Belgium 1991 (Jordan-Ford)

- 213 Grands Prix
- 1186 points scored
- Average per Grand Prix: 5.56
- 137 podiums
- 83 victories
- 36 2nd places
- 18 3rd places
- 8 4th places
- 7 5th places
- 5 6th places
- 2 7th places*
- 2 8th places*

- 63 pole positions
- 66 fastest laps
- 126 GP in the lead
- 21,954 kms in the lead
- 4,657 laps in the lead

\* Since 2003 and the attribution of points
to 7th and 8th places.

## Team-mates

1991: A. De Cesaris (Jordan-Ford) and N. Piquet (Benetton-Ford)
1992: M. Brundle
1993: R. Patrese
1994: J.-J. Lehto, J. Verstappen and J. Herbert
1995: J. Herbert
1996, 1997, 1998 and 1999: E. Irvine
2000, 2001, 2002, 2003 and 2004: R. Barrichello

## Qualifications 2004

M. Schumacher 13 / Barrichello 5

# QUESTIONS

# MICHAEL SCHUMACHER

**And the worst?**
The 1995 Benetton even if I've got great memories of that season. With experience you know how to drive any car.

**What's your best racing memory?**
Probably the 2000 World Championship especially when I crossed the finishing line at Suzuka.

**And your worst?**
Ayrton Senna's death at Imola in 1994 and my collision with Jacques Villeneuve at Jerez in 1997. That's still one of my biggest disappointments.

**Do you remember the first Grand Prix you saw on TV?**
I don't really remember very well. All I know is that Hans Stuck crashed. It was on the Nürburgring. When I was a kid I wasn't very interested in Formula 1, I preferred karting. When I watched sport on TV it was football.

**And the first one you attended?**
Yes I do. It was when I was racing in F3 during the German Grand Prix meeting at Hockenheim in 1989.

**What's your aim in racing?**
Win as many races as possible; the rest doesn't matter.

**What's your favourite circuit?**
I think it'd be a mixture of Spa and Suzuka. All the technical challenges are combined on those two circuits.

**And the one you dislike the most?**
Paradoxically I don't like Monaco very much. Although it's a great track, it's one of the most dangerous.

**Who's your favourite driver in the history of racing?**
Ayrton Senna. **And among those currently racing?**
My brother, naturally.

**Who's been your best team-mate?**
Without hesitation, I'd say Rubens Barrichello.

**If you were a team manager who would you pick?**
I'll never be a team manager!

**What was the first car you drove?**
A Fiat 500 when I was eight. The first time I drove it my foot slipped on the clutch pedal and we were parked facing a wall. Luckily, my father had enough time to pull the handbrake!

**And today?**
A Ferrari Enzo. I've also got a Fiat 500 which President Montezemolo gave me as a present.

**What is your favourite/dream car?**
The Ferrari Enzo is really awesome.

**What does your helmet design mean?**
I did the design myself. Originally, the base was white and I changed it at Ferrari when Barrichello arrived. I choose a very prominent red. I used the colours of the German flag and the upper part was blue with stars that represent the universe, but now it's red.

**What is your favourite racing car?**
Each time it's my Ferrari of the year in question.

**What do you love about this profession?**

Working with my team, making progress and then winning.

**What don't you like about it?**

It's a very artificial world.

**What's your favourite moment of a Grand Prix?**

It's difficult to say. Maybe the chequered flag or a good overtaking move or a lap of honour. It depends on the context.

**Do you always get into your car on the same side?**

Looking from the back of the car I get in on the left.

**When you stop racing, what then?**

There's nothing I love more or do better than racing. I don't know yet when I'll retire and I don't know what I'll do. I'd have liked to have been a professional footballer but I'm not good enough.

**What's your favourite dish?**

Italian cooking. Spaghetti with tomatoes 'quatro frommagio' and sushi.

**And the ones you dislike?**

Nothing really.

**What's your favourite drink?**

Apple juice and sparkling water.

**Do you like alcohol?**

To say I like it is a bit exaggerated. I like a glass of good wine but generally in winter.

**Have you ever smoked?**

Yes, quite often to be honest. I like smoking a good cigar after a good weekend's racing. It's pleasant.

**What sports do you do?**

I love playing football, my other passion. I do some cycling, mountain biking, rock climbing, deep-sea diving from time to time; jogging and of course a lot of physical training.

**And your favourite sports?**

I like all sports. I try to watch cycling and especially the "Tour de France" whenever I can.

**Who's your favourite sportsperson?**

When I was young I really admired Toni Schumacher, the FC Cologne goalkeeper and I tried to make my friends believe he was my uncle! In general, I admire sportspeople who stay at the top like Tiger Woods or Hermann Maier. There are many who impress me very much. As I love football I'd say Zidane; the guy's a real magician.

**What are your hobbies/interests outside racing?**

I like being with Corina and the kids.

**What are your favourite films?**

I like DVDs.

**And your favourite actors?**

Robert de Niro.

**What do you watch on TV?**

Mainly the news.

**What kind of music do you like?**

It depends on my mood.

**What do you like reading?**

Thrillers and spy novels.

**What's your favourite colour?**

In my professional life it's red, otherwise blue.

**What's your favourite holiday destination?**

Our chalet in Norway. I like going to Utah before Indianapolis.

**And your favourite place for shopping?**

I've no real preference.

**What do you collect?**

Omega watches. It's almost a drug. And I also collect the cars that I've raced for our karting centre in Kerpen.

**Have you got any animals?**

We've got four dogs, two horses and two poneys.

**Outside motor racing, whom do you admire?**

People that are capable of things like the Triathlon.

**If you were to go to a desert island, what would you bring?**

Without hesitation, Corina and the kids.

**What's your perfect day?**

It would have to last more than twenty-four hours! After a long night I like waking up slowly and then the children come and play with us on the bed. Then do some sport, lots of other things with the children, film them...

**What's been the greatest day of your life so far?**

Was it my marriage to Corina or the birth of Gina or Mick? The happiest day of my life has to be divided by three. I'm very lucky; I've got several happiest days of my life!

**What makes you laugh the most?**

Certainly my children who make us roar with laughter when they come up with a few home truths!

**If you were not a driver what would you have done?**

I think I would have been a car mechanic.

**What's the most important thing in life for you?**

My family's happiness.

**What are your best qualities?**

I don't like to talk about that. I'm really a normal guy. A husband and father.

**And your worst?**

People never stop spelling them out!

# RUBENS BARRICHELLO
## FERRARI *2

**Date and place of birth** May 23, 1972 in Sao Paolo (Brazil)
**Nationality** Brazilian
**Place of residence** Monte-Carlo
**Marital status** Married to Silvana, one son, Eduardo
**Height** 1.72m **Weight** 71kgs
**Internet** www.barrichello.com.br

## F1 results

Best F1 Championship result: 2nd in 2002 and 2004 (Ferrari)
Best F1 result: 1st (9 victories)
Best F1 qualification: 1st (13 pole positions)

1993: Jordan-Hart • 16 GP, 2 points, 17th
1994: Jordan-Hart • 15 GP, 19 points, 6th
1995: Jordan-Peugeot • 17 GP, 11 points, 11th
1996: Jordan-Peugeot • 16 GP, 14 points, 8th
1997: Stewart-Ford • 17 GP, 6 points, 14th
1998: Stewart-Ford • 16 GP, 4 points, 14th
1999: Stewart-Ford • 16 GP, 21 points, 7th
2000: Ferrari • 17 GP, 62 points, 4th
2001: Ferrari • 17 GP, 56 points, 3rd
2002: Ferrari • 17 GP, 77 points, 2nd
2003: Ferrari • 16 GP, 65 points, 4th
2004: Ferrari • 18 GP, 114 points, 2nd

Nicknamed Rubinho by his fellow-countrymen Barrichello, now starting his sixth season with the Scuderia, has been a model team-mate for Michael Schumacher. He has been runner-up in the world championship and has dreamed of winning the title for years, the triumph of optimism over experience, perhaps. The German driver has overshadowed him and even if he is very talented he can never do battle with his illustrious team-mate on an equal footing. He has occasionally been quicker than Michael but has always had to follow orders (the 2002 Austrian Grand Prix is the most glaring example). He was incontestably the best that day but had to allow Schumacher to win for a couple of points that had no bearing on the final outcome of the championship. Ferrari's team orders are not often to the taste of the public. Year after year the Scuderia bets on Schumacher. Nobody questions the supremacy of the most titled world champion in the history of the sport: so why impose strategies that tarnish the image of F1? Let them fight it out man to man. That's what racing is all about.

Rubens picks up the odd victory here and there and knows that when his team-mate has an off-day he can give full rein to his talent. The new regs may help him to win. In Australia when Schumacher was stuck in the middle of the field Barrichello was battling up front saving Ferrari's honour for once with a second place. Overall, he has built up a respectable set of results

## Titles

5 times Brazilian Karting Champion between 1981 and 1988.
- 1990: Euroseries Opel Lotus Series Champion.
- 1991: British F3 Champion.

## Career summary

Competition debut: 1981 (karting)
Grand Prix debut: South Africa 1993 (Jordan-Hart)

- 198 Grands Prix
- 451 points scored
- Average per Grand Prix: 2.27
- 57 podiums
- 9 victories
- 23 2nd places
- 24 3rd places
- 15 4th places
- 13 5th places
- 5 6th places
- 1 7th place*
- 1 8th place*

- 13 pole positions
- 15 fastest laps
- 42 GP in the lead
- 3,389 kms in the lead
- 699 laps in the lead

* Since 2003 and the attribution of points
  to 7th and 8th places.

## Team-mates

1993: I. Capelli, T. Boutsen, E. Naspetti, M. Apicella and E. Irvine
1994 and 1995: E. Irvine
1996: M. Brundle
1997: J. Magnussen
1998: J. Magnussen and J. Verstappen
1999: J. Herbert
2000, 2001, 2002, 2003 and 2004: M. Schumacher

## Qualifying 2004

Barrichello 5 / M. Schumacher 13

# QUESTIONS

# RUBENS BARRICHELLO

**What was the first car you drove?**
An old GM when I was six.

**And today?**
A Ferrari 575 Maranello and an Alfa Romeo 166.

**What is your favourite/dream car?**
The Ferrari Enzo.

**What does your helmet design mean?**
I've used this design since my early karting days. I did it in collaboration with the Brazilian painter Sid Mosca who advised me. Inigo Hoffman probably influenced me a bit in the choice of colours. I've not had many changes in my career except in Brazil in 1995 when I added Ayrton Senna's helmet's colours.

**What's been your best racing car so far?**
The Ferrari F 2004 was almost perfect.

**And the worst?**
The 1998 Stewart.

**What's your best racing memory?**
The period when I drove with Ayrton Senna at the start of my F1 career. In 2004, I'm happy to have won the first Chinese Grand Prix. Monza too was a great occasion when I came first in front of the Tifosi.

**And your worst?**
Imola 1994 will always be a nightmare.

**Do you remember the first grand prix you saw on TV?**
Monza 1977. I was five years old and I remember Mario Andretti winning the race.

**And the first one you attended?**
Brazil in 1979. We could see the track from my grandfather's house. It was just after the first corner and Arnoux won the race.

**What's your aim in racing?**
Become world champion.

**What's your favourite circuit?**
Interlagos in Brazil.

**And the one you dislike the most?**
Budapest is not one of my favourites, but generally speaking each circuit has its own charm.

**Who's your favourite driver in the history of racing?**
Ayrton Senna. He was my idol and was everything I dreamed of being.

**And among those currently racing?**
I like joking with Montoya and Alonso. We speak a kind of gibberish in Spanish and Portuguese! I get on well with all the Brazilian drivers without forgetting my team-mate, Michael Schumacher.

**Who's been your best team-mate?**

There have been many. I had great fun with Herbert and Magnussen. Now I get on very well with Michael. I must admit that I've been lucky enough to have always had good times with my team-mates.

**If you were a team manager what drivers would you choose?**

I'd choose quick, experienced drivers. Like Michael Schumacher and Rubens Barrichello for example!

**What do you love about this profession?**

The sensation of speed and the pleasure of winning.

**What don't you like about it?**

In F1 there are some truths that should not be expressed. I'd also like to cancel a few days' private testing between races.

**What's your favourite moment of a Grand Prix?**

Qualifying.

**Do you always get into your car on the same side?**

Yes, on the right. It doesn't mean much but it helps me to get more comfortable in the car. I was superstitious at the start. I always put my right foot on the floor when getting up.

**When you stop racing, what then?**

The day when I don't want to win, I'll go and do something else.

**What's your favourite dish?**

Pasta.

**And the ones you dislike?**

I don't like Mangoes.

**What's your favourite drink?**

Red Bull.

**Do you like alcohol?**

I like a glass of good wine from time to time.

**Have you ever smoked?**

No thank you!

**What sports do you do?**

Jogging, squash, jet ski, tennis, some surfing, golf and now the Triathlon.

**And your favourite sports?**

Football, jet ski and Motor Bike Grands Prix.

**Who's your favourite sportsperson?**

It"ll always be Ayrton Senna.

**What are your hobbies/interests outside racing?**

I like relaxing and living a quiet life in Brazil with my family.

**What are your favourite films?**

I like going to the cinema: it's always fun.

**And your favourite actors?**

Robert de Niro, Cameron Diaz and Robin Williams.

**What do you watch on TV?**

Variety programmes.

**What kind of music do you like?**

Biaggo Antonacci and Brazilian pop music. If I had time I'd like to learn to play the guitar.

**What do you like reading?**

Books on science. I read on the plane when I can't get to sleep. I read a book on reincarnation recently.

**What's your favourite colour?**

Blue.

**What's your favourite holiday destination?**

Brazil with the family. I really regret the fact that I spend only five weeks there every year.

**And your favourite place for shopping?**

Miami in the USA.

**What do you collect?**

I'm not really a collector, but I've got a few funny things that I've picked up during my travels like a kimono from Japan.

**Have you got any animals?**

I've got three Labradors in Brazil. I adore dogs.

**Outside motor racing, whom do you admire?**

My dad and my family. I've also got a lot of respect for Jackie Stewart who's played an important role in my career.

**If you were to go to a desert island, what would you bring?**

My wife Silvana and my son, Eduardo.

**What's your perfect day?**

Being with my family and friends in Brazil.

**What's been the greatest day of your life so far?**

My marriage with Silvana and the birth of our son, Eduardo.

**What makes you laugh the most?**

Funny stories and practical jokes.

**If you were not a driver what would you have done?**

I always wanted to be a racing driver.

**What's the most important thing in life for you?**

To be happy.

**What are your best qualities?**

Originality.

**And your worst?**

The pressure in the past sometimes got to me.

B.A.R 007

V10 Honda RA005E (90°)

Michelin

## LUCKY STRIKE B·A·R HONDA

Address: British American Racing
Operations Centre, Brackley,
Northants, NN13 7BD
Great Britain

Tel.: +44 (0) 1280 84 40 00
Fax: +44 (0) 1280 84 40 01
Internet: www.barf1.com

Team founded in 1997
Grand Prix debut: Australia 1999
Number of Grands Prix: 101

Number of victories: 0
Best result: 2nd (4 times)

Number of pole positions: San Marino 2004 (Button)
Number of pole positions: 1

Number of fastest laps: 0

First points scored: Australia 2000 (Villeneuve, 4th and Zonta, 6th)
Number of points scored: 189
Points average per race: 1.87

First podium: Spain 2001 (Villeneuve, 3rd)
Number of podiums: 13

Best classification in the Constructors' World Championship:
2nd in 2004
Best classification in the Drivers' World Championship:
3nd in 2004 (Button).

## Strengths

- Increased involvement by Honda.
- Button's ambition and motivation.
- Complementary drivers.
- Good technical staff.
- Highly motivated team.

## Weaknesses

- Engine's reliability.
- Small margin for progression.

## 2004 summary

- 2nd in the Constructors' World
  Championship
- Best result: 4 x 2nd
  (Button - San Marino, Monaco,
  Germany and China)
- 1 pole position
  (Button - San Marino)
- 119 points scored
  (Button 85, Sato 34)
- 27 finishes out of a possible 36
  (Button 16, Sato 11)
- 25 points scoring finishes
  (Button 16, Sato 9)
- 2 drivers used
  (Button and Sato).

# B·A·R-HONDA

**Nick Fry (GB)**
General manager

**Geoffrey Willis (GB)**
Technical director

**Matsu Tanaka (J)**
Honda Racing
President

**Anthony Davidson (GB)**
3rd driver

**Enrique Bernoldi (BR)**
Test driver

**Number of employees**
300

In 2004, the B.A.R-Honda team pulled off a memorable exploit by finishing the Constructors' championship in an unexpected second place behind the uncatchable Ferraris and ahead of Renault, Williams and McLaren. David Richards had fulfilled his mission and left to devote himself to Prodrive, his company that has its fingers in almost every area of motor racing. Reaching the top is difficult: staying there is even more so and nowhere is this truer than in F1. The team has opted for safety and the 2005 B.A.R-Honda is a simple evolution of the previous year's car. The season has got off to a bad start for the squad and in Australia an aerodynamic glitch upset the B.A.R 007's performance. It suffered from grip and turbulence problems and its drivers were never among the front-runners. In Malaysia the team exploited a loophole in the regulations and fitted new engines both of which self-destructed within the first three laps. This year Honda has intensified its efforts at every level. So far this has not really borne fruit. In 2004, the team looked a potential candidate for victory but its performance so far has been very unimpressive. Is it slipping inexorably back down the ladder to its former inglorious anonymity? This catastrophic start to the season also raises a question mark over Jenson Button's contract. If B.A.R-Honda does not improve he will be freed at the end of the year from his obligations and will be able to quit the team.

# JENSON BUTTON

## B.A.R
## HONDA *3

**Date and place of birth**
January 19, 1980 in Frome (Great Britain)
**Nationality** English
**Place of residence** Monte-Carlo
**Marital status** Engaged to Louise
**Height** 1.82m **Weight** 68.5kgs
**Internet** www.jensonbutton.com

## F1 results

Best F1 Championship result: 3rd in 2004 (B.A.R-Honda)
Best F1 result: 2nd (4 times)
Best F1 qualification: 1st (1 pole position)

2000: Williams-BMW • 17 GP, 12 points, 8th
2001: Benetton-Renault • 17 GP, 2 points, 17th
2002: Renault • 17 GP, 14 points, 7th
2003: B.A.R-Honda • 15 GP, 17 points, 9th
2004: B.A.R-Honda • 18 GP, 85 points, 3rd

Jenson Button is continuing with B.A.R-Honda despite the rather slap stick affair last season concerning his contract with Williams which spilled a lot of ink in magazines and newspapers. He showed considerable steadfastness and maturity while the lawyers were going at each other like rabid dogs!

Aged twenty-five he has confirmed all his early promise and is another pretender to Michael Schumacher's crown. Last year he finished in the points on fifteen occasions including many rostrum placings. Only a win has escaped him so far. After his headline grabbing performances at Williams in 2000 he was thrown off course by his sudden rise to fame and fell victim to 'Buttonmania.' He soon got back on track and has matured very quickly despite an unhappy period at Renault.

This year his team seems to be lagging behind its rivals in relation to 2004. If B.A.R-Honda doesn't get its act together and the results are not forthcoming he will be able to join the Williams team next year as stipulated in his contract, this time without problems.

Honda, though, is working flat out to recapture the glory that it enjoyed in the late 80s and early 90s with McLaren. If the company achieves this then there is no reason why Button should not bring them a few victories and become a member of that very closed circle of grand prix winners.

## Titles

- 1993, 1994, 1995, 1996, 1997 and 1998:
  British Karting Champion, Italian Karting Champion (once).
- 1998: British Formula Ford Champion.

## Career summary

Competition debut: 1989 (kart)
Grand Prix debut: Australia 2000 (Williams-BMW)

- 85 Grands Prix
- 130 points scored
- Average per Grand Prix: 1.52
- 10 podiums
- 0 victories
- 4 2nd places
- 6 3rd places
- 6 4th places
- 10 5th places
- 4 6th places
- 2 7th places*
- 5 8th places*

- 1 pole position
- 0 fastest laps
- 7 GP in the lead
- 358 kms in the lead
- 70 laps in the lead

* Since 2003 and the attribution of points
  to 7th and 8th places.

## Team-mates

2000: R. Schumacher
2001: G. Fisichella
2002: J. Trulli
2003: J. Villeneuve and T. Sato
2004: T. Sato

## Qualifications 2004

Button 11 / Sato 7

# QUESTIONS

# JENSON BUTTON

**What was the first car you drove?**
An Audi on a disused airport runway when I was eight.

**And today?**
A Honda NSX.

**What is your favourite/dream car?**
I really like the 1963 Corvette Stingray.

**What does your helmet design mean?**
The basis is the Union Jack, the British flag. This decoration dates from 1994 when I was racing karts. You can also see the initials of my name.

**What's been your best racing car so far?**
The 1999 Formula 3 car.

**And the worst?**
I've not really had a bad car.

**What's your best racing memory?**
The 2004 German Grand Prix at Hockenheim; it's been the best race of my life... so far.

**And your worst?**
When I lost a kart world championship by a few seconds. At Spa in my F1 debut year I was third on the grid and came home fifth. I was unhappy not to have made it onto the rostrum. My ten rostrum finishes in 2004 are some consolation!

**Do you remember the first Grand Prix you saw on TV?**
I must've been around four or five.

**And the first one you attended?**
I was fourteen and it was at Silverstone.

**What's your aim in racing?**
Become world champion.

**What's your favourite circuit?**
Difficult to choose but I'd say the grand prix layout at Silverstone

**And the one you dislike the most?**
Imola as I've never been lucky there.

**Who's your favourite driver in the history of racing?**
Ayrton Senna and Alain Prost.

**And among those currently racing?**
I've got a lot of respect for Michael Schumacher.

**Who's been your best team-mate?**
Giancarlo Fisichella.

**If you were a team manager what drivers would you choose?**
Jacques Villeneuve and myself.

**What do you love about this profession?**
The sensation of speed, the competitive spirit and sharing the life of a team.

**What don't you like about it?**
You go from hero to zero from one race to another.

**What's your favourite moment of a Grand Prix?**
The start.

**Do you always get into your car on the same side?**
Yes, but I'm really not superstitious.

**When you stop racing, what then?**
I'd like to stay in racing; it's my life.

**What's your favourite dish?**
Pasta and English roast beef on a Sunday. I love meat. In Brazil I really enjoy myself in the Currascherias. I like fish too especially the Mahi-mahi from the Bahamas.

**And the ones you dislike?**
Heavy food and raw meat.

**What's your favourite drink?**
Water.

**Do you like alcohol?**
I appreciate good wines and I'm beginning to recognise them. I like Italian wines very much especially the Sassicaia. I also like a good Tequila from time to time.

**Have you ever smoked?**
No, never.

**What sports do you do?**
Swimming, body board, all kinds of cycling and surfing.

**And your favourite sports?**
The big football matches and cross-country biking. My girlfriend's family is involved in the Arsenal football club so I've become a supporter of the team.

**Who's your favourite sportsperson?**
Lance Armstrong's done some incredible things in his sport.

**What are your hobbies/interests outside racing?**
Surfing the net. I like computer games too and shopping with my girlfriend, Louise.

**What are your favourite films?**
Man on Fire.

**And your favourite actors?**
Bryan Felipe and Julia Roberts.

**What do you watch on TV?**
I only watch sports reports.

**What kind of music do you like?**
A lot of things. I like ballads like Angels or Robbie Williams. I also listen to Lenny Kravitz and Maxwell.

**What do you like reading?**
I only read motor sport magazines. I like biographies too, Lance Armstrong's for example.

**What's your favourite colour?**
Black.

**What's your favourite holiday destination?**
I love Cancun in Mexico. The beaches are fantastic.

**And your favourite place for shopping?**
Sloane street in Chelsea in London.

**What do you collect?**
I like clothing and cars

**Have you got any animals?**
I like dogs very much. I had one and I'd like to have another when I've got more time

**Outside motor racing, whom do you admire?**
My dad and Louise.

**If you were to go to a desert island, what would you bring?**
My girlfriend, Louise, a boat and motor car mags.

**What's your perfect day?**
Going shopping with Louise and relaxing in Monaco.

**What's been the greatest day of your life so far?**
The day I was born.

**What makes you laugh the most?**
Formula 1 as there are a whole of crazy things to try.

**If you were not a driver what would you have done?**
I'd like to have been a film producer.

**What's the most important thing in life for you?**
Health and happiness.

**What are your best qualities?**
I think I'm a nice guy. I"m fairly laid-back and I don't like judging others. I'm impulsive and intuitive.

**And your worst?**
I love racing too much and I can sometimes be a bit arrogant.

# TAKUMA SATO

## B.A.R
## HONDA *4

**Date and place of birth** January 28, 1977 in Tokyo (Japan)
**Nationality** Japanese
**Place of residence** Marlow (Great Britain)
**Marital status** Single
**Height** 1.63m **Weight** 58kgs
**Internet** www.takumasato.com

## F1 results

Best F1 Championship result: 8th in 2004 (B.A.R-Honda)
Best F1 result: 3rd (USA 2004)
Best F1 qualification: 2nd (Europe 2004)

2002: Jordan-Honda • 17 GP, 2 points, 15th
2003: B.A.R-Honda • 1 GP, 3 points, 18th
2004: B.A.R-Honda • 18 GP, 34 points, 8th

Takuma Sato is probably the best of the small contingent of Japanese drivers in the history of Formula 1. Last year he emulated Auguri Suzuki (3rd at Suzuka in 1990) by finishing third in the USA GP at Indianapolis. However, he has been more consistent and aggressive than the latter. He has put on some fantastic displays in front of his home crowd and in 2004 he showed that Honda had made the right choice by his performances all over the world. He finished eighth overall in the Drivers' Championship and provided a lot of excitement with some excellent drives combining dash and a fair dose of courage. The ever-smiling Takuma has become very popular with the public, helped no doubt by occasional overtaking manoeuvres that have a touch of the kamikaze about them. He is now familiar with the little world of F1 and fears nobody, not even his team-mate, Button, whom he has pushed to the limit on several occasions.

## Titles

- 1996 and 1997: Japanese Karting Champion.
- 2001 British Formula 3 Champion, 1st Marlboro Masters (Zandvoort), 1st Macao F3.

## Career summary

Competition debut: 1996 (karting)
Grand Prix debut: Australia 2002 (Jordan-Honda)

- 36 Grands Prix
- 39 points scored
- Average per Grand Prix: 1.08
- 1 podium
- 0 victories
- 1 3rd place
- 2 4th places
- 3 5th places
- 4 6th places
- 3 8th places*

- 0 pole positions
- 0 fastest laps
- 1 GP in the lead
- 10 kms in the lead
- 2 laps in the lead

* Since 2003 and the attribution of points to 7th and 8th places.

## Team-mates

2002: G. Fisichella
2003 and 2004: J. Button

## Qualifications 2004

Sato 7 / Button 11

# QUESTIONS

# TAKUMA SATO

**What was the first car you drove?**
A Honda Civic when I was eighteen.

**And today?**
An old Mini in England.

**What is your favourite/dream car?**
All the Porsches fascinate me. I'd like to find a Honda S 800 in a good state but it's not easy.

**What does your helmet design mean?**
I'm quite proud as I designed it myself. It's got no particular signification. It's designed around the T of my Christian name plus the colours I like.

**What's been your best racing car so far?**
The F3 Dallara I drove in the 2001 British Championship.

**And the worst?**
My kart in 1997; I never liked karts.

**What's your best racing memory?**
My fifth place at Suzuka in 2002 and more recently my rostrum finish at Indy and my second place on the starting grid at the Nürburgring.

**And your worst?**
My accident in Austria in 2002.

**Do you remember the first Grand Prix you saw on TV?**
Yes, very well. I followed Ayrton Senna's exploits at Lotus and then McLaren.

**And the first one you attended?**
The 1987 Japanese Grand Prix.

**What's your aim in racing?**
To become F1 World Champion.

**What's your favourite circuit?**
I go very well at Spa and Suzuka.

**And the one you dislike the most?**
None really.

**Who's your favourite driver in the history of racing?**
I was a great admirer of Ayrton Senna.

**And among those currently racing?**
I don't really want to have role models. I want to be myself.

**Who's been your best team-mate?**
Anthony Davidson whom I've known since my karting days. I've never had any problems with my team-mates be they Giancarlo Fisichella or Jenson Button.

**If you were a team manager what drivers would you choose?**
There's no way I'll ever be a team manager!

**What do you love about this profession?**
Driving.

**What don't you like about it?**
The politics and special interests.

**What's your favourite moment of a Grand Prix?**
Achieving a good result in front of my home crowd which supports me 100%.

**Do you always get into your car on the same side?**
Out of habit on the left-hand side putting my right foot first.

**When you stop racing, what then?**
I have not thought about it yet.

**What's your favourite dish?**
I like all kinds of cooking especially Japanese.

**And the ones you dislike?**
There's nothing I really dislike.

**What's your favourite drink?**
Fruit juice and a beer from time to time.

**Do you like alcohol?**
A beer, or some red wine or sake.

**Have you ever smoked?**
Never.

**What sports do you do?**
Jogging, muscle building, skiing and cycling.

**And your favourite sports?**
I like watching the Tour de France. Unfortunately, there are a lot of GPs in July.

**Who's your favourite sportsperson?**
Lance Armstrong is exceptional; he 's won the Tour de France six times, an unheard of exploit.

**What are your hobbies/interests outside racing?**
I like going for a walk with my friends.

**What are your favourite films?**
Recently I saw Man on Fire with Denzel Washington.

**And your favourite actors?**
Nicolas Cage and Bridget Fonda.

**What do you watch on TV?**
Sports programmes like cycling.

**What kind of music do you like?**
A bit of everything. I like some Japanese singers and folk music.

**What do you like reading?**
Books and magazines written in Japanese. It's relaxing.

**What's your favourite colour?**
Blue.

**And your favourite place for shopping?**
Countries where it's hot like the south of Spain, Thailand, Malaysia and I also adore the south of Japan.

**What do you collect?**
Nowhere in particular.

**What do you collect?**
I'm not a collector. Clothes perhaps.

**Have you got any animals?**
A cat and a dog.

**Outside motor racing, whom do you admire?**
My parents.

**If you were to go to a desert island, what would you bring?**
My girlfriend.

**What's your perfect day?**
Feeling at ease and to be able to relax.

**What's been the greatest day of your life so far?**
The day of my birth.

**What makes you laugh the most?**
I laugh easily.

**If you were not a driver what would you have done?**
I've no idea!

**What's the most important thing in life for you?**
To be human and a reliable and faithful friend.

**What are your best qualities?**
I never give up.

**And your worst?**
Sometimes it's a defect.

Renault R25

V10 Renault RS25 (72°)

Michelin

Address: Renault F1 UK
Whiteways Technical Centre,
Endstone, Oxon 0X74EE,
Great Britain

Tel.: +44(0)1608 678 000
Fax: +44(0)1608 678 809

Internet: www.renaultf1.com

Team founded in 1973
Grand Prix debut: Great Britain 1977
Number of Grands Prix: 174

First victory: France 1979 (Jabouille)
Number of victories: 17

First pole position: South Africa 1979 (Jabouille)
Number of pole positions: 36

First fastest lap: France 1979 (Arnoux)
Number of fastest laps: 19

First points scored: United States 1978 (Jabouille, 4th)
Number of points scored: 528
Points average per race: 3.03

First podium: France 1979 (Jabouille, 1st and Arnoux 3rd)
Number of podiums: 47

Best classification in the Constructors' World Championship:
2nd in 1983.
Best classification in the Drivers' World Championship:
2nd in 1983 (Prost).

Renault F1 France
1-15, avenue du Pdt Kennedy
91177 Viry-Châtillon
France

Tel.: +33 (0)1 69 12 58 00
Fax: +33 (0)1 69 12 58 17

## Strengths

- Excellent driver pairing.
- Desire to win.
- Car is easy on its tyres.
- Stable and skilled technical team.
- Competitive chassis and engine.
- Excellent interseason tests.

## Weaknesses

- Driver rivalry
- Under pressure to deliver
- Departure of Mark Smith (engineer)

## 2004 summary

- 3rd in the Constructors' World
  Championship

- 1 victoiry
  (Trulli - Monaco)

- 3 pole positions
  (Trulli 2, Alonso 1)

- 105 points scored
  (Alonso 59, Trulli 46)

- 28 finishes out of a possible 36
  (Alonso 13, Trulli 12, Villeneuve 3)

- 21 points scoring finishes
  (Alonso 12, Trulli 9)

- 3 drivers used
  (Alonso, Trulli and Villeneuve)

# RENAULT

**Patrick Faure (F)**
Managing director
Renault F1

**Flavio Briatore (I)**
Team principal

**Bob Bell (GB)**
Technical director
(Chassis)

**Robert White (GB)**
Technical director
(Engine)

**Franck Montagny (F)**
3rd driver

**Number of employees**
Renault F1 UK: 390
Renault F1 France: 280

When the R25 was presented on 1st February in Monte Carlo Patrick Faure and Flavio Briatore both said that this year they were out for ultimate victory. Last year Renault lost the runner-up spot in the Constructors' Championship to BAR due to its somewhat crass dismissal of Jarno Trulli followed by the heavily publicised – and unsuccessful - return of Jacques Villeneuve. This faux pas was not enough to unbalance the team which, in 2005, has pursued its climb to the top of the F1 ladder with a couple of early season victories shared by its two drivers, Fisichella and Alonso. Their respective talents complement each other and it is reminiscent of 1982 when Prost and Arnoux dominated their rivals early on. Renault has certainly been helped by Ferrari's poor start to the championship which has made the blue and yellow cars look even more dominant.

The French team has numerous aces up its sleeve this year. The engine and chassis are a perfect marriage and enable the Michelin tyres to achieve optimum efficiency and the two drivers are supported by a highly skilled organisation.

Giancarlo Fisichella is considered to be one of the best of the current pack and he knows that he has been thrown a once in a lifetime chance. His team-mate, Fernando Alonso, is certainly one of tomorrow's great champions. Finally, puppet master, Flavio Briatore, runs it all behind the scenes with diabolical cunning!

# FERNANDO ALONSO
## RENAULT *5

**Date and place of birth** July 29, 1981 in Oviedo (Spain)
**Nationality** Spanish
**Place of residence** Oviedo (Spain) and Oxford (Great Britain)
**Marital status** Single
**Height** 1.71m **Weight** 68kgs
**Internet** www.fernandoalonso.com

## F1 results

Best F1 Championship result: 4th in 2004 (Renault)
Best F1 result: 1st (1 victory, Hungary 2003)
Best F1 qualification: 1st (3 pole positions)

2001: Minardi-European • 17 GP, 0 point, 23rd
2003: Renault • 16 GP, 55 points, 6th
2004: Renault • 18 GP, 59 points, 4th

The Spaniard is the youngest-ever pole man and winner of an F1 grand prix. He is also one of the most serious challengers for the 2005 title and behind the scenes rumours are already going round that he will replace Michael Schumacher in the Scuderia. He's made of the right stuff.

He did a season with Minardi in 2001 after which he was the Renault test driver for a year. He was then integrated into the French squad in 2003. This is his third year with the team and its rise to the top provides him with the ideal opportunity to show off his talent, which he did in Malaysia with a dominating victory. He has what it takes in every area and he has now achieved a certain maturity. His trendy looks, long hair and laid-back attitude have made him the idol of a whole nation. He has shone in every formula in his short but brilliant career, and is looked after by Flavio Briatore, a man who knows better than most the ins and outs of the paddock. He is a real fighter and his pugnacity has been rewarded by two rostrum finishes so far (3rd and 1st) in the first two GPs. However, he has to remain vigilant. In F1 there is no place for sentiment and last year he had a tough battle with Jarno Trulli so he has to keep a weather eye on his team-mate, Fisichella.

## Titles

- 1994, 1996 and 1997: Spanish karting Champion (serie A).
- 1996: Karting World Champion.
- 1999: Formula Euro Open Nissan Champion

## Career summary

Competition debut: 1988 (karting)
Grand Prix debut: Australia 2001 (Minardi-European)

- 51 Grands Prix
- 114 points scored
- Average per Grand Prix: 2.23
- 8 podiums
- 1 victory
- 2 2nd places
- 5 3rd places
- 7 4th places
- 3 5th places
- 2 6th places
- 2 7th places*
- 1 8th place*

- 3 pole positions
- 1 fastest lap
- 13 GP in the lead
- 718 kms in the lead
- 157 laps in the lead

* Since 2003 and the attribution of points
  to 7th and 8th places.

## Team-mates

2001: T. Marques and A. Yoong
2003: J. Trulli
2004: J. Trulli and J. Villeneuve

## Qualifications 2004

Alonso 7 / Trulli 8
Alonso 2 / Villeneuve 1

# QUESTIONS

# FERNANDO ALONSO

**What was the first car you drove?**

A Nissan, when I was seventeen. My father never wanted me to drive without a driving licence. Before that I drove a 4-wheeled vehicle with an engine that my father built for me when I was two.

**And today?**

I've got a Renault Vel Satis in Spain and a Mégane CC.

**What is your favourite/dream car?**

A Renault.

**What does your helmet design mean?**

I've had this design since my karting days. Of, course, there's the Spanish flag.

**What's been your best racing car so far?**

The 2003 Renault 25 and now I'd say the R 25.

**And the worst?**

The F3000 Lola.

**What's your best racing memory?**

My win in the 1996 World Championship for Karts. Now, of course, it's my first F1 victory in Hungary.

**And your worst?**

In a kart in during the 1995 European Championship. I was in the lead when the accelerator cable snapped.

**Do you remember the first Grand Prix you saw on TV?**

I must've have been about thirteen.

**And the first one you attended?**

I never attended a Grand Prix until I was actually racing in one!

**What's your aim in racing?**

To become world champion.

**What's your favourite circuit?**

Valencia.

**And the one you dislike the most?**

I'm not very keen on Monaco.

**Who's your favourite driver in the history of racing?**

I liked Ayrton Senna but he wasn't a hero.

**And among those currently racing?**

I get on well with Jarno Trulli. He's a good bloke. Fisichella is a charming guy, too.

**Who's been your best team-mate?**

Tarso Marques, and I've known Jarno Trulli since my karting days.

**If you were a team manager what drivers would you choose?**

Young, aggressive ones. I'd go for the Latins.

**What do you love about this profession?**

Driving's a pleasure. I also love F1 single-seaters.

**What don't you like about it?**

The crazy schedule between races with private testing and promotional work in the four corners of the world.

**What's your favourite moment of a Grand Prix?**

Qualifying.

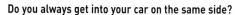

**Do you always get into your car on the same side?**

Always. In fact, that depends on which side the mechanics are working. I'm superstitious. I always put on my left sock and glove before the right ones!

**When you stop racing, what then?**

I'd like to remain in the racing milieu but in what field I don't really know yet.

**What's your favourite dish?**

Pasta.

**And the ones you dislike?**

Many things like rice, fish, paëlla.

**What's your favourite drink?**

Mineral water.

**Do you like alcohol?**

I've never touched the stuff!

**Have you ever smoked?**

Never.

**What sports do you do?**

Cycling, tennis, football and swimming.

**And your favourite sports?**

Cycling, football and tennis.

**Who's your favourite sportsperson?**

When I was a bit younger, the cyclist Miguel Induran was my hero. Now, I've got a lot of admiration for Lance Armstrong. I'm also a passionate supporter of Real Madrid.

**What are your hobbies/interests outside racing?**

I like watching sport and good films on TV. I also like computers and the little digital cameras. Since I was a kid I've always liked doing card tricks.

**What are your favourite films?**

I I like 'Aviator. In Spain I have to come in in the middle of the showing when the lights are down. If not I can't see the film. People takes photos of me and ask me for autographs until the middle of the movie!

**And your favourite actors?**

There are a lot. I like Jim Carey because he makes me laugh.

**What do you watch on TV?**

Funny films, sport and certain comedies.

**What kind of music do you like?**

Everything. I really like Spanish rock groups.

**What do you like reading?**

I don't read much. I like specialised magazines.

**What's your favourite colour?**

Black.

**What's your favourite holiday destination?**

Being at home in Oviedo. I like the Canaries too.

**And your favourite place for shopping?**

Japan and Singapore.

**What do you collect?**

Nothing! Ah yes. Now I want to collect victories!

**Have you got any animals?**

I've got a cocker in Oviedo whose name in lame after my first kart!

**Outside motor racing, whom do you admire?**

I've got a lot of respect for the King of Spain, Juan Carlos. He always calls me before a grand prix.

**If you were to go to a desert island, what would you bring?**

A beautiful girl and an F1....!

**What's your perfect day?**

I'm a loner. I like to rest, to think.

**What's been the greatest day of your life so far?**

Christmas at home with my family and grandparents.

**What makes you laugh the most?**

I like funny stories.

**If you were not a driver what would you have done?**

I don't know. At the age of 3 I was already sitting in a kart. Other wise I'd have done cycling or football. I'm part of the Drivers' football team with Michael and Giancarlo.

**What's the most important thing in life for you?**

My family is more important than my career. If I had to choose I'd prefer to give my parents another two hundred years' life than to be world champion.

**What are your best qualities?**

Honesly.

**And your worst?**

I I'm a Latin. I get angry too often and I'm far too impatient. I want everything yesterday!

# GIANCARLO FISICHELLA

## RENAULT *6

**Date and place of birth** January 14, 1973 in Rome (Italy)
**Nationality** Italian
**Place of residence** Rome (Italy) and Monte-Carlo
**Marital status** Married to Luna, a daughter Carlotta and a son Christopher
**Height** 1.72m **Weight** 66kgs
**Internet** www.giancarlofisichella.com

## F1 results

Best F1 Championship result: 6th in 2000 (Benetton-Supertec)
Best F1 result: 1st (1 victory, Brazil 2003)
Best F1 qualification: 1st (1 pole position)

1996: Minardi-Ford • 8 GP, 0 point, not classified
1997: Jordan-Peugeot • 17 GP, 20 points, 8th
1998: Benetton-Mecachrome • 16 GP, 16 points, 9th
1999: Benetton-Supertec • 16 GP, 13 points, 9th
2000: Benetton-Supertec • 17 GP, 18 points, 6th
2001: Benetton-Renault • 17 GP, 8 points, 11th
2002: Jordan-Honda • 16 GP, 7 points, 11th
2003: Jordan-Ford • 16 GP, 12 points, 12th
2004: Sauber-Petronas • 18 GP, 22 points, 11th

*"It's just the right moment to be at Renault,"* crows Giancarlo Fisichella. *"They want to win races. Me too. Being in a top team that has the means to win is a very important factor for a driver."* The Italian grabbed the chance offered to him with both hands in the Australian Grand Prix. During the presentation of the Renault R25 in Monte Carlo Flavio Briatore spelled it out loud and clear: *"this is going to be his year."* In Melbourne he added, *"before he had the talent but not the car. Now he's got both!"*

At the end of 2001 Giancarlo was thrown out of the Benetton-Renault team but he is back in with a bang beginning his tenth year in F1. Aged thirty-two he is one of the most experienced drivers in the paddock and many consider the little man from Rome to be one of the quickest of his generation. He has never been able to fulfil his dream of driving a Ferrari. This year he has a car that will enable him to do battle with the red cars on an equal footing.

It is a just reward for one of the nicest guys in F1 who has always been in the wrong place at the wrong time. Until 2005!

## Titles

- 1994: Italian Formula 3 Champion and Winner of the F3 Monaco Grand Prix.

## Career summary

Competition debut: 1984 (karting)
Grand Prix debut: Australia 1996 (Minardi-Ford)

- 141 Grands Prix
- 116 points scored
- Average per Grand Prix: 0.82
- 10 podiums
- 1 victory
- 5 2nd places
- 4 3rd places
- 6 4th places
- 9 5th places
- 7 6th places
- 3 7th places*
- 3 8th places*

- 1 pole position
- 1 fastest lap
- 4 GP in the lead
- 176 kms in the lead
- 36 laps in the lead

\* Since 2003 and the attribution of points to 7th and 8th places.

## Team-mates

1996: P. Lamy
1997: R. Schumacher
1998, 1999 and 2000: A. Wurz
2001: J. Button
2002: T. Sato
2003: R. Firman and Z. Baumgartner
2004: F. Massa

## Qualifications 2004

Fisichella 11 / Massa 7

# QUESTIONS

# GIANCARLO FISICHELLA

**What was the first car you drove?**

A Fiat 127 when I was five.

**And today?**

I've got a Renault Mégane coupe/cabriolet.

**What is your favourite/dream car?**

I'm lucky enough to have it. But that's a secret!

**What does your helmet design mean?**

It doesn't have any particular meaning. A friend designed it for me when I was doing karting and I've kept the green and yellow since then. Now the base isn't white but grey. I felt like a change.

**What's been your best racing car so far?**

My F1s in general.

**And the worst?**

The F3 Ralt RT 36.

**What's your best racing memory?**

All my rostrums are good memories. I have very good memories of my F3 win in Monaco in 1994 and my first day in F1. Obviously, my victory in Brazil has a very special place.

**And your worst?**

When I retired while in the lead in the Benetton in the 1999 Grand Prix on the Nürburgring.

**Do you remember the first Grand Prix you saw on TV?**

I was very small. I remember Niki Lauda in a Brabham so it must've been in 1979.

**And the first one you attended?**

When I raced in Monaco in D F3 in 1993.

**What's your aim in racing?**

To become world champion.

**What's your favourite circuit?**
Imola.

**And the one you dislike the most?**
Maybe Silverstone because the weather's always bad there.

**Who's your favourite driver in the history of racing?**
Niki Lauda and then Ayrton Senna.

**And among those currently racing?**
I like Michael Schumacher.

**Who's been your best team-mate?**
Alexander Wurz.

**If you were a team manager what drivers would you choose?**
Schumacher and Fisichella.

**What do you love about this profession?**
I feel good when I'm behind the wheel.

**What don't you like about it?**
Not having a competitive car.

**What's your favourite moment of a Grand Prix?**
Qualifying and the start. Then the plane on Sunday evening!

**Do you always get into your car on the same side?**
Usually on the left but it's only out of habit.

**When you stop racing, what then**
I'd like to stay in racing. Enrico Zanarini, my manager, and I have created Fisichella Motor Sport in F3000 Italy to help young drivers.

**What's your favourite dish?**
"Bucatini alla matriciana", a pasta special "alla romaine."

**And the ones you dislike?**
Curry and Sushi.

**What's your favourite drink?**
Coca Cola and orange juice.

**Do you like alcohol?**
Red wine, caipirinha and rostrum champagne!

**Have you ever smoked?**
Never. It doesn't interest me.

**What sports do you do?**
Football, VTT, skiing, tennis and gymnastics.

**And your favourite sports?**
I'm interested in all sports including football and especially la Roma.

**Who's your favourite sportsperson?**
Lance Armstrong and Hermann Maier who made an incredible comeback after his terrible motorbike accident. They're two miraculous survivors.

**What are your hobbies/interests outside racing?**
I love river fishing and playing billiards.

**What are your favourite films?**
I like watching cartoons with my daughter. Recently I liked 'Shark Tale' which I saw on the plane going to Australia.

**And your favourite actors?**
I love Robert Benigni.

**What do you watch on TV?**
A bit of everything.

**What kind of music do you like?**
Everything. I like Elton John, Claudia Baglioni, Renato Zero, Madonna and Robbie Williams.

**What do you like reading?**
I don't read much. I like short texts!

**What's your favourite colour?**
Yellow and red.

**What's your favourite holiday destination?**
I like going to the Maldives with my family especially at the end of the season.

**And your favourite place for shopping?**
Rome and Milan in Italy.

**What do you collect?**
I like beautiful cars.

**Have you got any animals?**
In Monte Carlo I've got an aquarium and love birds. I like dogs and cats as well.

**Outside motor racing, whom do you admire?**
My family.

**If you were to go to a desert island, what would you bring?**
My family.

**What's your perfect day?**
Going fishing and winning the pools!

**What's been the greatest day of your life so far?**
The birth of my two children. It was extraordinary.

**What makes you laugh the most?**
I like having a good laugh.

**If you were not a driver what would you have done?**
I'd have been a mechanic in a garage.

**What's the most important thing in life for you?**
Health and being happy with my loved ones.

**What are your best qualities?**
I'm pleasant.

**And your worst?**
I'm not nasty enough!

Williams FW27

V10 BMW P84/5 (90°)

Michelin

Address: WilliamsF1
Grove, Wantage, Oxfordshire
OX12 0DQ,
Great Britain

Tel.: +44 (0)1235 777 700
Fax: +44 (0)1235 764 705
Internet: www.bmw.williamsf1.com

Team founded in 1969
Grand Prix debut: Argentina 1975 (Arg. 1973, with ISO)
Number of Grands Prix: 496 (30 with ISO)

First victory: Great Britain 1979 (C. Regazzoni)
Number of victories: 113

First pole position: Great Britain 1979 (Jones)
Number of pole positions: 124

First fastest lap: Austria 1973 (Ganley) with ISO,
United States West 1978 (Jones)
Number of fastest laps: 127

First points scored: Holland 1973 (Van Lennep, 6th) with ISO,
Germany 1975 (Laffite, 2nd)
Number of points scored: 2,429.5 (2,435.5 with ISO)
Points average per race: 4.89

First podium: Germany 1975 (Laffite, 2nd)
Number of podiums: 286

Constructors' World Titles: 9
(1980, 1981, 1986, 1987, 1992, 1993, 1994, 1996 and 1997).
Drivers' World Titles: 7
(Jones: 1980, Rosberg: 1982, Piquet: 1986, Mansell: 1992,
Prost: 1993, D. Hill: 1996, J. Villeneuve: 1997).

## Strenghts
- Performance and reliability of the
  BMW engine.
- Motivation.
- Good budget.
- Good drivers.

## Weaknesses
- Relations between the drivers.
- They must deliver.
- Relationships between drivers and team.
- Difficult to get back to the top.

## 2004 summary
- 4th in the Constructors' World Championship

- 1 victory
  (Montoya - Brazil)

- 1 pole position
  (R. Schumacher - Canada)

- 88 points scored
  (Montoya 58, R. Schumacher 24, Pizzonia 6)

- 29 finishes out of a possible 36
  (Montoya 16, R. Schumacher 8,
  Pizzonia 3, Gené 2)

- 22 points scoring finishes
  (Montoya 13, R. Schumacher 6, Pizzonia 3)

- 4 drivers used
  (Montoya, R. Schumacher, Gené and
  Pizzonia).

# WILLIAMS-BMW

**Frank Williams (GB)**
Managing director &
team principal

**Sam Michael (GB)**
Technical director

**Patrick Head (GB)**
Director of
engineering

**Mario Theissen (D)**
BMW Motorsport
director

**Antonio Pizzonia (BR)**
Test driver

**Number of employees**
Williams: 500
BMW: 250

Williams makes no bones about it. 2004 was a setback. Montoya saved the team's bacon with his victory in the last round in Brazil and then went off to McLaren. Frank Williams is still at the helm of a team whose structure has undergone a few modifications especially in the technical department. Patrick Head has stepped down and young Sam Michael's position as technical director has been strengthened. Driverwise both Montoya and Ralf Schumacher have quit the Grove man-of-war, and after the Jenson Button fiasco the team has taken on a couple of drivers who have everything to prove. Mark Webber is still a stranger to the rostrum and his team-mate Nick Heidfeld

from Germany has been there only once, some time ago. He learned of his appointment on the morning of the presentation of the new car. He certainly owes his seat to heavy pressure from BMW and has been preferred to Brazilian, Antonio Pizzonia.

The 2004 FW26 with its original nose was a setback and the team has followed a more conventional route with the FW 27. It seems to be working as Nick Heidfeld came home in a strong third place in Malaysia. This is more like what Williams is used to and augurs well for the rest of the season for the blue and white cars.

# MARK WEBBER

## WILLIAMS
## BMW *7

**Date and place of birth**
August 27, 1976 in Queanbeyan, NSW, (Australia)
**Nationality** Australian
**Place of residence** Buckinghamshire (Great Britain)
**Marital status** Engaged to Ann
**Height** 1.84m **Weight** 74kgs
**Internet** www.markwebber.com

## F1 results

Best F1 Championship result: 10th in 2003 (Jaguar)
Best F1 result: 5th (Australia 2002)
Best F1 qualification: 2nd (Malaysia 2004)

2002: Minardi-Asiatech • 16 GP, 2 points, 16th
2003: Jaguar • 16 GP, 17 points, 10th
2004: Jaguar • 18 GP, 7 points, 13th

In his fourth season in F1 Mark Webber has joined Williams, one of the top teams, and his days of running midfield are over. He made a big impact at the very start of his career becoming one of the few drivers to score points in his first grand prix in 2002 on his home patch in Australia. He scored two points in his Minardi going one better than his idol, Alain Prost, who came sixth in Brazil in 1980. He also had a couple of good races in the two years he spent at Jaguar: enough to impress Frank Williams who gave him a seat. He is effectively the Williams no.1, a tough task. His team-mate, Nick Heidfeld, will be out to profit from any slip-ups on the part of the Australian. However, Mark is one of the quickest drivers in the 2005 field but will he be able to bear the pressure that weighs on his shoulders? In 1980, his fellow-countryman Alan Jones won the F1 World title with Williams and Mark is hoping to follow in his footsteps. On his debut he was backed up by rugby star David Campese: now he has to convert the try, to use an obvious metaphor.

At present Williams is going through a rough period and may not be able to give him the right car to do the job. This, though, is not really part of his worries. For the first time in his career he has a car capable of fighting at the front of the field and he knows that his reputation is on the line. In Australia he proved his worth by finishing in a fighting fifth place egged on by his home crowd.

## Titles

- 1992: Karting: NSW and ACT Champion.
- 1996: Winner of the Formula Ford Festival.
- 1998: Five wins with Mercedes-Benz in Endurance (with Bernd Schneider).

## Career summary

Competition debut: 1991 (karting)
Grand Prix debut: Australia 2002 (Minardi-Asiatech)

- 50 Grands Prix
- 26 points scored
- Average per Grand Prix: 0.52
- 0 podiums
- 0 victories
- 1 5th place
- 4 6th places
- 5 7th places*
- 2 8th places*

- 0 pole positions
- 0 fastest laps
- 1 GP in the lead
- 8 kms in the lead
- 2 laps in the lead

* Since 2003 and the attribution of points
  to 7th and 8th places.

## Team-mates

2002: A. Yoong and A Davidson
2003: A. Pizzonia and J. Wilson
2004: C. Klien

## Qualifications 2004

Webber 15 / Klien 3

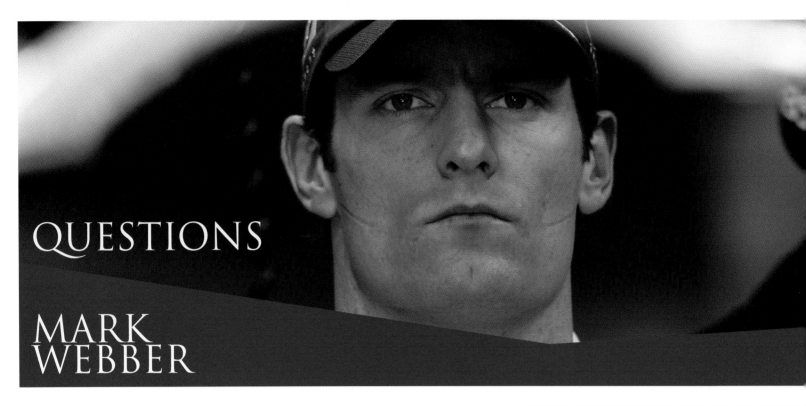

# QUESTIONS

# MARK WEBBER

**What was the first car you drove?**
A Toyota Corona in 1989.

**And today?**
A Series 5 BMW Touring. I'm waiting for the new M5.

**What is your favourite/dream car?**
I like the BMW M5 and the Mercedes-Benz SLR.

**What does your helmet design mean?**
I've had this design that I did myself since I was eighteen. On the top are yellow and green the colours worn by all Australian sports people. On the side I wanted to put the colours of the national flag. Maybe it's not that original, but I like it.

**What's been your best racing car so far?**
My 1997 F3 Dallara 397.

**And the worst?**
The F3000 Lola.

**What's your best racing memory?**
My F3000 win in Monaco and my two points in Melbourne in 2002.

**And your worst?**
Le Mans 1999 and my two accidents when my Mercedes took off and went over the railings.

**Do you remember the first Grand Prix you saw on TV?**
The 1997 Monaco Grand Prix.

**And the first one you attended?**
The 1997 Australian Grand Prix.

**What's your aim in racing?**
Winning.

**What's your favourite circuit?**
Spa.

**And the one you dislike the most?**
Barcelona and the A1-Ring in Austria.

**Who's your favourite driver in the history of racing?**
Alain Prost.

**And among those currently racing?**
I've a lot of respect for Michael Schumacher.

**Who's been your best team-mate?**
Bernd Schneider with Mercedes-Benz in Endurance.

**If you were a team manager what drivers would you choose?**
Michael Schumacher and Kimi Räikkönen.

**What do you love about this profession?**
The travel, the hotels and the fact that the drivers are always on call. Among other things I regret being so far away from my family in Australia.

**What don't you like about it?**
Travelling, hotels and the excessive number of requests that drivers have to comply with.

**What's your favourite moment of a Grand Prix?**
Crossing the line like I did in Melbourne for my first Grand Prix.

**Do you always get into your car on the same side?**
Always on the left because in karting the engine is on the right.

**When you stop racing, what then?**
I'll involve myself in a lot of charity work.

**What's your favourite dish?**

Pasta, pizzas, chocolate, ice creams and desserts.

**And the ones you dislike?**

Sushi.

**What's your favourite drink?**

Apple juice, lemonade and sparkling water.

**Do you like alcohol?**

A drop of red wine from time to time.

**Have you ever smoked?**

I've tried it.

**What sports do you do?**

I do as much sport as possible: cycling, mountain biking, skiing in Austria and a lot of hard physical workouts. A bit over a year ago I did a very exhausting raid in Tasmania for the Battle against Cancer.

**And your favourite sports?**

Tennis, squash and all kinds of cycling.

**Who's your favourite sportsperson?**

The motor bike rider, Mike Doohan, and the cyclist Lance Armstrong. Last year after Brazil I went to his place in Austin Texas to play football. He's an exceptional guy. There's also the Manchester United footballer Roy Keane.

**What are your hobbies/interests outside racing?**

I like remote controlled planes and helicopters, and video games like Playstation.

**What are your favourite films?**

I don't like the cinema much.

**And your favourite actors?**

Jack Nicholson.

**What do you watch on TV?**

Some documentaries and sports reports.

**What kind of music do you like?**

INXS, U2, some hits and relaxing music.

**What do you like reading?**

Autobiographies and biographies. I also like some Autobiographies and biographies. I also like thrillers.

**What's your favourite colour?**

Blue.

**What's your favourite holiday destination?**

In Australia and Austria for skiing.

**And your favourite place for shopping?**

Montreal and Italian towns.

**What do you collect?**

I'm not a collector.

**Have you got any animals?**

No, but I'd like to have a dog later on.

**Outside motor racing, whom do you admire?**

All those who overcome adversity.

**If you were to go to a desert island, what would you bring?**

A lot of chocolate!

**What's your perfect day?**

I'd begin with a good breakfast, then a little gymnastics. After a light meal I'd go and drive an F1 in qualifying set up. Then back home and spend a quiet evening zapping on TV.

**What's been the greatest day of your life so far?**

The 2002 Australian Grand Prix. Finishing in the points in my first race and in front of my home crowd is something I'll never forget.

**What makes you laugh the most?**

When I'm with friends; it's always fun.

**If you were not a driver what would you have done?**

I'd have been a plumber.

**What's the most important thing in life for you?**

My family. I regret not being able to see my parents and my sister who live in Australia.

**What are your best qualities?**

I'm honest and I think I've got my feet on the ground.

**And your worst?**

Sometimes I'm too impatient.

# NICK HEIDFELD

## WILLIAMS BMW *8

**Date and place of birth**
May 10, 1977 in Mönchengladbach (Germany)
**Nationality** German
**Place of residence** Monte-Carlo
**Marital status** Engaged to Patricia
**Height** 1.64m **Weight** 59kgs
**Internet** www.nick-heidfeld.com

## F1 results

Best F1 Championship result: 8th in 2001 (Sauber-Petronas)
Best F1 result: 3rd (Brazil 2001)
Best F1 qualification: 4th (Austria 2003)

2000: Prost-Peugeot • 16 GP, 0 point, not classified
2001: Sauber-Petronas • 17 GP, 12 points, 8th
2002: Sauber-Petronas • 17 GP, 7 points, 10th
2003: Sauber-Petronas • 16 GP, 6 points, 14th
2004: Jordan-Ford • 18 GP, 3 points, 18th

Like Jenson Button in 2000 Nick Heidfeld only learned of his arrival at Williams a few minutes before the official announcement. He was up against Antonio Pizzonia for the seat and it was Frank Williams himself who told the press that his team had decided on the little German. BMW obviously had a hand in the decision but whatever the reasons it is a fitting reward for the self-effacing Heidfeld. It is also a revenge. He was a product of the Mercedes-Benz nursery and it looked like he was destined for McLaren. After driving for Prost Grand Prix he continued with Sauber while awaiting the call. It never came as McLaren chose his team-mate Räikkönen instead. It was the end of a dream and he found himself at the back of the grid in a Jordan which boded ill for his future. Throughout the winter he battled with Pizzonia and finally he got the drive. In his Williams powered by BMW, Mercedes-Benz's direct rival, he will be out to beat his former mentors.

## Titles

- 1994: German Formula Ford 1600 Champion.
- 1995: German Formula Ford 1800 Champion.
- 1996: Winner of the Macao F3 Grand Prix.
- 1997: German F3 Champion.
- 1999: F3000 Champion.

## Career summary

Competition debut: 1986 (karting)
Grand Prix debut: Australia 2000 (Prost-Peugeot)

- 84 Grands Prix
- 28 points scored
- Average per Grand Prix: 0.33
- 1 podium
- 0 victories
- 1 3rd place
- 2 4th places
- 2 5th places
- 7 6th places*
- 1 7th place*
- 3 8th places*

- 0 pole positions
- 0 fastest laps
- 0 kms in the lead
- 0 laps in the lead

\* Since 2003 and the attribution of points to 7th and 8th places.

## Team-mates

2000: J. Alesi
2001: K. Raïkkönen
2002: F. Massa and H-H. Frentzen
2003: H-H. Frentzen
2004: G. Pantano and T. Glock

## Qualifications 2004

Heidfeld 11 / Pantano 3
Heidfeld 3 / Glock 0

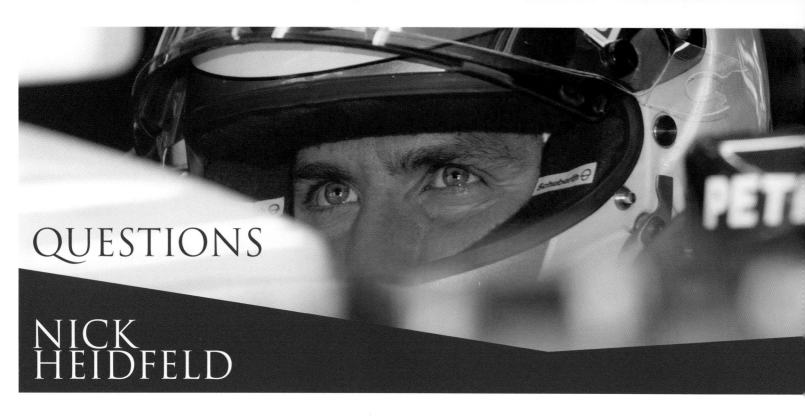

# QUESTIONS

# NICK HEIDFELD

**What was the first car you drove?**

I was about ten. It was in a car park at the Nürburgring and I was on my father's knees. But I don't remember the make of car.

**And today?**

I've got a BMW X5.

**What is your favourite/dream car?**

I like many but I don't dream about them.

**What does your helmet design mean?**

My favourite colours are blue and yellow so I tried to do something with the German flag at the rear. Apart from minor touches the design hasn't changed very much except to make room for sponsors.

**What's been your best racing car so far?**

The 2001 Sauber, the 1997 F3 Dallara and my F3000 Lola at Imola in 1999. The Williams is on another level.

**And the worst?**

The Prost AP 03 of 2001.

**What's your best racing memory?**

My third place in Brazil with Sauber in 2001, my F3000 title in 1999 and the Monaco races which I won in F3 and F3000.

**And your worst?**

The 1994 Formula Ford Festival, Monaco 1999 and the Nürburgring in 2000.

**Do you remember the first Grand Prix you saw on TV?**

I remember that Niki Lauda was driving but I couldn't put a year to it.

**And the first one you attended?**

Monaco 1988.

**What's your aim in racing?**

Being happy doing what I like. Maybe one day it'll be something else.

**What's your favourite circuit?**

City circuits like Monaco and Macao, and the Nürburgring.

**And the one you dislike the most?**

I don't like Spa and circuits laid out on airports.

**Who's your favourite driver in the history of racing?**

Ayrton Senna and Alain Prost.

**And among those currently racing?**

No one in particular.

**Who's been your best team-mate?**

It's personal. I'd rather not say.

**If you were a team manager what drivers would you choose?**

I'll never be a team manager. I'm not interested in this type of reconversion.

**What do you love about this profession?**

Driving above all.

**What don't you like about it?**
Doing things that have nothing to do with my job.
I don't like the politics in F1 and the uncertainty
like this winter before I signed with Jordan.
It's very hard to put up with.

**What's your favourite moment of a Grand Prix?**
I like everything. When you have a good car it's
fun working with the engineers.

**Do you always get into your car on the same side?**
I get in on the left but it's really not important.

**When you stop racing, what then?**
I haven't thought about it.

**What's your favourite dish?**
Pasta and tasty hors d'oeuvres.

**And the ones you dislike?**
I like just about everything except caviar
and oysters.

**What's your favourite drink?**
Orange juice and fizzy water.

**Do you like alcohol?**
Certain cocktails like caipirinha and Red Bull
with Vodka.

**Have you ever smoked?**
Yes, occasionally.

**What sports do you do?**
I love tennis, golf, beach volleyball baseball,
basketball, gym, cycling and surfing.

**And your favourite sports?**
I like all sports.

**Who's your favourite sportsperson?**
The basketball player Michael Jordan.

**What are your hobbies/interests outside racing?**
I need to do sport. I used to ride motor bikes but it's
too dangerous. I like music and the cinema too.

**What are your favourite films?**
Recently I adored the cartoon 'Shark Tales' which I
saw coming back from Australia.

**And your favourite actors?**
Robert de Niro, Al Pacino and Robert Norton.

**What do you watch on TV?**
Motor Sports above all, big football matches
and boxing.

**What kind of music do you like?**
Hits, jazz, pop and hip hop.

**What do you like reading?**
Car magazines. I don't read a lot of books.

**What's your favourite colour?**
Blue and yellow.

**What's your favourite holiday destination?**
I like Australia very much. It's a bit far away, though.

**And your favourite place for shopping?**
Sydney but it's not exactly next-door.

**What do you collect?**
I collect certain models of Swatch watches.

**Have you got any animals?**
I love animals. I don't have any because I'm never
at home. I prefer birds, cheetahs and dolphins.
Patrica has two horses.

**Outside motor racing, whom do you admire?**
No one really.

**If you were to go to a desert island, what would
you bring?**
My girlfriend Patrica, thousands of cans of Coca
Cola and a genie to get me out of there!

**What's your perfect day?**
I'd like to be on a sunny island with Patricia and
my friends. I'd be relaxed, do a little sport, surfing
and some beach volleyball. In the evening we'd have
a good barbeque and I'd drink two or three beers.

**What's been the greatest day of your life so far?**
When I met Patricia.

**What makes you laugh the most?**
Lots of things. A satirical programme on
German TV.

**If you were not a driver what would you have done?**
I'd certainly have done another sport.
I like competition.

**What's the most important thing in life for you?**
To be happy.

**What are your best qualities?**
I'm realistic and I think I analyse things well. I try to
respect others.

**And your worst?**
Like everybody I've got a lot.

McLaren MP4/20

V10 Mercedes FO 110R (90°)

Michelin

WEST McLAREN MERCEDES

Address: McLaren International Ltd
Woking Business Park,
Albert Drive, Sheerwater
Woking, Surrey GU21 5JY,
Great Britain

Tel.: +44 (0) 1483 711 117
Fax: +44 (0) 1483 711 119
Internet: www.mclaren.com

Team founded in 1963
Grand Prix debut: Monaco 1966
Number of Grands Prix: 577

First victory: Belgium 1968 (McLaren)
Number of victories: 138

First pole position: Canada 1972 (Revson)
Number of pole positions: 115

First fastest lap: South Africa 1970 (Surtees)
Number of fastest laps: 114

First points scored: Great Britain 1966 (McLaren, 6th)
Number of points scored: 2,856.5 (2,862.5)
Points average per race: 4.95

First podium: Spain 1968 (Hulme, 2nd)
Number of podiums: 367

Constructors' World Titles: 8
(1974, 1984, 1985, 1988, 1989, 1990, 1991 and 1998).

Drivers' World Titles: 11
(E. Fittipaldi: 1974, Hunt: 1976, Lauda: 1984,
Prost: 1985, 1986 and 1989, Senna: 1988, 1990 and 1991,
Häkkinen: 1998 and 1999).

## Strengths

- Excellent driver pairing.
- Ample budget.
- Strong motivation.
- Good technical team.
- Very good test drivers.

## Weaknesses

- Driver rivalry.
- Keeping the peace between them.

## 2004 summary

- 5th in the Constructors' World Championship

- 1 victory
  (Räikkönen - Belgium)

- 1 pole position
  (Räikkönen - Great Britain)

- 69 points scored
  (Räikkönen 45, Coulthard 24)

- 24 finishes out of a possible 36
  (Coulthard 14, Räikkönen 10)

- 18 point scoring finishes
  (Räikkönen 9, Coulthard 9)

- 2 drivers used
  (Coulthard and Räikkönen).

# McLAREN-MERCEDES

**Ron Dennis (GB)**
CEO McLaren group

**Martin Whitmarsh (GB)**
General manager

**Adrian Newey (GB)**
Technical director

**Norbert Haug (D)**
Vice president
Mercedes-Benz
Motorsport

**Pedro de la Rosa (E)**
Test driver
**Alexander Wurz (A)**
3rd driver

**Number of employees**
520

Not in the twenty-one years since Ron Dennis took over the team in 1983 had McLaren finished so far down the championship ratings than in 2004. Fifth was tantamount to humiliation for the Woking squad, which hopes to phoenix in 2005. The boss has taken the risk of combining the opposing temperaments of Räikkönen and Montoya – ice against fire – which looks like a re-run of the Prost-Senna saga of the late eighties.

Another vital element in McLaren's climb back to the top of the ladder is a good car, something that has been sadly lacking in the last two years. The MP4-20 penned by Adrian Newey has shown promise in testing meeting the ambitions of both its drivers and the McLaren management. As the team did not finish in the first four in 2004 it has the right to enter a third car in the Friday practice session. Last year B.A.R owed part of its success to this advantage.

Mercedes-Benz cannot content itself with a walk-on role and seems to have overcome the early-season engine fragility shown in 2004.

At the start of August McLaren will give up smoking after many years ending its long-time reliance on the weed; this will be replaced by Johnny Walker, the famous brand of whisky. During the interseason Michael Schumacher stated that he considered McLaren as being his most dangerous rival. This threat has yet to materialise and Renault has dominated the Woking outfit in the opening grands prix, its best result being Montoya's fourth place in Malaysia.

# KIMI RAIKKÖNEN

## McLAREN MERCEDES *9

**Date and place of birth** October 17, 1979 in Espoo (Finland)
**Nationality** Finnish
**Place of residence**
Espoo (Finland), Wollerau (Switzerland) and Chigwell (GB)
**Marital status** Married to Jenni
**Height** 1.75m **Weight** 63kgs
**Internet** www.kimiraikkonen.com

## F1 results

Best F1 Championship result: 2nd in 2003 (McLaren-Mercedes)
Best F1 result: 1st (2 victories)
Best F1 qualification: 1st (3 pole positions)

2001: Sauber-Petronas • 17 GP, 9 points, 10th
2002: McLaren-Mercedes • 17 GP, 24 points, 6th
2003: McLaren-Mercedes • 16 GP, 91 points, 2nd
2004: McLaren-Mercedes • 18 GP, 45 points, 7th

He is nicknamed the 'Ice Man' a slogan that he openly displays on his helmet. Maybe some of his nocturnal escapades in nightclubs during the interseason give lie to the above! Wanting to sink his teeth into the very stuff of existence he has behaved like any man. And who could blame him? Well, McLaren for one whose bosses got on their high horse because of these capers that are incompatible with their team's reputation. Räikkönen was furious and said that he liked doing things his way. "*If somebody doesn't appreciate me, I don't give a damn.*"

Flavio Briatore never misses an opportunity for a dig at his rivals: "*if Kimi had been one of my drivers, he'd have had no problems! A young guy isn't a robot. He has to let off steam provided he doesn't get up to mischief the night before a race!*"

The Finn's character is in stainless steel. If his private life is a bit turbulent, on the track he is as cool as a cucumber. The fact that he is up against the fiery Montoya seems to have helped him mature. Last year he was plagued by his McLaren's reliability, or rather lack of it. This season he seems to have the car to take him to the top. McLaren is counting on the healthy rivalry between the two to get back to where it thinks it belongs. In 2003, Räikkönen put Schumacher under a lot of pressure during the final grand prix of the season, and he will do the same again should the opportunity present itself.

## Titles
- 1998: Karting Formule A Champion (Finland and Scandinavia).
- 1999: Winner of the Formula Renault Winter Series.
- 2000: British Formula Renault Champion.

## Career summary
Competition debut: 1990 (karting)
GP debut: Australia 2001 (Sauber-Petronas)

- 68 Grands Prix
- 169 points scored
- Average per Grand Prix: 2.48
- 18 podiums
- 2 victories
- 10 2nd places
- 6 3rd places
- 6 4th places
- 2 5th place
- 4 6th places
- 1 7th places [*]
- 1 8th place [*]

- 3 pole positions
- 6 fastest laps
- 16 GP in the lead
- 1071 kms in the lead
- 209 laps in the lead

\* Since 2003 and the attribution of points
  to 7th and 8th places.

## Team-mates
2001: N. Heidfeld
2002, 2003 and 2004: D. Coulthard

## Qualifications 2004
Räikkönen 12 / Coulthard 6

# QUESTIONS

# KIMI RAIKKÖNEN

**What was the first car you drove?**
A Lada in Finland.

**And today?**
A Mercedes-Benz ML 55 AMG in Switzerland and a C32 AMG in Finland.

**What is your favourite/dream car?**
Lamborghinis and the Ferrari Modena.

**What does your helmet design mean?**
A Finnish painter did it. I wanted the colours of the Finnish flag. Since last year he's added a red band. I've changed decorations several times in my career.

**What's been your best racing car so far?**
Driving the McLaren was a dream.

**And the worst?**
The Formula Ford.

**What's your best racing memory?**
My first rostrum finish in Australia in 2002 is a good one. My first victory in Malaysia in 2003 has a special place in my memory and the one at Spa in 2004 is also very special after a difficult start to the season.

**And your worst?**
In general, I try to be positive and erase any disappointments from my memory.

**Do you remember the first Grand Prix you saw on TV?**
I must've been very young.

**And the first one you attended?**
I never saw a Grand Prix before my debut in 2001.

**What's your aim in racing?**
I always wanted to be an F1 driver.

**What's your favourite circuit?**
Donington and Spa.

**And the one you dislike the most?**
I like all the circuits. Each one is unique and deserves to stay in the championship. I've always had a problem with the first corner on the Suzuka track.

**Who's your favourite driver in the history of racing?**
Ayrton Senna.

**And among those currently racing?**
I liked Mika Häkkinen. I chat to all the drivers before the parade but in F1 you can't really have friends.

**Who's been your best team-mate?**
No one in particular.

**If you were a team manager what drivers would you choose?**
I've never asked myself that question.

**What do you love about this profession?**
Fighting to win.

**What don't you like about it?**
The overbearing influence of the medias and the promotions that go with F1. I know, alas, that that's part of my job.

**What's your favourite moment of a Grand Prix?**
Being on the limit in the car.

**Do you always get into your car on the same side?**
No, I'm not superstitious.

**When you stop racing, what then?**
I can imagine myself sun tanning on a beach and going snowboarding.

**What's your favourite dish?**
Pasta with mushroom sauce. I like chicken in all its forms and a typical Finnish dish based on reindeer.

**And the ones you dislike?**
None especially.

**What's your favourite drink?**
Pineapple juice, Coca Cola and water.

**Do you like alcohol?**
No.

**Have you ever smoked?**
No.

**What sports do you do?**
Snowboard, moto cross, ice hockey, jogging, cycling and gymnastics.

**And your favourite sports?**
The ones I do and all forms of motor sports.

**Who's your favourite sportsperson?**
I've got a lot of respect for some athletes who excel in their field. I'd also mention Michael Johnson and Tiger Woods, but nobody in particular really.

**What are your hobbies/interests outside racing?**
I love racing too much. I've just set up my own F3 team in England with my manager Steve Roberts: it's called Räikkönen Robertson Racing. I'm not doing it for money but to help youngsters.

**What are your favourite films?**
Generally I like action movies. I liked 'Million Dollar Baby' with Clint Eastwood.

**And your favourite actors?**
I don't really have any. In this movie I liked Clint Eastwood.

**What do you watch on TV?**
All forms of motor sport.

**What kind of music do you like?**
Eminem.

**What do you like reading?**
Motor racing magazines. I never read books because I don't like reading.

**What's your favourite colour?**
Blue.

**What's your favourite holiday destination?**
I'm not very keen on going on holiday. I like spending my free time at home in Switzerland or in Epsoo in Finland.

**And your favourite place for shopping?**
I like going to Metzgen, to Hugo Boss.

**What do you collect?**
All snowboarding gadget.

**Have you got any animals?**
I haven't got any as I travel too much but I love animals.

**Outside motor racing, whom do you admire?**
I've got a lot of respect for my parents.

**If you were to go to a desert island, what would you bring?**
A lot of food, my wife Jenny and a helicopter.

**What's your perfect day?**
Being with Jenny and relaxing at home in Switzerland or Finland.

**What's been the greatest day of your life so far?**
I'm sure it's still to come.

**What makes you laugh the most?**
Jokes and taking the mickey!

**If you were not a driver what would you have done?**
I'd have been a professional ice hockey player.

**What's the most important thing in life for you?**
To make your dreams come true.

**What are your best qualities?**
Maybe you should ask my mother!

**And your worst?**
I'm too serious!

# JUAN PABLO MONTOYA

## McLAREN MERCEDES *10

**Date and place of birth**
September 20, 1975 in Bogota (Colombia)
**Nationality** Colombian
**Place of residence** Monte-Carlo, Oxford (GB) and Madrid (E)
**Marital status** Married to Connie, one son, Sebastien
**Height** 1.68m  **Weight** 66kgs
**Internet** www.jpmontoya.com

## F1 Results

Best F1 championship result: 3rd in 2002 and 2003 (Williams-BMW)
Best F1 result: 1st (3 victories)
Best F1 qualification: 1st (11 pole-positions)

2001: Williams-BMW • 17 GP, 31 points, 6th
2002: Williams-BMW • 17 GP, 50 points, 3rd
2003: Williams-BMW • 16 GP, 82 points, 3rd
2004: Williams-BMW • 18 GP, 58 points, 5th

In the USA he was simply known as Juan. Having won the Cart title and the Indianapolis 500 Miles he no longer had anything left to prove over there and came back to Europe to tackle the challenge of F1 preceded by a flattering reputation. His four years at Williams were not as successful as expected yielding only 4 victories. He has certainly lacked consistency and his Latin temperament has not helped either.

He left Williams on a winning note thanks to his victory in 2004 Brazilian Grand Prix. If it inspired any regrets in Frank Williams, he did not show it and did little to try to hang on to the Colombian. His transfer to McLaren was probably the earliest ever announced in the history of F1 (over a year). The battle between himself and Kimi Räikkönen should add a lot of spice to the season given their completely different temperaments: what they have in common is driving ambition. Juan Pablo has lost weight and physically is in better shape than ever before; he wants to be at the head of the field despite the threat of his team-mate. At present he seems to have adapted well to his new team, and his boss, the enigmatic Ron Dennis, reckons that the Colombian has not yet fulfilled his potential. The McLaren MP4-20 showed a lot of promise in pre-race testing so he has the ideal weapon to make it to the top. Now the time has come for him to live up to his reputation. Should he fail to do so then his F1 career will inevitably go into decline.

## Titles

- 1991 and 1992: Junior Karting World Champion.
- 1998: F3000 International Champion.
- 1999: CART Champion (USA).
- 2000: Winner of the Indy 500 Miles.

## Career summary

Competition debut: 1981 (karting)
Grand Prix debut: Australia 2001 (Williams-BMW)

- 68 Grands Prix
- 221 points scored
- Average per Grand Prix: 3.25
- 23 podiums
- 4 victories
- 13 2nd places
- 3 3rd places
- 8 4th places
- 6 5th places
- 1 6th place
- 2 7th places*
- 2 8th places*

- 11 pole positions
- 11 fastest laps
- 24 GP in the lead
- 1792 kms in the lead
- 382 laps in the lead

\* Since 2003 and the attribution of points
  to 7th and 8th places.

## Team-mates

2001 and 2002: R. Schumacher
2003: R. Schumacher and M. Gené
2004: R. Schumacher, M. Gené and A. Pizzonia

## Qualifications 2004

Montoya 9 / R. Schumacher 3
Montoya 2 / Gené 0
Montoya 3 / Pizzonia 1

# QUESTIONS

# JUAN PABLO MONTOYA

**What was the first car you drove?**

My dad's car when I was fourteen.

**And today?**

I drive a Mercedes-Benz SL.

**What is your favourite/dream car?**

I'd love to have driven Graham Hill's Lotus 49.
It must've been wild! I've got my dream car but it's
not a BMW.

**What does your helmet design mean?**

The overall outline was created with my father's
help. Since my debut I've hardly changed it.
Of course, there are the colours of the Colombian
flag and the base, which was white, is now chrome.

**What's been your best racing car so far?**

The Williams FW 19 when I was test driver in 1998.

**And the worst?**

No comment.

**What's your best racing memory?**

The 1999 CART title and my Indy victory in 2000 first
time out. In Formula 1 my win in Monaco in 2003
gave me a great deal of pleasure.

**And your worst?**

Mistakes are always a help for the future; that's my
philosophy on this subject.

**Do you remember the first grand prix you saw on
TV?**

I don't really remember but it was a long time ago. I
admired Senna's exploits. It was at the end of the
eighties.

**And the first one you attended?**

In Jerez in 1997 when Villeneuve won the title. I
came to sign my contract with Williams as a test
driver.

**What's your aim in racing?**

It's simple: win!

**What's your favourite circuit?**

None in particular.

**And the one you dislike the most?**

I don't like Barcelona; it's not that interesting from a
driving point of view.

**Who's your favourite driver in the history of
racing?**

I admired Ayrton Senna.

**And among those currently racing?**

I like joking with Rubens Barrichello before the
parade.

**Who's been your best team-mate?**
I've never had problems with my team-mates.

**If you were a team manager what drivers would you choose?**
Luckily, I'm not a team manager.

**What do you love about this profession?**
It's the permanent challenge.

**What don't you like about it?**
All the incompetent people that you find in the paddock.

**What's your favourite moment of a Grand Prix?**
I like qualifying when you push the car right to the limit.

**Do you always get into your car on the same side?**
No, I'm not superstitious.

**When you stop racing, what then?**
The idea hasn't even crossed my mind.

**What's your favourite dish?**
Pasta.

**And the ones you dislike?**
I don't like vegs.

**What's your favourite drink?**
Orange juice.

**Do you like alcohol?**
A glass of red wine from time to time.

**Have you ever smoked?**
No.

**What sports do you do?**
I like going for a bike ride. I play some squash and do some jogging. I don't like gyms. They stink!

Generally speaking I like all forms of water sports. Surfing is my favourite pastime whenever I go to Miami. I also like water skiing.

**And your favourite sports?**
Anything with an engine.

**Who's your favourite sportsperson?**
I like motor sports: really there aren't any others, which give me a buzz.

**What are your hobbies/interests outside racing?**
Computers and video games. I have over 100 of them, mainly football games.

**What are your favourite films?**
Recently, I've seen 'Aviator.'

**And your favourite actors?**
Andy McDowell and Will Smith are very funny.

**What do you watch on TV?**
I don't like TV.

**What kind of music do you like?**
I like rock and some Colombian musicians.

**What do you like reading?**
I only read motor sport magazines.

**What's your favourite colour?**
Blue and white.

**What's your favourite holiday destination?**
Miami beach where I have a house. I can do surfing, jet ski and water skiing.

**And your favourite place for shopping?**
It's also Miami.

**What do you collect?**
I've got a lot of video games most of which have been sent to me for free. On the other hand I can lash out a lot of money on a watch. I've got twenty and they've cost me a small fortune!

**Have you got any animals?**
I haven't got any and I hate dogs and cats.

**Outside motor racing, whom do you admire?**
Maybe some sports people.

**If you were to go to a desert island, what would you bring?**
My wife, Connie.

**What's your perfect day?**
Keep my feet on the ground. I like being together with Connie or with friends. I like being laid back, calm, playing some Playstation.

**What's been the greatest day of your life so far?**
I'm still waiting for it.

**What makes you laugh the most?**
When I joke with Connie. We sometimes laugh a lot with certain video games.

**If you were not a driver what would you have done?**
Been an architect like my dad.

**What's the most important thing in life for you?**
Respect others.

**What are your best qualities?**
I'm persevering.

**And your worst?**
I don't know.

Sauber C24

V10 Petronas 05A /
Ferrari 054 (90°)

Michelin

Address: Sauber Motorsport AG
Wildbachstrasse 9
CH-8340 Hinwil
Switzerland

Tel.: +41 (0)1-937 90 00
Fax: +41 (0)1-937 90 01
Internet: www.sauber-petronas.com

Team founded in 1970
Grand Prix debut: South Africa 1993
Number of Grands Prix: 197

Number of victories: 0
Best result: 3$^{rd}$ (6 times)

Number of pole positions: 0
Best qualification: 2$^{nd}$ (2 times)

Number of fastest laps: 0

First points scored: South Africa 1993 (Lehto, 5$^{th}$)
Number of points scored: 175
Points average per race: 0.88

First podium: Italy 1995 (Frentzen, 3$^{rd}$)
Number of podiums: 6

Best classification in the Constructors' World Championship:
4$^{th}$ in 2001
Best classification in the Drivers' World Championship:
8$^{th}$ in 2001 (Heidfeld)

## Strengths

- Close collaboration with Ferrari.
- Arrival of Villeneuve.
- Massa's ambition.
- Good technical staff.
- Arrival of Michelin.
- Desire to progress.

## Weaknesses

- Enough cash?
- No major manufacturer.
- Test driver?

## 2004 summary

- 6$^{th}$ in the Constructors' World Championship
- Best result: 4$^{th}$
  (Fisichella - Canada, Massa - Belgium)
- Best qualification: 4$^{th}$
  (Massa - China and Brazil)
- 34 points scored
  (Fisichella 22, Massa 12)
- 30 finishes out of a possible 36
  (Fisichella 16, Massa 14)
- 14 points scoring finishes
  (Fisichella 9, Massa 5)
- 2 drivers used
  (Fisichella and Massa)

# SAUBER-PETRONAS

**Peter Sauber (CH)**
Team principal

**Willy Rampf (CH)**
Technical director

**Jacky Eeckelaert (B)**
Development
director

**Neel Jani (CH)**
Test driver

**Number of employees**
270

On the grid for the Malaysian Grand Prix Mario Thiessen, BMW's engineering director, took a close look at one of the Saubers and scribbled down some notes in a small notebook. Rumour has it that a partnership is in the offing between the Munich giant and the little Swiss team indicating that the relationship between Sauber and Ferrari is over. The exorbitant price charged by the Italian firm for its engines probably has something to do with this.

With the departure of its faithful sponsor, Red Bull, determined to go its own way, Peter Sauber and his men seem to be at a turning point in their history and they well know that a team nourishing any long-term ambition today needs the support of a major manufacturer.

Discrete is the best adjective to describe Peter Sauber but the arrival of Jacques Villeneuve created a media frenzy around his team. The presence of the world champion, who is still scrabbling for grip, is an obvious advantage for Sauber. His team-mate, Felipe Massa, is still as quick as ever and seems to have calmed down so the team should be able to pick up some points. The new wind tunnel has come on stream and this allied to good tyres (Michelin) and the Ferrari engine opens up promising horizons for the Hinwill outfit. If Sauber chooses to enter a third car for Friday's practice it could help them gain valuable information.

The C25 is considered as being one of the most evolved machines of the 2005 field but it still needs fettling in to enable its drivers to get the best out of it.

# JACQUES VILLENEUVE

## SAUBER PETRONAS *11

**Date and place of birth**
April 9, 1971 in St-Jean-sur-Richelieu, Québec (Canada)
**Nationality** Canadian
**Place of residence** Monte-Carlo (Monaco)
**Marital status** Engaged to Ellen
**Height** 1.71m **Weight** 63kgs
**Internet** www.jv-world.com

## F1 results

Best F1 Championship result: World Champion in 1997, (Williams)
Best F1 result: 1st (11 victories)
Best F1 qualification: 1st (13 pole positions)

1996: Williams-Renault • 16 GP, 78 pts, 2nd
1997: Williams-Renault • 17 GP, 81 pts, World Champion
1998: Williams-Mecachrome • 16 GP, 21 pts, 5th
1999: B.A.R-Supertec • 16 GP, 0 pt, 21st
2000: B.A.R-Honda • 17 GP, 17 pts, 7th
2001: B.A.R-Honda • 17 GP, 12 pts, 7th
2002: B.A.R-Honda • 17 GP, 4 pts, 12th
2003: B.A.R-Honda • 15 GP, 6 pts, 16th
2004: Renault • 3 GP, 0 pt, 21st

At the end of 2003 Jacques Villeneuve decided to take a year off after five very tough seasons at BAR. The 1997 world champion allowed himself to be tempted by Renault at the end of 2004 after Trulli's eviction and came back for the last three grands prix. Although he was dominated by Alonso he managed to get himself taken on by Sauber and began the 2005 championship rarin' to go. Villeneuve's name is known throughout the world and F1 needs people like him. He is as motivated as when he made his debut and in tiptop physical form. During winter testing he gradually dialled himself back in although overshadowed by his team-mate Felipe Massa. He brings enormous experience acquired in both the USA and Europe to his team and hopefully this will help Sauber move up the F1 ladder. He is driven by the same burning determination as his team and he is hoping to recapture the panache that has become part of his legend. He is capable of awesome exploits and on his debut in 1996 in Australia he snatched pole. A year later after a memorable skirmish with Michael Schumacher's Ferrari at Jerez he become world champion.

His return to the F1 fold should be cause for rejoicing for all die-hard enthusiasts.

## Titles
- 1995: CART Champion (United States) and Winner of the Indy 500 Miles.
- 1997: Formula 1 World Champion.

## En bref...
Competition debut: 1986 (Jim Russel School)
Grand Prix debut: Australia 1996 (Williams-Renault)

- 134 Grands Prix
- 219 points scored
- Average per Grand Prix: 1.63
- 23 podiums
- 11 victories
- 5 2nd places
- 7 3rd places
- 11 4th places
- 6 5th places
- 6 6th places

- 13 pole positions
- 9 fastest lap
- 20 GP in the lead
- 2,965 kms in the lead
- 533 laps in the lead

## Team-mates
1996: D. Hill
1997 and 1998: H.H. Frentzen
1999 and 2000: R. Zonta
2001 and 2002: O. Panis
2003: J. Button
2004: F. Alonso

## Qualifications
Villeneuve 1 / Alonso 2

# QUESTIONS

# JACQUES VILLENEUVE

**What was the first car you drove?**

It was a Fiat Uno. I'd just turned eighteen and I upset a policeman after going through a red light.

**And today?**

I've got a Subaru Legacy.

**What is your favourite/dream car?**

I like the American cars of the sixties.

**What does your helmet design mean?**

I designed my own motif at the start of my career. I wanted something a bit unusual. I like these colours. Among my sources of inspiration was my father's helmet's decoration.

**What's been your best racing car so far?**

The Williams FW 19 in which I won the Drivers' World Championship in 1997.

**And the worst?**

The 1999 BAR; it was a real truck, a nightmare.

**What's your best racing memory?**

My world title at Jerez in 1997 and my win in the Indy 500 Miles in 1995.

**And your worst?**

It was in Formula Atlantic in Phoenix in 1994. I crashed and my car was cut in half. My first season with BAR in 1999 is also a bad memory: we didn't even score a point!

**Do you remember the first Grand Prix you saw on TV?**

No, I don't. I grew up on the circuits with my parents.

**And the first one you attended?**

I don't remember, as I was very young. Probably my father's first drive in a Ferrari at the end of 1977 but I'm not really sure. Otherwise it was at the start of 1978.

**What's your aim in racing?**

To win.

**What's your favourite circuit?**

Elkhart Lake in the USA.

**And the one you dislike the most?**

The Detroit circuit and I'm not that keen on Interlagos.

**Who's your favourite driver in the history of racing?**

I had a lot of idols when I was a kid. It doesn't have much meaning for me today.

**And among those currently racing?**

David Coulthard is a good mate. I also liked Olivier Panis when we were at BAR.

**Who's been your best team-mate?**

Olivier Panis.

**If you were a team manager what drivers would you choose?**

I must admit that the question has never even crossed my mind.

**What do you love about this profession?**

The notion of danger. Being on the razor's edge, driving at the limit.

**What don't you like about it?**

I don't like the importance of politics in the sport and certain egos in the paddock. I sometimes feel that I'm in a kiddies' playground. Also I'm not very keen on public relations.

**What's your favourite moment of a Grand Prix?**
If you are in the lead, the finish is the best moment of a grand prix because you've won.

**Do you always get into your car on the same side?**
I nearly always get in on the same side because the mechanics are on the other. It's not superstition; it's practical.

**When you stop racing, what then**
I'd like to have children.

**What's your favourite dish?**
Pasta.

**And the ones you dislike?**
I hate spicy food and onions.

**What's your favourite drink?**
Milk and root beer.

**Do you like alcohol?**
I like having a glass of red wine or a beer. A cocktail in the evening from time to time also goes down well.

**Have you ever smoked?**
No.

**What sports do you do?**
I took advantage of my break to do a lot of skiing and ice hockey. I'm crazy about these sports. Otherwise I do a lot of roller-skating and physical training.

**And your favourite sports?**
Downhill skiing and ice hockey.

**Who's your favourite sportsperson?**
People who aren't afraid to take risks like downhill skiers.

**What are your hobbies/interests outside racing?**
Play the guitar, write and listen to music. I'm also mad about anything that's electronic.

**What are your favourite films?**
There are a lot I like at present. 'Elvis GratonXXX', a Canadian film, 'Wanted' and 'Der Schuh des Manitou' two Austrian movies.

**And your favourite actors?**
Nobody in particular.

**What do you watch on TV?**
The MTV musical channel and clips.

**What kind of music do you like?**
I love the piece Who Killed by The Zutons, the Maroons and Natalia Imbruglia's second album.

**What do you like reading?**
Nothing special at present.

**What's your favourite colour?**
If I had to choose, I'd go for blue. But I don't really have a favourite colour.

**What's your favourite holiday destination?**
In my Chalet in Villars in the Swiss Alps. In summer I like being on a boat on the Med.

**And your favourite place for shopping?**
I don't like shopping unless it's for CDs or books.

**What do you collect?**
Everything that involves music and the world of computers.

**Have you got any animals?**
I've got a cat called Eartha Kitten!

**Outside motor racing, whom do you admire?**
Nobody in particular.

**If you were to go to a desert island, what would you bring?**
I wouldn't like to be alone.

**What's your perfect day?**
Have a good breakfast, being in the sun, relaxing. Then have a good meal that goes on and on, have a coffee, laze about, the 'Dolce Vita!'.

**What's been the greatest day of your life so far?**
I hope it's still to come.

**What makes you laugh the most?**
Satire and black humour. I like films such as Austin Powers and cartoons like Beavis and Buthead.

**If you were not a driver what would you have done?**
I'd probably have gone into music. But I'd have to make a lot of progress to earn my living. If not, skiing, my other passion.

**What's the most important thing in life for you?**
To be happy.

**What are your best qualities?**
I like being myself.

**And your worst?**
I'm very badly organised and above all very selfish!

# FELIPE MASSA

## SAUBER PETRONAS *12

**Date and place of birth** April 25, 1981 in São Paolo (Brazil)
**Nationality** Brazilian
**Place of residence** Hinwil (Switzerland)
**Marital status** Engaged to Rafaela
**Height** 1.66m  **Weight** 59kgs
**Internet** www.felipemassa.com

### F1 results

Best F1 Championship result: 12th in 2004 (Sauber-Petronas)
Best F1 result: 4th (Belgium 2004)
Best F1 qualification: 4th (China and Brazil 2004)

2002: Sauber-Petronas • 16 GP, 4 points, 13th
2004: Sauber-Petronas • 18 GP, 12 points, 12th

In 2002, the little Brazilian made his debut with Sauber. His very loose fling-it-about style quickly caught the pundits' attention. The following year he became a Ferrari test driver and as he was not under pressure he was able to develop his concentration and emerged a transformed individual from his stint with the Scuderia. In 2004, he was back with the Swiss team and his performances had little to envy those of Fisichella.

His outright speed has not suffered and this season it will be interesting to compare him with his much more experienced team-mate, Jacques Villeneuve. If he wants to reach the top he has to beat the illustrious Canadian.

He is at a critical turning point in his career as his contract runs out at the end of 2005 so his aim must be one of the top teams. His excellent relationship with the Scuderia could be a help and his manager is Nicolas Todt, Jean's son. When Michael Schumacher decides to hang up his helmet, this could play in his favour.

He is another championship pretender. He is a real fighter behind the wheel but when he gets out of the car he is a calm, smiling individual with a twinkle in his eyes. Like many he awaits his hour of glory.

## Titles

- 1999: Brazilian Formula Chevrolet-Opel Champion.
- 2000: European and Italian Formula Renault Champion.
- 2001: European Italian F3000 Champion.

## Career summary

Competition debut: 1990 (karting).
Grand Prix debut: Australia 2002 (Sauber-Petronas)

- 34 Grands Prix
- 16 points scored
- Average per Grand Prix: 0.47
- 0 podiums
- 0 victories
- 1 4th place
- 2 5th places
- 2 6th places
- 3 8th places[*]

- 0 pole positions
- 0 fastest laps
- 1 GP in the lead
- 9 kms in the lead
- 2 laps in the lead

* Since 2003 and the attribution of points
  to 7th and 8th places.

## Team-mates

2002: N. Heidfeld
2004: G. Fisichella

## Qualifications 2004

Massa 7 / Fisichella 11

# QUESTIONS

## FELIPE MASSA

**What's been your best racing car so far?**
Last year's Sauber in which I had some good qualifying results and also at Spa during the race. The Sauber C 23 was a great car.

**And the worst?**
The Chevrolet-Opel Formula in Brazil in 1999. I don't have good memories of the Sauber in Monaco in 2002 either.

**What's your best racing memory?**
My fourth place at Spa in the Sauber. And my fourth place in qualifying in Brazil was another exceptional memory.

**And your worst?**
My accident in the first corner in my first Grand Prix in Australia in 2002.

**Do you remember the first Grand Prix you saw on TV?**
I must've been about four.

**And the first one you attended?**
I think it was at Interlagos in 1988. I remember Senna in the McLaren.

**What's your aim in racing?**
Become Formula 1 World Champion.

**What's your favourite circuit?**
Fast circuits like Spa and Mugello.

**And the one you dislike the most?**
I hate Varano in Italy. It's a Mickey Mouse track.

**Who's your favourite driver in the history of racing?**
I was thirteen when Senna was killed at Imola. I was too young to follow his exploits. I also liked Nelson Piquet very much.

**What was the first car you drove?**
I must've been around eight or nine. I really don't remember the car but I'm sure I gave it a good hammering!

**And today?**
I've just changed Subarus. I've now got a Legacy instead of an Imprezza.

**What is your favourite/dream car?**
The Ferrari Enzo.

**What does your helmet design mean?**
A painter called Sid in Brazil did it. He copied the colours of my father's helmet just replacing the orange with yellow. The design includes a big M like our name.

**And among those currently racing?**
I've a lot of admiration for Michael Schumacher whom I was lucky enough to get to know last year at Ferrari.

**Who's been your best team-mate?**
I think it's Nick Heidfeld.

**If you were a team manager what drivers would you choose?**
Michael Schumacher and me.

**What do you love about this profession?**
The sensation of speed and the adrenaline.

**What don't you like about it?**
Not much, really.

**What's your favourite moment of a Grand Prix?**
The opening laps of a race and being well-placed to battle it out for a good finishing position.

**Do you always get into your car on the same side?**
I always get in on the left-hand side.

**When you stop racing, what then?**
Keep on racing even if it's in other categories.

**What's your favourite dish?**
Any kind of pasta, meat and Brazilian cooking like Churrascaria.

**And the ones you dislike?**
None really.

**What's your favourite drink?**
Rostrum champagne.

**Do you like alcohol?**
Sometimes, on big occasions.

**Have you ever smoked?**
No. I hate it.

**What sports do you do?**
Jogging, cycling, muscle building, swimming and tennis.

**And your favourite sports?**
Football, jet skiing and water skiing.

**Who's your favourite sportsperson?**
I really like football. I follow the performances of Sao Paolo, Barcelona, Real Madrid and Milan AC. I like Ronaldhino who gets the FC Barcelona all fevered up. I've also got a lot of admiration for bike rider Valentino Rossi and Roger Federer in tennis.

**What are your hobbies/interests outside racing?**
Going to the cinema, listening to music and going out with friends. Nothing special really.

**What are your favourite films?**
Recently I saw Aviator with Leonardo di Caprio. I also liked Troy with Brad Pitt.

**And your favourite actors?**
How about Brad Pitt and Angelina Jolie!

**What do you watch on TV?**
Mainly films and some sports documentaries.

**What kind of music do you like?**
I like black music and the latest hits.

**What do you like reading?**
Motor Car magazines and those dealing with general information.

**What's your favourite colour?**
Blue.

**What's your favourite holiday destination?**
Brazil, of course. I like going to Angra dos Reis and Ilhabela.

**And your favourite place for shopping?**
London, Paris and Milan.

**What do you collect?**
Watches. I've got some pretty nice ones including a Richard Mille. Otherwise clothes.

**Have you got any animals?**
I've got two Labradors in Brazil.

**Outside motor racing, whom do you admire?**
My family.

**If you were to go to a desert island, what would you bring?**
My girl-friend, Rafaela, and a gun to blow my brains out if I found myself alone with no way of getting off!

**What's your perfect day?**
A day's holiday.

**What's been the greatest day of your life so far?**
I hope it's still to come.

**What makes you laugh the most?**
A lot of things make me laugh. I laugh easily. I'm not difficult to please!

**If you were not a driver what would you have done?**
I haven't got the slightest idea!

**What's the most important thing in life for you?**
My family and the races.

**What are your best qualities?**
I'm a pretty happy-go-lucky kind of guy. I like talking to people and I think I'm easily approachable.

**And your worst?**
No, of course not!! (laughs).

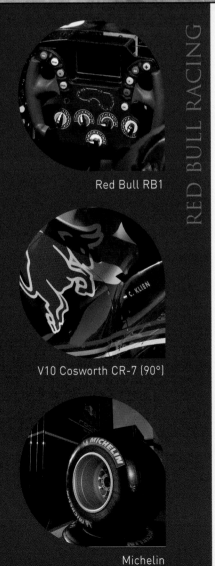

Red Bull RB1

V10 Cosworth CR-7 (90°)

Michelin

Address: Red Bull Racing
Bradbourne Drive, Tilbrook,
Milton Keynes, MK7 8BJ,
Great Britain

Tel.: +44 (0)1908 27 97 00
Fax: +44 (0)1908 27 97 11
Internet: www.redbullf1.com

Team founded in 2004
Grand Prix debut: Australia 2005

## Strengths

- Coulthard's experience.
- Battle between Klien and Liuzzi.
- Good Cosworth engine.
- Hungry for success.

## Weaknesses

- New team.
- Rivalry between Klien and Liuzzi.
- Enough cash?
- Inexperienced technical staff.
- No major manufacturer.

# RBR-COSWORTH

**Dietrich Mateschitz (AUT)**
Owner

**Helmut Marko (AUT)**
General manager

**Christian Horner (GB)**
Team manager

**Günther Steiner (I)**
Technical director

**Vitantonio Liuzzi (I)**
3rd driver

**Number of employees**
270

The big surprise of the start of the 2005 season! Red Bull, producer of the eponymous energetic drink, was a long-time sponsor of Sauber, until its boss, Dietrich Mateschitz, decided to fulfil his dream and bought the Jaguar team dropped by Ford. Suddenly it has all come together and the cars now painted blue, an evolution of last year's model, have found a hitherto unsuspected level of performance. David Coulthard and a restructured management team have given a new lease of life to the previously moribund team, which hit the ground running right from the first grand prix. The car's reliability and performance have enabled the Scot and Christian Klien to score points in both early season races. David has certainly been one of the movers and shakers behind this success. Liberated from the politically correct shackles at McLaren he has sunk his teeth into this new challenge and is driving as well if not better than ever before. His immense experience is of great benefit to his young team-mates. What could cause problems is the team's policy in this area. Klien has made a great start to the season but may be replaced by Vitantonio Liuzzi after the Bahrain Grand Prix. Such a policy of driver swapping is liable to put a lot of unnecessary pressure on inexperienced shoulders. Dietrich Mateschitz has long dreamed of having an F1 team with a strong American flavour to it and young US coming man, Scott Speed, could well be the first link in the chain. Finally, Red Bull has injected a note of irreverence and freshness into the stodgy atmosphere of the paddock as Eddie Jordan did in 1991.

# DAVID COULTHARD

## RBR COSWORTH *14

**Date and place of birth**
March 27, 1971 in Twynholm (Scotland)
**Nationality** Scottish
**Place of residence** Monaco
**Marital status** Single
**Height** 1.82m **Weight** 72.5kgs
**Internet** www.davidcoulthard-f1.com

## F1 results

Best F1 Championship result: 2nd in 2001 (McLaren-Mercedes)
Best F1 result: 1st (13 victories)
Best F1 qualification: 1st (12 pole positions)

1994: Williams-Renault • 8 GP, 14 points, 8th
1995: Williams-Renault • 17 GP, 49 points, 3rd
1996: McLaren-Mercedes • 16 GP, 18 points, 7th
1997: McLaren-Mercedes • 17 GP, 36 points, 3rd
1998: McLaren-Mercedes • 16 GP, 56 points, 3rd
1999: McLaren-Mercedes • 16 GP, 45 points, 4th
2000: McLaren-Mercedes • 17 GP, 73 points, 3rd
2001: McLaren-Mercedes • 17 GP, 65 points, 2nd
2002: McLaren-Mercedes • 17 GP, 41 points, 5th
2003: McLaren-Mercedes • 16 GP, 51 points, 7th
2004: McLaren-Mercedes • 18 GP, 24 points, 10th

Just over a year ago McLaren announced the arrival of Juan Pablo Montoya. It was a rather inelegant way of telling David Coulthard that his time was up, and announced the end of a 9-year collaboration during which the Scot had racked up a good series of results. He never showed quite the same consistency as the two 'Flying Finns,' Mika Häkkinen and Kimi Räikkönen, who always had the whip hand over him. Of course, he was convinced that one day it would all come good; that next year was going to be his year, and never had he been better prepared to win the world championship. Alas, his dream never came true.

This winter David found himself at a crossroads. He did not want to go into semi-retirement and turned down a testing role at Ferrari. A few weeks later he signed as no.1 with new arrival, Red Bull. His enormous experience will be very useful to the fledgling outfit; he is not afraid of the responsibility involved in getting the team up and running and is counting on his young team-mates to help him fulfil this delicate mission. In Melbourne he finished in an excellent fourth place. He is in top form and his rage to win is stronger than ever.

Although he has a one-year contract the idea of hanging up his helmet does not seem to have crossed his mind. Released from the shackles of McLaren DC has changed his look and his pugnacious chin now sports a few days' growth dappled with grey.

## Titles
- 1989: Formula Ford 1600 Junior Champion .
- 1991: Winner of the F3 Macao and Marlboro Masters race.

## Career summary
Competition debut: 1983 (karting)
Grand Prix debut: Spain 1994 (Williams-Renault)

- 175 Grands Prix
- 475 points scored
- Average per Grand Prix: 2.71
- 60 podiums
- 13 victories
- 26 2nd places
- 21 3rd places
- 9 4th places
- 16 5th places
- 11 6th places
- 4 7th places*
- 1 8th place*

- 12 pole positions
- 18 fastest laps
- 58 GP in the lead
- 4195 Kms in the lead
- 894 laps in the lead

\* Since 2003 and the attribution of points
to 7th and 8th places.

## Team-mates
1994 and 1995: D. Hill
1996, 1997, 1998, 1999, 2000 and 2001: M. Häkkinen
2002, 2003 and 2004: K. Räikkönen

## Qualifications 2004
Coulthard 6 / Räikkönen 12

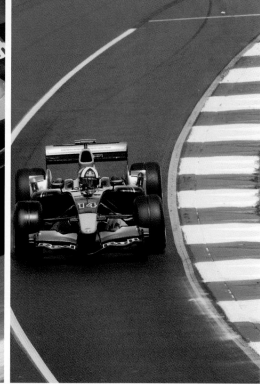

# QUESTIONS

# DAVID COULTHARD

**What does your helmet design mean?**
I've always used this helmet decoration since my debut. My dad's transport company helped a driver who created the design for my helmet. In fact, it's just the Scottish flag.

**What's been your best racing car so far?**
Difficult to make a choice between all my F1s since 1994.

**And the worst?**
The 1990 Vauxhall Lotus.

**What's your best racing memory?**
My next victory. Otherwise Macao in F3 in 1991 and my first F1 win at Estoril in 1995.

**And your worst?**
Always the last race I didn't win.

**Do you remember the first Grand Prix you saw on TV?**
No, I don't.

**And the first one you attended?**
At Paul Ricard in 1990 when there was a Vauxhall Lotus race.

**What's your aim in racing?**
Become world champion. Before I dreamed of becoming a pilot.

**What's your favourite circuit?**
Spa which I'm glad we'll be racing on again.

**And the one you dislike the most?**
I'm not very keen on Budapest.

**Who's your favourite driver in the history of racing?**
Jackie Stewart and Alain Prost, two great champions that I've been lucky enough to get to know.

**And among those currently racing?**
Jacques Villeneuve. We're motor home neighbours during the European Grands Prix. I'm glad to see him back.

**What was the first car you drove?**
It was when I was on my father's knees. I must've been about eight.

**And today?**
I drive a Mercedes E55AMG Estate and a Smart when I'm in Monaco. The E55 is a great car; it's got a lot of room and its performance is unbelievable for a road car. The cops have caught me on a couple of occasions for being slightly over the speed limit! The Smart is very practical for town use. I've also got an old Mercedes 280SL Pagoda that I've had restored in the Stuttgart factory. It's in a perfect state and I love driving it.

**What is your favourite/dream car?**
The McLaren F1 road car designed by Gordon Murray.

**Who's been your best team-mate?**
I've had good relations with them all.

**If you were a team manager what drivers would you choose?**
Schumacher and me.

**What do you love about this profession?**
Speed. I love racing.

**What don't you like about it?**
There's too much politics today. And I don't like the magnetic turnstile we have to go through to get into the paddock.

**What's your favourite moment of a Grand Prix?**
The start of a Grand Prix.

**Do you always get into your car on the same side?**
No, but I'm a bit superstitious. I've got lucky socks!

**When you stop racing, what then?**
Stay in the world of racing. But I don't see myself continuing after 40. Maybe I'll become a journalist to criticise the others.

**What's your favourite dish?**
Pasta.

**And the ones you dislike?**
Dishes based on liver.

**What's your favourite drink?**
Tea and mineral water.

**Do you like alcohol?**
Vodka.

**Have you ever smoked?**
Yes, of course, but I don't like it.

**What sports do you do?**
I love cycling. I always have one with me. Otherwise, I like golf, sailing, jogging, physical training and swimming.

**And your favourite sports?**
I like following athletics.

**Who's your favourite sportsperson?**
I don't really have a favourite. I admire a lot of people. I judge them on their performances or their character. I like watching a big football match or a boxing match, but really I don't have a favourite.

**What are your hobbies/interests outside racing?**
To be free. I love water and being on my boat called 'Highlander.' I also like music and the cinema.

**What are your favourite films?**
I watch a lot of films on DVD in my motor home. Lately I've seen The Aviator in which Leonardo di Caprio's acting is great and Howard Hughes' story is fascinating. Great story, great movie.

**And your favourite actors?**
That depends on the role they play. Before seeing The Aviator I never considered Leonardo di Caprio a great actor. You have to admire guys like Robert de Niro who can play any part in a film; he's done it for years.

**What do you watch on TV?**
I don't watch TV programmes.

**What kind of music do you like?**
At present I listen to Maroon 5 and the Scissors Sisters a lot.

**What do you like reading?**
Ian Banks's novels and biographies. I don't have a lot of time for reading.

**What's your favourite colour?**
Blue.

**What's your favourite holiday destination?**
In the Carribean on a boat, in my house in Monaco or in Scotland.

**And your favourite place for shopping?**
London, Milan, Paris and New York.

**What do you collect?**
I'm not really a collector.

**Have you got any animals?**
I had a little Maltese terrier called Moody.

**Outside motor racing, whom do you admire?**
I've got a lot of respect for my father.

**If you were to go to a desert island, what would you bring?**
I'd like to be with the girl I love!

**What's your perfect day?**
Not to have to get up early. Then go for a boat trip with friends, have a drink, have a siesta in a creek in a corner of St Tropez for example.

**What's been the greatest day of your life so far?**
It's still to come, I hope.

**What makes you laugh the most?**
Silly stories.

**If you were not a driver what would you have done?**
My parents have a transport business. I'd also like to have played music.

**What's the most important thing in life for you?**
Good health and to be able to assuage my passion.

**What are your best qualities?**
I'm not the person to ask.

**And your worst?**
Oh, a lot.

# CHRISTIAN KLIEN

## RBR COSWORTH *15

**Date and place of birth**
February 7, 1983 in Hohenems (Austria)
**Nationality** Austrian
**Place of residence** Hohenems (Austria)
**Marital status** Single
**Height** 1.68m **Weight** 64kgs
**Internet** www.christian-klien.com

## F1 results

Best F1 Championship result: 16th in 2004 (Jaguar)
Best F1 result: 6th (Belgium 2004)
Best F1 qualification: 10th (Canada 2004)

2004: Jaguar • 18 GP, 3 points, 16th

Thanks to the help of his main sponsor, Red Bull, Christian Klien made his F1 debut last year in the Jaguar team. He was the best rookie and had a few good drives but blotted his copybook with his off on the first lap in the Monaco Grand Prix, which was down to inexperience. Thanks to Dietrich Mateschitz's purchase of the team his future in F1 looks assured. He is the youngest driver in the field and alongside him is David Coulthard. Nonetheless, a sword of Damocles hovers over his head in the person of Vitantonio Liuzzi, the team's reserve driver who is ready to profit from Klien's slightest slip-up. The Italian is champing at the bit to show what he can do. Liuzzi is rumoured to be starting a series of three races at Imola. American, Scott Speed, another product of the Red Bull nursery, is also going to test and is another potential rival.

Christian Klien has his back to the wall. In Melbourne he really went for it and finished in a promising seventh place not far behind Coulthard. He knows he has to shine to keep his seat so there is a lot of pressure on his young shoulders. He is only twenty-two and he needs to keep a cool head to cope with the Darwinian struggle for survival that is F1.

## Titles
- 1996: Swiss Karting Champion.
- 2002: German Formula Renault Champion.
- 2003: Winner of the Marlboro F3 event at Zandvoort.

## Career summary
Competition debut: 1996 (kart)
Grand Prix debut: Australia 2004 (Jaguar)

- 18 Grands Prix
- 3 points scored
- Average per Grand Prix: 0.16
- 0 podiums
- 0 victories
- 1 6th place
- 0 pole positions
- 0 fastest laps
- 0 GP in the lead
- 0 kms in the lead
- 0 laps in the lead

## Team-mates
2004: M. Webber

## Qualifications 2004
Klien 3 / Webber 15

# QUESTIONS

# CHRISTIAN KLIEN

**What was the first car you drove?**
I think it was a VW Golf.

**And today?**
A Jaguar.

**What is your favourite/dream car?**
A Porsche Turbo.

**What does your helmet design mean?**
They're the colours of my sponsor, Red Bull. I've been wearing them for eight seasons.

**What's been your best racing car so far?**
My 2003 F3 Dallara.

**And the worst?**
The 1999 Formula Koenig car.

**What's your best racing memory?**
My win in the F3 Marlboro Masters at Zandvoort in 2003 and my sixth place at Spa in F1 in 2004.

**And your worst?**
In Formula Renault at home in Austria on the Salzburgring. I was in the lead and I went off all by myself. Last year's Monaco Grand Prix wasn't too good either. I crashed on lap1.

**Do you remember the first Grand Prix you saw on TV?**
In 1989, I must've been around six or seven.

**And the first one you attended?**
The 1991 German Grand Prix on the Hockenheim circuit.

**What's your aim in racing?**
I want to do everything possible to achieve the aims I've set myself.

**What's your favourite circuit?**
I don't really have one. I like the Bugatti circuit and Zandvoort.

**And the one you dislike the most?**
Well, I'm not very keen on Zolder.

**Who's your favourite driver in the history of racing?**
Ayrton Senna. My dad is an F1 fanatic and we managed to get into the paddock at Hockenheim in 1993. My father took a photo of me with Ayrton.

I had a poster made from it and it hung in my bedroom for a long time.

**And among those currently racing?**
Montoya.

**Who's been your best team-mate?**
Markus Winkelhock in F3 in 2003.

**If you were a team manager what drivers would you choose?**
Michael Schumacher and Kimi Räikkönen.

**What do you love about this profession?**
Speed and teamwork.

**What don't you like about it?**
Driving in pouring rain.

**What's your favourite moment of a Grand Prix?**
Taking the chequered flag as winner.

**Do you always get into your car on the same side?**
No, I'm not superstitious.

**When you stop racing, what then?**
I'm too young to think about that.

**What's your favourite dish?**
All Italian cooking.

**And the ones you dislike?**
Nothing, really.

**What's your favourite drink?**
Apple juice with sparkling water.

**Do you like alcohol?**
During the odd party some Red Bull with vodka.

**Have you ever smoked?**
No, never.

**What sports do you do?**
I do a lot of skiing: there are ski runs just ten minutes from the house. Otherwise I do a lot of cross-country biking and fitness training.

**And your favourite sports?**
Grand Prix bike racing and ice hockey.

**Who's your favourite sportsperson?**
Hermann Maier. His comeback after his motor bike accident is just unbelievable. In 2004 he was in the lead in the World Cup general classification. It's awesome!

**What are your hobbies/interests outside racing?**
Internet excites me. I like sport in general and skiing on a frozen lake in Lech Zürs.

**What are your favourite films?**
Actor movies. I recently saw Oceans Twelve; it was presented in Monaco with Brad Pitt and George Clooney.

**And your favourite actors?**
Beautiful girls and Arnold Schwarzenegger.

**What do you watch on TV?**
News and sport.

**What kind of music do you like?**
None in particular. I like Rhythm and Blues.

**What do you like reading?**
Motor sport magazines. Books are too long!

**What's your favourite colour?**
Blue.

**What's your favourite holiday destination?**
South America, Cuba and Mexico.

**And your favourite place for shopping?**
London.

**What do you collect?**
Scale model F1 cars, Ferraris and Porsches. I also collect watches.

**Have you got any animals?**
No.

**Outside motor racing, whom do you admire?**
Nobody in particular.

**If you were to go to a desert island, what would you bring?**
A beautiful girl and a toothbrush.

**What's your perfect day?**
Getting up on a beautiful day when it's hot and I have a race ahead of me.

**What's been the greatest day of your life so far?**
The day I signed with Jaguar.

**What makes you laugh the most?**
I laugh easily.

**If you were not a driver what would you have done?**
I wanted to be a racing driver.

**What's the most important thing in life for you?**
Work to achieve one's aims and be happy.

**What are your best qualities?**
I'm obstinate.

**And your worst?**
Sometimes I'm blinkered. I don't take other people's advice into account enough.

# VITANTONIO LIUZZI

## RBR
## COSWORTH *15

**Date and place of birth**
August 6, 1981 in Locorotondo (Italy)
**Nationality** Italian
**Place of residence** Pescara (Italy)
**Marital status** Single
**Height** 1.69m **Weight** 68kgs
**Internet** www.liuzzi.com

Vitantonio Liuzzi won the 2004 F3000 Championship in a canter and looks to have a brilliant F1 career ahead of him. In 2002, he had a promising test with Williams on the Valencia circuit. Backed by Red Bull he was introduced to Peter Sauber last year at Monza and a few days later he tested at Jerez. With Giancarlo Fisichella leaving for Renault the young Italian thought he had the seat sewn up. However, Jacques Villeneuve snatched the drive from under his nose and signed for the Swiss team. All his hopes seemed to vanish in an instant and after being linked to Ferrari, BAR and Williams he found himself out in the cold. Luckily, Red Bull's purchase of Jaguar gave him a fresh opportunity. He has been Dietrich Mateschitz's protégé for several years and this has helped put his career back on the rails. The evaluation tests between the two drivers continued up to mid-February. Finally, Klien was chosen as he knew the first three circuits of the season unlike Liuzzi. It may be a whole different story when the circus comes back to Europe.

Vitantonio won the Karting World Championship and in 2001 he beat Michael Schumacher on his home ground in Kerpen. He is a bit different from the usual run of drivers and awaits his hour – impatiently. Christian Horner, the Red Bull team manager, knows Liuzzi well as the latter won last year's F3000 title with his team, Arden Racing.

## Titles
- 1993: Italian karting champion.
- 1995: Victory in the Lonato Winter Cup (kart).
- 1996: Italian karting champion.
- 1999: European karting champion (Formula Super A).
- 2001: Karting World Champion (FIA/CIK).
- 2004: International F3000 Champion.

## Career summary
Competition debut: 1991 (karting)
Grand Prix debut: San Marino 2005 (RBR-Cosworth)

# QUESTIONS

# VITANTONIO LIUZZI

**What was the first car you drove?**

A Mitsubishi. I think I was about eleven.

**And today?**

I've got an Audi A3.

**What is your favourite/dream car?**

I'd have a hard job choosing. Maybe a Hummer; it's monstrous!

**What does your helmet design mean?**

It's adapted to the Red Bull colours but they're my own choice.

**What's been your best racing car so far?**

The 2004 F3000 Arden.

**And the worst?**

The F3 BSR that I had in 2002.

**What's your best racing memory?**

For the moment it's my F3000 win in Monaco in 2004.

**And your worst?**

It was at the Sachsring in F3 in 2002. I wasn't quick enough.

**Do you remember the first Grand Prix you saw on TV?**

No, not exactly. I must have been around eight.

**And the first one you attended?**

Imola in 2001.

**What's your aim in racing?**

Win the world championship.

**What's your favourite circuit?**

Spa. No doubt about that.

**And the one you dislike the most?**

I don't like Estoril.

**Who's your favourite driver in the history of racing?**

Ayrton Senna.

**And among those currently racing?**

Michael Schumacher. What he does is just incredible.

**Who's been your best team-mate?**
Robert Doornbos at Arden in F3000 in 2004. I was also on good terms with Auinger and Heupel before that.

**If you were a team manager what drivers would you choose?**
Kimi Räikkönen and Fernando Alonso.

**What do you love about this profession?**
The adrenaline and the battle.

**What don't you like about it?**
No, for the moment everything's fine.

**What's your favourite moment of a Grand Prix?**
The start.

**Do you always get into your car on the same side?**
No, it's not important.

**When you stop racing, what then?**
No...

**What's your favourite dish?**
Pizza and pasta.

**And the ones you dislike?**
I don't like fish.

**What's your favourite drink?**
Coca Cola and Red Bull.

**Do you like alcohol?**
Very little.

**Have you ever smoked?**
No.

**What sports do you do?**
Physical fitness in the gym, fotball with my friends, skiing, cycling and skateboarding.

**And your favourite sports?**
Football and the Milan Inter in particular. I also like watching the Motor Cycle Grands Prix.

**Who's your favourite sportsperson?**
David Beckham.

**What are your hobbies/interests outside racing?**
Whenever I've got the time, I like doing a bit of karting.

**What are your favourite films?**
I liked the Passion of Christ. Otherwise I like funny films.

**And your favourite actors?**
Angelina Jolie.

**What do you watch on TV?**
The music channels, above all.

**What kind of music do you like?**
Rhythm and Blues and pop music.

**What do you like reading?**
I don't like reading. I glance at the sports newspapers.

**What's your favourite colour?**
After a lot of thought, I'd say blue.

**What's your favourite holiday destination?**
Many. I like staying at home. I also like towns like London and Paris.

**And your favourite place for shopping?**
All the towns attract me: there are too many.

**What do you collect?**
I love clothes. I'm crazy about them; I've got loads at home.

**Have you got any animals?**
I've got a dog called Mike.

**Outside motor racing, whom do you admire?**
My dad.

**If you were to go to a desert island, what would you bring?**
A girl and a car.

**What's your perfect day?**
Being at a circuit and racing.

**What's been the greatest day of your life so far?**
The day I signed my first F1 contract.

**What makes you laugh the most?**
My friends.

**If you were not a driver what would you have done?**
A football player or dancer.

**What's the most important thing in life for you?**
Friendship means a lot to me.

**What are your best qualities?**
I think I'm a loyal friend.

**And your worst?**
I'm too nice!

Toyota TF105

V10 Toyota RVX-05 (90°)

Michelin

Address: Toyota Motorsport GmbH
Toyota-Allee 7
50858 Cologne
Germany

Tel.: +49 (0)223 418 23 444
Fax: +49 (0)223 418 23 37
Internet: www.toyota-f1.com

Team founded in 1999
Grand Prix debut: Australia 2002
Number of Grands Prix: 51

Number of victories: 0
Best result: 5th (Germany 2003 and USA 2004)

Number of pole positions: 0
Best qualification: 3rd (United States and Japan 2003)

Number of fastest laps: 0

First points scored: Australia 2002 (Salo, 6th)
Number of points scored: 27
Points average per race: 0.52

Number of podiums: 0

Best classification in the Constructors' World Championship:
8th in 2003 and 2004
Best classification in the Drivers' World Championship:
13th in 2003 (Da Matta)

## Strengths

- Very good technical staff.
- Excellent drivers.
- Powerful and reliable engine.
- Large budget.
- Desire to succeed.
- Very good test driver.

## Weaknesses

- Must deliver the goods.
- Under heavy pressure.
- Chassis hard on tyres?
- Too much red tape.
- Internal ambience.

## 2004 summary

- 8th in the Constructors' World Championship

- Best result: 5th
  (Panis - USA)

- Best qualification: 6th
  (Trulli - Japan)

- 9 points scored
  (Panis 6, Da Matta 3)

- 25 finishes out of a possible 36
  (Panis 14, Da Matta 8, Trulli 2, Zonta 1)

- 4 points scoring finishes
  (Panis 3, Da Matta 1)

- 4 drivers used
  (Panis, Da Matta, Zonta and Trulli)

# TOYOTA

**Tsutomu Tomita (J)**
Chairman and
team principal

**Mike Gascoyne (GB)**
Technical director
(chassis)

**Luca Marmorini (I)**
Technical director
(engine)

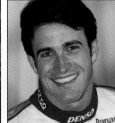

**Ricardo Zonta (BR)**
3rd driver

**Olivier Panis (F)**
Test driver

**Number of employees**
580

Jarno Trulli's performance in the Malaysian inferno of Sepang was deliverance for Toyota and after the race the team's management breathed a huge sigh of relief. The atmosphere was beginning to get very strained, as despite its huge investment the Japanese giant was unable to make any headway. The swirl of engineers and drivers through the corridors of its Cologne factory did not seem to do the trick. Then 18 months ago Toyota hired Mike Gascoyne, one of the most brilliant engineers in F1. He was nicked from Renault for a record amount of dollars. The Japanese manufacturer then hired Jarno Trulli and Ralf Schumacher, two leading drivers, to

stack the cards in its favour. It was the moment of truth and the directors of the huge company no longer wanted just to make up the numbers: they wanted results. A sword of Damocles hung over the team.

Will 2005 be Toyota's year? It is beginning to look like it. In Australia, Jarno Trulli shone in practice and fifteen days later he confirmed that it was no fluke by finishing second in Mayalsia, the first rostrum placing for the team after four difficult years.

By starting from a blank sheet and deciding to build its own chassis and engine Toyota has not chosen the easiest route. Just ask Ferrari and Renault!

# JARNO TRULLI

## TOYOTA *16

**Date and place of birth** July 13, 1974 in Pescara (Italy)
**Nationality** Italian
**Place of residence** Monte-Carlo, Pescara and St-Moritz (Switzerland)
**Marital status** Married to Barbara
**Height** 1.73m **Weight** 60kgs
**Internet** www.jarnotrulli.com

### F1 results

Best F1 Championship result: 6th in 2004 (Renault / Toyota)
Best F1 result: 1st (Monaco 2004)
Best F1 qualification: 1st (2 pole positions)

1997: Minardi-Hart and Prost-Mugen Honda • 14 GP (7+7), 3 points, 15th
1998: Prost-Peugeot • 16 GP, 1 point, 15th
1999: Prost-Peugeot • 16 GP, 7 points, 11th
2000: Jordan-Mugen Honda • 17 GP, 6 points, 10th
2001: Jordan-Honda • 17 GP, 12 points, 9th
2002: Renault • 17 GP, 9 points, 8th
2003: Renault • 16 GP, 33 points, 8th
2004: Renault and Toyota • 17 GP (15+2), 46 points, 6th

Why Jarno Trulli was shown the door by Renault remains a mystery. After his brilliant Monaco victory and his pole at Spa it was goodbye. Luckily he was snapped up by Toyota and drove the last two grands prix of the season for the Japanese team providing him with useful experience in view of 2005. He is one of the nicest guys in the F1 paddock and is always pleasant with a permanent smile on his face. His Monaco victory sent a wave of joy through the normally cynical ranks of the media. He has often been hit by bad luck so it was a just reward.

He is an excellent test driver and his whole life revolves around racing. He did nine years' karting before changing to single-seaters: now aged thirty he already has seven F1 seasons under his belt. His experience will be of great help to his new employer. His team-mate is Ralf Schumacher also given the boot by Williams so they are both out for revenge. Jarno made a brilliant debut for Toyota in Australia by grabbing second place on the grid after practice had been perturbed by rain. In Malaysia, he finished second behind Alonso to the great joy of his employer. He is filled with a burning desire to make it to the top and has all the necessary qualities to give his former team a few frights.

## Titles

- 1988, 1989 and 1990: Italian Karting Champion.
- 1991: World Karting Champion (Class 100 FK).
- 1994: European and North American Champion in FSA Class 100 karts, World Champion in Class 125 FC Class Karts, Winner of the Ayrton Senna World Cup in Class 100 FSA karts.
- 1995: Italian Champion in Class 100 FA Karts, Winner of the Ayrton Senna World Cup in Class 100 FSA karts.
- 1996: German F3 Champion.

## Career summary

Competition debut: 1983 (mini-karting)
Grand Prix debut: Australia 1997 (Minardi-Hart)

- 130 Grands Prix
- 117 points scored
- Average per Grand Prix: 0.90
- 4 podiums
- 1 victory
- 1 2$^{nd}$ place
- 2 3$^{rd}$ places
- 11 4$^{th}$ places
- 9 5$^{th}$ places
- 8 6$^{th}$ places
- 2 7$^{th}$ places*
- 2 8$^{th}$ places*

- 2 pole positions
- 0 fastest laps
- 7 GP in the lead
- 574 kms in the lead
- 141 laps in the lead

\* Since 2003 and the attribution of points to 7$^{th}$ and 8$^{th}$ places.

## Team-mates

1997: U. Katayama (Minardi-Hart) and
       S. Nakano (Prost-Mugen Honda)
1998 and 1999: O. Panis
2000: H.-H. Frentzen
2001: H.-H. Frentzen and J. Alesi
2002: J. Button
2003: F. Alonso
2004: F. Alonso (Renault), O. Panis and R. Zonta (Toyota)

## Qualifications 2004

Trulli 8 / Alonso 7
Trulli 1 / Panis 0
Trulli 1 / Da Matta 0

# QUESTIONS

# JARNO TRULLI

**What was the first car you drove?**
A Renault Clio when I was eighteen.

**And today?**
A V8 Lexus Coupe SC 430.

**What is your favourite/dream car?**
My old Fiat 500 that I have in Pescara.

**What does your helmet design mean?**
It goes back to my karting days. I designed it with a friend. He used the colours of the Italian flag and the initials of my name. Then last year I felt like changing. I decided on something very simple. The base is chrome and the rest is decorated according to sponsors' requirements.

**What's been your best racing car so far?**
The 1996 Dallara 396 and of course, the Renault R24 in Monte Carlo.

**And the worst?**
The 1998 AP 02 Prost.

**What's your best racing memory?**
My karting successes, my victory in the 1996 German F3 Championship and of course, my win in Monaco in 2004.

**And your worst?**
Among others I regret I did not win the F3 Monaco and Macao Grands Prix in 1996 but my Monaco F1 victory is ample compensation!

**Do you remember the first Grand Prix you saw on TV?**
I must've been four.

**And the first one you attended?**
I never attended one before my debut in 1997. I may have been to a Grand Prix at Monza but I don't remember the year.

**What's your aim in racing?**
Reach the top.

**What's your favourite circuit?**
Monaco is too small for F1. But since I've won there...!

**And the one you dislike the most?**
Monaco is too tight for F1 cars and I don't like Buenos Aires.

**Who's your favourite driver in the history of racing?**
Niki Lauda and Alain Prost.

**And among those currently racing?**
I don't really have one. Olivier Panis is a good friend and I get on well with Fernando Alonso whom I've known since my karting days.

**Who's been your best team-mate?**
Panis and Alonso.

**If you were a team manager what drivers would you choose?**
Alonso... and Trulli!

**What do you love about this profession?**
Driving and the fact that the team is like a second family.

**What don't you like about it?**
Many things. There's too much to do outside the car.

**What's your favourite moment of a Grand Prix?**
I like everything.

**Do you always get into your car on the same side?**
No, I'm not superstitious.

**When you stop racing, what then?**
Not for the moment. My little karting factory and my vineyard in Montepulciano will certainly keep me busy.

**What's your favourite dish?**
A good pizza.

**And the ones you dislike?**
Liver.

**What's your favourite drink?**
Coca Cola.

**Do you like alcohol?**
Red wine occasionally like the Montepulciano from my vineyard.

**Have you ever smoked?**
No.

**What sports do you do?**
Karting, cycling, jogging, sea canoeing and gymnastics. I'd like to be able to do more training for the New York marathon, which I've already competed in.

**And your favourite sports?**
Downhill skiing, Motor Bike Grands Prix and kart races.

**Who's your favourite sportsperson?**
I've got good friends in bike racing like Biaggi, Melandri, Capirossi and Laconi.

**What are your hobbies/interests outside racing?**
I've always got a laptop with me. It's an excellent way to escape. Recently I bought a small vineyard in Montepulciano in Itally and that really excites me. I also look after my small karting factory.

**What are your favourite films?**
I like movies but I soon forget the titles.
In fact, I don't go to the cinema very often.

**And your favourite actors?**
Cinema is entertainment for me. I'm not a really a fan.

**What do you watch on TV?**
I watch the news to see what's happening in Italy.

**What kind of music do you like?**
I like everything, pop, rock, jazz and blues.

**What do you like reading?**
I read the papers a little to keep up to date, but I don't like reading much.

**What's your favourite colour?**
Red.

**What's your favourite holiday destination?**
I never go on holiday. I prefer staying at home in Pescara. I discovered St Moritz five years ago. I like the sea but I think I prefer the mountains. It's nature and you feel free.

**And your favourite place for shopping?**
I like buying watches and shoes but I don't have a favourite town for that.

**What do you collect?**
Watches, shoes and scale model cars. I'm not a real collector.

**Have you got any animals?**
In Pescara my family has four dogs and two cats.

**Outside motor racing, whom do you admire?**
My family.

**If you were to go to a desert island, what would you bring?**
A kart, a set of overalls and a helmet.

**What's your perfect day?**
When I'm in Monaco I do some cycling, biking, canoeing or rock climbing on the sides of La Turbie. I also like playing with my computer, I send emails, surf the net and go and see my friends.

**What's been the greatest day of your life so far**
It hasn't happened yet.

**What makes you laugh the most?**
Good films and good jokes.

**If you were not a driver what would you have done?**
I've been doing karting since I was eight.

**What's the most important thing in life for you?**
To feel good, and my family which is everything for me.

**What are your best qualities?**
I don't know.

**And your worst?**
I'm too much of a perfectionist and I'm never satisfied.

# RALF SCHUMACHER
## TOYOTA *17

**Date and place of birth**
June 30, 1975 in Hurth-Hermühlheim (Germany)
**Nationality** German
**Place of residence** Hallwang (Salzburg) (Austria)
**Marital status** Married to Cora, one son, David
**Height** 1.78m **Weight** 73kgs
**Internet** www.ralf-schumacher.net

## F1 results

Best F1 Championship result: 4th in 2001 and 2002 (Williams-BMW)
Best F1 result: 1st (6 victories)
Best F1 qualification: 1st (4 pole positions)

1997: Jordan-Peugeot • 17 GP, 13 points, 11th
1998: Jordan-Mugen Honda • 16 GP, 14 points, 10th
1999: Williams-Supertec • 16 GP, 35 points, 6th
2000: Williams-BMW • 17 GP, 24 points, 5th
2001: Williams-BMW • 17 GP, 49 points, 4th
2002: Williams-BMW • 17 GP, 42 points, 4th
2003: Williams-BMW • 15 GP, 58 points, 5th
2004: Williams-BMW • 12 GP, 24 points, 9th

When Ralf Schumacher had his big accident at Indianapolis he was on the way out at Williams having already signed for Toyota. He was forced to miss several grands prix due to serious injuries to his vertebrae and did not come back until the season was nearing its end. Like Trulli he is out to prove a point at Toyota which can no longer be content just to make up numbers. The company's management is beginning to show signs of impatience and wants results. It is just the right situation for Michael's younger brother to enhance his reputation. He is not psychologically as tough as the reigning world champion and his career has been marked by a lack of consistency and steadiness. On a good day he is as quick as the best but does not have the same never-say die attitude as Michael.

His 3-year contract should provide him with the time to build up a good set of results. Toyota, though, has not been noted for its understanding attitude to its drivers who have come and gone with disconcerting regularity. Ralf is at a turning point in his career and has to overcome this challenge. It is an exciting one and full of risk.

He has been overshadowed by his brother's success and now it is time for him to stand on his own two feet. He has got what it takes to win races. Toyota seems to be up to speed at last so Ralf has no longer any margin for error.

## Titles
- 1995: Winner of the Macao F3 race.
- 1996: Japanese F3000 Champion.

## Career summary
Competition debut: 1974 (karting)
Grand Prix debut: Australia 1997 (Jordan-Peugeot)

- 127 Grands Prix
- 259 points scored
- Average per Grand Prix : 2.03
- 24 podiums
- 6 victories
- 6 2nd places
- 12 3rd places
- 16 4th places
- 16 5th places
- 6 6th places
- 3 7th place*
- 1 8th place*

- 5 pole positions
- 7 fastest laps
- 19 GP in the lead
- 1858 kms in the lead
- 357 laps in the lead

\* Since 2003 and the attribution of points
  to 7th and 8th places.

## Team-mates
1997: G. Fisichella
1998: D. Hill
1999: A. Zanardi
2000: J. Button
2001, 2002, 2003 and 2004: J.P. Montoya

## Qualifications 2004
R. Schumacher 3 / Montoya 9

# QUESTIONS

# RALF
# SCHUMACHER

**If you were a team manager what drivers would you choose?**
That's not my job.

**What do you love about this profession?**
Driving.

**What don't you like about it?**
Media hysteria and political intrigue.

**What's your favourite moment of a Grand Prix?**
I like all aspects of racing.

**Do you always get into your car on the same side?**
I'm not superstitious.

**When you stop racing, what then?**
For the moment I'm concentrating on racing.

**What's your favourite dish?**
Pasta and Austrian cooking.

**What was the first car you drove?**
A Fiat 500 when I was seven.

**And today?**
I've got a Lexus SC 430 V8.

**What is your favourite/dream car?**
There are many I like.

**What does your helmet design mean?**
My main wish was to include the German colours. I've had this decoration since my single-seater debut. A designer did it with the help of my brother.

**What's been your best racing car so far?**
The 2001 Williams FW 23 and the 1998 Jordan.

**And the worst?**
It would not be correct to make any comment about people who've trusted me.

**What's your best racing memory?**
My title in Japan in 1996 and my F1 wins.

**And the worst?**
I do everything to erase them from my mind. It's obvious that I don't have good memories of the 2004 season and my accident at Indy.

**Do you remember the first Grand Prix you saw on TV?**
I don't remember exactly. I can't really give you a date.

**And the first one you attended?**
I think I went to Hockenheim with my brother in 1993.

**What's your aim in racing?**
To have panache.

**What's your favourite circuit?**
Monaco.

**And the one you dislike the most?**
Spa is dangerous, but then so is Monaco.

**Who's your favourite driver in the history of racing?**
Nobody.

**And among those currently racing?**
My brother, Michael.

**Who's been your best team-mate?**
I got on very well with Alex Zanardi. He's a really good bloke. I admire him for coming back to racing.

**And the ones you dislike?**
There's nothing I really dislike.

**What's your favourite drink?**
Apple juice with fizzy water.

**Do you like alcohol?**
A beer from time to time.

**Have you ever smoked?**
An occasional cigar.

**What sports do you do?**
Tennis, cycling, horse riding, karting and physical preparation.

**And your favourite sports?**
The Olympic Games, basketball and the major athletics meetings.

**Who's your favourite sportsperson?**
I've got a lot of admiration for top level sports people who dominate their category.

**What are your hobbies/interests outside racing?**
I love playing backgammon.

**What are your favourite films?**
I liked "X-Men" very much.

**And your favourite actors?**
Bill Crosby.

**What do you watch on TV?**
I look at it above all to change my ideas.

**What kind of music do you like?**
Soft rock.

**What do you like reading?**
I've read all the "Harry Potters" recently.

**What's your favourite colour?**
I like dark colours.

**What's your favourite holiday destination?**
In Austria or on the beach.

**And your favourite place for shopping?**
Singapore.

**What do you collect?**
I'm not a collector.

**Have you got any animals?**
A dog, a bull, cows and a horse.

**Outside motor racing, whom do you admire?**
My brother and my family.

**If you were to go to a desert island, what would you bring?**
A boat to get out of there quick!

**What's your perfect day?**
Being at home with Cora and David.

**What's been the greatest day of your life so far?**
I hope it's still to come.

**What makes you laugh the most?**
Good jokes and English humour.

**If you were not a driver what would you have done?**
I think I'd have been a businessman.

**What's the most important thing in life for you?**
Health first of all, earn a good living even though money is not an obsession. Achieve the aims you've set yourself.

**What are your best qualities?**
I think that I'm strong mentally.

**And your worst?**
I'm too selfish but then all drivers are.

Jordan EJ15

V10 Toyota RVX-05 (90°)

Bridgestone

Address: Jordan Grand Prix Ltd
Buckingham Road,
Silverstone, Northants NN12 8TJ,
Great Britain

Tel.: +44 (0)1327 850 800
Fax: +44 (0)1327 857.993
Internet: www.f1jordan.com

Team founded in 1981
Grand Prix debut: United States 1991
Number of Grands Prix: 231

First victory: Belgium 1998 (D. Hill)
Number of victories: 4

First pole position: Belgium 1994 (Barrichello)
Number of pole positions: 2

First fastest lap: Hungary 1991 (Gachot)
Number of fastest laps: 2

First points scored: Canada 1991 (De Cesaris, 4th and Gachot, 5th)
Number of points scored: 279
Points average per race: 1.20

First podium: Pacific 1994 (Barrichello, 3rd)
Number of podiums: 18

Best classification in the Constructors' World Championship: 3rd in 1999.
Best classification in the Drivers' World Championship: 3rd in 1999 (Frentzen).

## Strengths

- Purchase of a team that was on the way out.
- Desire to bounce back.
- Good Toyota engine.
- Fast, ambitious drivers.

## Weaknesses

- Drivers are F1 debutants.
- Chassis' competitiveness.
- Very little private testing.
- No major manufacturer.
- Inexperienced technical staff.

## 2004 summary

- 9th in the Constructors' World Championship
- Best result: 7th
  (Heidfeld - Monaco, Glock - Canada)
- Best qualification: 13th
  (Heidfeld - Europe)
- 5 points scored
  (Heidfeld 3, Glock 2)
- 21 finishes out of a possible 36
  (Heidfeld 11, Pantano 6, Glock 4)
- 3 points scoring finishes
  (Heidfeld 2, Glock 1)
- 3 drivers used
  (Heidfeld, Pantano and Glock).

# JORDAN-TOYOTA

**Alex Shnaider (CDN)**
Owner

**Colin Kolles (GB)**
Managing Director

**Trevor Carlin (GB)**
Sporting Director

**Robert Doornbos (MC)**
3rd driver

**Number of employees**
200

On 25th February 2005 a strange kind of ceremony took place on Moscow's Red Square: it was a kind of instant reincarnation! From the ashes of Eddie Jordan Racing arose the new Phoenix, Midland-Jordan. 2005 sees old rocker, Eddie Jordan, starting his final world tour. The difficult economic situation did for this likeable team.

It should not be forgotten that Jordan was responsible for giving the Schumacher brothers, Irvine and Barrichello among others their F1 break. Eddie is proud of the fact that four world champions have driven his cars. In 1999, Jordan Racing finished third in the Constructors' Championship but it was not enough to attract the full-blown support of a major manufacturer, the only way to ensure long-term survival in Formula 1. At the end of this season after fifteen years his name will disappear from the F1 roll call like Prost, Arrows and Jaguar in the recent past. The Jordan moniker will have a hollow ring in its swansong season bereft of its glamour that once lit up the paddock's gloom. Eddie Jordan had his back to the wall despite the agreement with Toyota for an engine supply and he had to sell to Alex Shnaider, a Canadian millionaire of Russian origins and chairman of the Midland Group. The latter has got himself a great financial deal and a racing team into the bargain, and is not obliged to put up the outlandish 50-million dollar guarantee required for the creation of a new team. His original intention was to come in in 2006 with a chassis constructed by Dallara powered by a Ferrari engine. However, he decided to bring his debut forward and purchased Jordan during the winter so everything had to be speeded up. The budget was found in a few weeks with the help of a couple of pay-drivers.

The powerful Toyota engine will be a great boost to the team to help it pick up a few points when circumstances play in its favour.

# TIAGO MONTEIRO

## JORDAN
## TOYOTA *18

**Date and place of birth** July 24, 1976 in Oporto (Portugal)
**Nationality** Portuguese
**Place of residence** Oporto (Portugal)
**Marital status** Single
**Height** 1.74m **Weight** 64kgs
**Internet** www.tiagoracing.com

## Titles

- 1997: French Porsche Carrera Cup B Champion.

## F1 Tests

- 2002: Renault practice (Renault Driver Development driver).
- 2004: Minardi test driver.

## Career summary

Competition debut: 1997 (Porsche Carrera Cup).
Grand Prix debut: Australia 2005 (Jordan-Toyota).

Tiago Monteiro from Portugal is fulfilling his dream. Last year he was present in Melbourne at the presentation of the Minardi as test driver. Little did he realise that twelve months later he would be on the starting grid making his entry into the very select club of F1 grand prix drivers.

He has raced in various formulas all over the world, a bit like his team-mate Karthikeyan. His debut came in the French F3 Championship in which he was beaten by Sébastien Bourdais against whom he competed in F3000. He has also raced with in endurance events like Le Mans and Spa and tried his hand in the Cart Championship in the USA plus Formula Nissan in all of which he met with some success. In addition, he has been a test driver for Minardi and Renault.

His experience will serve him well in the Jordan team, which is undergoing a complete makeover. He is an intelligent, affable individual who speaks five languages fluently making him an excellent ambassador for his team. Like David Coulthard he has just the right profile to do excellent PR work for his sponsors. He is out to show that he is no slouch on the track despite a relatively uncompetitive car. His ability as a test driver should stand him in good stead because he is under pressure to deliver straight away. Robert Doornbos, the team's third driver, has a well-filled wallet: always a strong argument in modern-day F1.

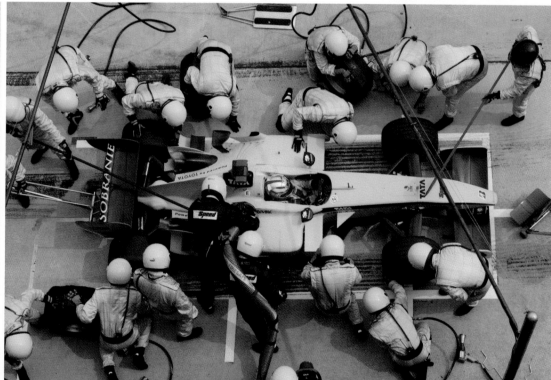

# QUESTIONS

# TIAGO MONTEIRO

**What's your favourite circuit?**

Spa.

**And the one you dislike the most?**

I don't like Imola.

**Who's your favourite driver in the history of racing?**

Senna and Prost.

**What was the first car you drove?**

It was with my granddad. I was around 12 and the car was a Citroën Mehari.

**And today?**

A Chevrolet Tahoe.

**What is your favourite/dream car?**

The Aston Martin DB7.

**What does your helmet design mean?**

I did it myself six years ago and I update it every season.

**What's been your best racing car so far?**

Je pense à la Reynard du Team Fittipaldi ou bien à la Dallara de World Nissan en 2004.

**And the worst?**

La Lola de SuperNova en F3000.

**What's your best racing memory?**

There are several. First of all my first F3 victory in 1999, then my F1 test with Renault and finally my signing with Jordan for 2005.

**And your worst?**

There are so many.

**Do you remember the first Grand Prix you saw on TV?**

No.

**And the first one you attended?**

I went to Spa when I was seven or eight.

**What's your aim in racing?**

Always go quicker...

**What do you like reading?**
The American author Dan Brown's Da Vinci Code among others
**What's your favourite colour?**
Red, yellow and blue.
**What's your favourite holiday destination?**
A desert island.

**And among those currently racing?**
They're not really heroes but I've got a lot of admiration for Michael Schumacher, Montoya and Villeneuve.
**Who's been your best team-mate?**
I've had a lot of good times with Bernard Tréluyer, Julien Beltoise and Sébastien Dumez in F3.
**If you were a team manager what drivers would you choose?**
Schumacher and myself.
**What do you love about this profession?**
The speed and the adrenaline. And you can also meet people from all over the world.
**What don't you like about it?**
Travelling a lot keeps you away from your friends, your family and your girlfriend. I don't like all the hypocrites you meet so often.
**What's your favourite moment of a Grand Prix?**
Overtaking.
**Do you always get into your car on the same side?**
Yes.
**When you stop racing, what then?**
No. I've got a lot of ideas about what I could do but I haven't yet taken a decision.

**What's your favourite dish?**
Asian cooking: Japanese, Thai and Indian.
**And the ones you dislike?**
I hate garlic.
**What's your favourite drink?**
I used to like Coca Cola, now I drink fizzy drinks.
**Do you like alcohol?**
No, not really.
**Have you ever smoked?**
I can't stand it.
**What sports do you do?**
I do a lot but not the most dangerous.
**And your favourite sports?**
A lot: motorbikes, surfing, snowboard, diving.
**Who's your favourite sportsperson?**
Lance Armstrong is awesome.
**What are your hobbies/interests outside racing?**
A lot of sport, cinema, reading and photography.
**What are your favourite films?**
I like 'Closer' with Julia Roberts and the 24 Series.
**And your favourite actors?**
Brad Pitt, Robert de Niro, Al Pacino.
**What do you watch on TV?**
Nothing!
**What kind of music do you like?**
I like to change. I must have around three thousand things on my ipod.

**And your favourite place for shopping?**
New York.
**What do you collect?**
I collect watches but less nowadays.
**Have you got any animals?**
I've got a Labrador called Buddy.
**Outside motor racing, whom do you admire?**
That's personal!
**If you were to go to a desert island, what would you bring?**
My computer and my ipod.
**What's your perfect day?**
Spend time with my family in Porto, with my girlfriend in London or with my best friends in Paris.
**What's been the greatest day of your life so far?**
There are many but they concern my family.
**What makes you laugh the most?**
Many things...
**If you were not a driver what would you have done?**
Probably hotel management.
**What's the most important thing in life for you?**
Trust and love.
**What are your best qualities?**
Honesty and to be worthy of trust.
**And your worst?**
I'm impatient and probably a bit stubborn.

# NARAIN KARTHIKEYAN

## JORDAN TOYOTA *19

**Date and place of birth**  January 14, 1977 in Chennai (India)
**Nationality**  Indian
**Place of residence**  Coimbatore (India)
**Marital status**  Married to Pavarna
**Height**  1.64m  **Weight**  64kgs
**Internet**  www.narainracing.com

### Titles
- 1994: British Formula Ford Winter Series Champion.
- 1996: Formula Asia Champion.

### F1 Tests
- 2001: Tests with Jaguar and Jordan.
- 2003: Test with Minardi.

### Career summary
Competition debut: 1992 (Ecole Winfield, France).
Grand Prix debut: Australia 2005 (Jordan-Toyota).

'The fastest Indian in the world.' That's the opening sentence on Narain Karthikeyan's web site. No beating about the bush here! The young and rather reserved Kathikeyan can count on the support of over a billion fellow-countrymen. He is backed by some of the biggest firms in a country that is undergoing massive expansion for which he is an ambassador. *"My aim's always been to get into F1 one day. No other Indian has ever achieved this. I've got the hopes of a nation riding on my shoulders and I can't let them down."* India is intent on organising a grand prix by 2007 and Bernie Ecclestone is giving the promoters a helping hand.

Narain is a quick driver whose impetuousness often worked against him in the past. He graduated from the Winfield School in France in 1992 and then raced in different formulas all over the world. His best results came in the Spanish World Series by Nissan. His personal sponsors have helped him break into F1 and when he arrived in Jordan he saw a few familiar faces including team manager, Trevor Carlin, for whom he raced in F3 in England. *"I competed against Jenson Button and Takumo Sato and I beat them both on several occasions. Today they're both doing well in F1 and that encourages me to think that I can be competitive too."*

Narain is all fired up and ready to go. He is under no illusions about his car's speed and his lack of experience. Hope springs eternal but he is lucid enough to know that he is faced with a tough challenge.

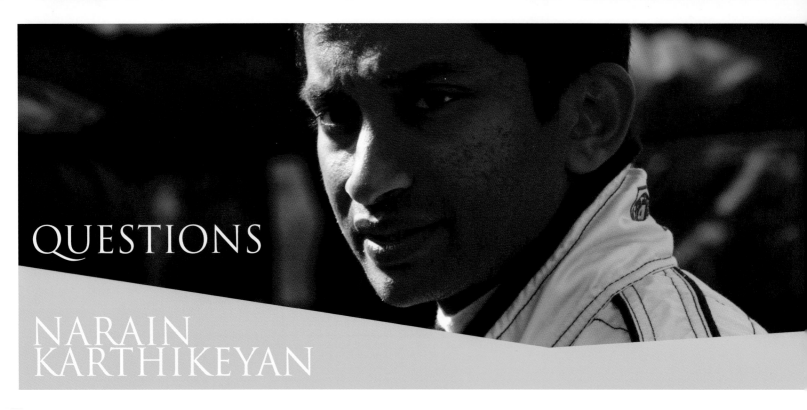

# QUESTIONS

# NARAIN KARTHIKEYAN

**Who's been your best team-mate?**
Bruce Jouanny in the World Series.

**If you were a team manager what drivers would you choose?**
Young, quick drivers.

**What do you love about this profession?**
An F1 qualifying session with little fuel.

**What don't you like about it?**
Driving when it's very hot like in Malaysia.

**What's your favourite moment of a Grand Prix?**
The start is the most exciting moment.

**Do you always get into your car on the same side?**
This detail is not important.

**When you stop racing, what then?**
It'll be in motor sport.

**What was the first car you drove?**
An 800 cc Suzuki on my cousin's farm.

**And today?**
A Tata Safari, a model made by one of my sponsors in India.

**What is your favourite/dream car?**
There are a lot.

**What does your helmet design mean?**
I did it myself using the Indian flag colours as inspiration.

**What's been your best racing car so far?**
The Jordan, of course, and the Formula Nippon.

**And the worst?**
The Formula Suzuki.

**What's your best racing memory?**
My first F3 victory on the Brands Hatch circuit in England in 1999.

**And your worst?**
I started on pole in the 2000 F3 Macao Grand Prix and went off in the first corner!

**Do you remember the first Grand Prix you saw on TV?**
I think it was in 1992.

**And the first one you attended?**
The Portuguese Grand Prix at Estoril in 1994.

**What's your aim in racing?**
Drive at 100%.

**What's your favourite circuit?**
Macao, Monza and Suzuki.

**And the one you dislike the most?**
The F3 circuit in Korea despite my win there in 2000.

**Who's your favourite driver in the history of racing?**
Ayrton Senna.

**And among those currently racing?**
Michael Schumacher.

**What are your favourite films?**
'Saving Private Ryan' with Tom Hanks.
**And your favourite actors?**
I don't really have one.
**What do you watch on TV?**
I zap a lot. One thing's for sure I never watch 'Friends!'
**What kind of music do you like?**
I like everything.
**What do you like reading?**
Motor Sport magazines and newspapers. I never read books.
**What's your favourite colour?**
Black.
**What's your favourite holiday destination?**
In India. Not too far from where I live there's a magnificent holiday centre.
**And your favourite place for shopping?**
London is the easiest for me.
**What do you collect?**
I'm not much of a collector.
**Have you got any animals?**
Yes, I've got a dog.

**Outside motor racing, whom do you admire?**
Many people deserve admiration.
**If you were to go to a desert island, what would you bring?**
A camel.
**What's your perfect day?**
To drive perfectly.
**What's been the greatest day of your life so far?**
Achieve your aims.
**What makes you laugh the most?**
A lot of things.
**If you were not a driver what would you have done?**
I don't really know.
**What's the most important thing in life for you?**
To succeed in what you do.
**What are your best qualities?**
Loyalty.
**And your worst?**
I've never thought about this question.

**What's your favourite dish?**
Indian cooking.
**And the ones you dislike?**
I don't like Chinese cooking.
**What's your favourite drink?**
Orange juice.
**Do you like alcohol?**
Not much.
**Have you ever smoked?**
No.
**What sports do you do?**
Apart from fitness training I play tennis.
**And your favourite sports?**
I like watching tennis matches.
**Who's your favourite sportsperson?**
Sachin Tendulkar, the best cricket player in the world. He's a friend.
**What are your hobbies/interests outside racing?**
Video games, PlayStation and films.

Minardi PS04B /PS05

V10 Cosworth CR-7 (90°)

Bridgestone

Address: Minardi Team SpA
Via Spallanzani, 21
48018 Faenza (RA)
Italy

Tel.: +39 0 546 696 111
Fax: +39 0 546 620 998
Internet: www.minardi.it

Team founded in 1974
Grand Prix debut: Brazil 1985
Number of Grands Prix: 321

Number of victories: 0
Best result: 4th (2 times)

Number of pole positions: 0
Best qualification: 2nd (once)

Number of fastest laps: 0

First points scored: United States East 1988 (Martini, 6th)
Number of points scored: 31
Points average per race: 0.09

Number of podiums: 0

Best classification in the Constructors' World Championship:
7th in 1991.
Best classification in the Drivers' World Championship:
7th in 1991 (Martini).

## Strengths

- A team of real enthusiasts.
- Rapid and ambitious drivers.
- Good Cosworth engine.
- Excellent mechanics.

## Weaknesses

- Drivers' lack of experience.
- Very tight budget.
- Chassis's competitiveness?
- No major manufacturer.

## 2004 summary

- 10th in the Constructors' World Championship

- Best result: 8th
  (Baumgartner - United States)

- Best qualification: 16th
  (Bruni - Malaysia)

- 1 point scored
  (Baumgartner)

- 20 finishes out of a possible 36
  (Baumgartner 11, Bruni 9)

- 1 grand prix in the points
  (Baumgartner)

- 2 drivers used
  (Bruni and Baumgartner)

# MINARDI-COSWORTH

**Paul Stoddart (AUS)**
Team principal

**Gabriele Tredozi (I)**
Technical director

**Gian Carlo Minardi (I)**
General director

**Chanoch Nissany (IL)**
Test driver

**Number of employees**
148

Bellicose Australian businessman, Paul Stoddart, has been the owner of Minardi since 2001. He made a lot of money in the aviation business, which has been hard-hit by the current recession. Paul soldiers on and has stuck in there despite the slings and arrows of outrageous fortune. Minardi is the last of the truly artisan teams and has managed to continue in F1 without the backing of either an engine manufacturer or major sponsor. Stoddart would not be out of place in an automobile remake of the 'Mutiny on the Bounty!' He has castigated Ferrari for not agreeing to the 30-day test period accepted by all the other teams. He is a wily politician and has spoken out against the unequal way in which the F1 cake is distributed. He refused to bend himself to the new rules and wanted to race in the opening grands prix with cars complying with the 2004 regs. In Melbourne he was finally obliged to knuckle under and put his cars in 2005 configuration.

The F1 minnow deserves respect. Its budget in comparison with its rivals is almost laughable and yet the Minardi's performances are never ridiculous. The big-hearted, very professional squad from Firenze has been responsible for giving current top of the heap drivers like Alonso, Trulli, Webber and Fisichella their chance in F1.

The new car, the PS 05, will make its debut in the opening grand prix in Europe. And you can count on Paul to come up with something special!

# PATRICK FRIESACHER

## MINARDI COSWORTH *20

**Date and place of birth**
September 26, 1980 in Wolfsberg / Corinthia (Austria)
**Nationality** Austria
**Place of residence** Wolfsberg / Corinthia (Austria)
**Marital status** Single
**Height** 1.78m **Weight** 68kgs
**Internet** www.friesacher.com

## Titles
- 2003: F3000 victory (Budapest)
- 2004: F3000 victory (Budapest)

## F1 tests
- 2004: Test Driver (Minardi).

## Career summary
Competition debut: 1985 (Motocross Junior)
GP debut: Australia 2005 (Minardi)

The battle for the last seat in F1 in 2005 was a hotly disputed one. Although the perspective for results was limited there were many applicants. Less than a month before the kick-off in Melbourne Paul Stoddart chose Patrick Friesacher. The latter received considerable backing from his region and a few well-heeled sponsors and joined his fellow-countryman, Christian Klien, in the premier formula in the world.

Patrick's career began in France with the 'Filière Campus' followed by F3 in both of which he finished third. He was backed by Red Bull and graduated to F3000 where he stayed for four years scoring two wins in Budapest in 2003 and 2004.

At the end of last year Minardi tested him together with several drivers. During the winter he managed to amass sufficient cash to get the seat. He arrived in Melbourne having only done a few laps at Imola.

Paul Stoddart's battle with the FIA lost him a day's practice and despite this he managed to finish the race. Given that the new engine and tyre regs may produce the odd surprise he may yet pick up a few crumbs from the rich men's tables.

# QUESTIONS
# PATRICK FRIESACHER

**And among those currently racing?**
Schumacher, of course, but there are other good drivers too.

**Who's been your best team-mate?**
André Lotterer.

**If you were a team manager what drivers would you choose?**
I'd give a young driver his chance and I'd be his team-mate.

**What do you love about this profession?**
It's my dream. I love racing. It's a special feeling.

**What don't you like about it?**
Sometimes there's too much politicking.

**What's your favourite moment of a Grand Prix?**
The start and the opening laps.

**Do you always get into your car on the same side?**
No.

**What was the first car you drove?**
It was my father's Mercedes-Benz 190. My first car was a Renault when I was 18 or 19.

**And today?**
An Alfa Romeo 166.

**What is your favourite/dream car?**
Oh, a lot. Probably a BMW M6.

**What does your helmet design mean?**
I'd been wearing the Red Bull colours for nine years. When we broke off our collaboration I designed my own helmet colours, which don't really have any particular meaning.

**What's been your best racing car so far?**
The F 1 Minardi.

**And the worst?**
The Formula Campus.

**What's your best racing memory?**
My two F3000 victories in Hungary in 2003 and 2004.

**And your worst?**
It was my first F3 season. I was a bit lost after coming from Formula Campus.

**Do you remember the first Grand Prix you saw on TV?**
I must have been around 8 or 9.

**And the first one you attended?**
The 1997 Austrian Grand Prix. I was in a wheelchair after a karting accident.

**What's your aim in racing?**
Become world champion.

**What's your favourite circuit?**
Monaco, Imola and Budapest.

**And the one you dislike the most?**
None of them.

**Who's your favourite driver in the history of racing?**
Ayrton Senna.

**What's your favourite colour?**
Blue.
**What's your favourite holiday destination?**
I've found a great place in Mexico called Playa del Carmen.
**And your favourite place for shopping?**
There are a lot.

**What do you collect?**
I've got a few watches.

**When you stop racing, what then?**
I don't know.
**What's your favourite dish?**
Pasta and pizza.
**And the ones you dislike?**
Cheese.
**What's your favourite drink ?**
Red Bull.
**Do you like alcohol?**
No.
**Have you ever smoked?**
No.
**What sports do you do?**
Cycling in all its forms, karting and Jet Ski.
**And your favourite sports?**
All kinds of motor sport.
**Who's your favourite sportsperson?**
Lance Armstrong and his exploits.
**What are your hobbies/interests outside racing?**
Fashion, what's trendy. I don't have much time. I like relaxing with my friends.
**What are your favourite films?**
Comedies which amuse me.
**And your favourite actors?**
Johnny Depp and Angelina Jolie.

**What do you watch on TV?**
Sport.
**What kind of music do you like?**
I like rock a lot.
**What do you like reading?**
Recently I read Lance Armstrong's biography. Otherwise I just glance at the daily news.

**Have you got any animals?**
My brother's got a cat. When I was small I had a tortoise.
**Outside motor racing, whom do you admire?**
Nobody really.
**If you were to go to a desert island, what would you bring?**
My girlfriend Evi.
**What's your perfect day?**
A day with no worries.
**What's been the greatest day of your life so far?**
The day I signed my contract with Minardi.
**What makes you laugh the most?**
Funny stories and comedies.
**If you were not a driver what would you have done?**
I'd probably have been a parachutist.
**What's the most important thing in life for you?**
At present it's racing and then my family and Evi.
**What are your best qualities?**
I'm very single-minded and I go for my objectives.
**And your worst?**
I think they're also shortcomings!

# CHRISTIJAN ALBERS

## MINARDI COSWORTH *21

**Date and place of birth**
April 16, 1979 in Eindhoven (Netherlands)
**Nationality** Dutch
**Place of residence** Laren (Netherlands)
**Marital status** Single
**Height** 1.76m **Weight** 68kgs
**Internet** www.christijan.com

## Titles

- 1997: Dutch karting champion (ICA 100ccs).
- 1997: Belgian and Dutch Formula Ford 1800 Champion.
- 1997: Winner of the Marlboro Masters Megane.
- 1999: German F3 Champion.

## F1 tests

- 2001: European Minardi test driver.
- 2002: KL Minardi-Asiatech test driver.
- 2004: Test with Jordan.

## Career summary

Competition debut: 1997 (Karting)
F1 debut: Australia 2005 (Minardi-Cosworth)

For F1 fans in the Netherlands Christmas came early. On 23rd December 2004 to be exact when Minardi announced that Christijan Albers was joining the team. It was a godsend for Dutch supporters who had not had much to cheer about since Jos Verstappen's sojourn at Arrows in 2001, apart from Robert Doornbos's brief appearance with Jordan last year. Albers is a very talented driver and he has won in every formula in which he has raced. He came first in the German F3 Championship in 1999 and then went into F3000 where he drove for Paul Stoddart. In 2001, the Australian bought the Minardi team and offered Albers a place as test driver. After a couple of years he left to try his luck in the DTM, the prestigious German Touring Car Championship, in which he finished second and third overall with Mercedes. Thanks to the backing of a few national companies Christijan has been able to fulfil his dream. Of course, he is well aware that the Minardi will never be quick enough to allow him to do battle up front. However, he also knows that many other drivers in front of him on the grid like Alonso, Webber, Trulli and Fisichella all began their F1 careers with the little Italian team.

# QUESTIONS

# CHRISTIJAN ALBERS

**What was the first car you drove?**
A Peugeot 205.

**And today?**
I've got a Porsche 997.

**What is your favourite/dream car?**
A Porsche Carrera GT.

**What does your helmet design mean?**
I like the colours.

**What's been your best racing car so far?**
The F1 Minardi and the DTM Mercedes-Benz.

**And the worst?**
The F3000 Lola in 2000; it was a real truck!

**What's your best racing memory?**
My German title in 1999.

**And your worst?**
I try not to think of them.

**Do you remember the first Grand Prix you saw on TV?**
It was in 1997.

**And the first one you attended?**
Silverstone in 1997.

**What's your aim in racing?**
Win championships.

**What's your favourite circuit?**
Zandvoort.

**And the one you dislike the most?**
None really.

**Who's your favourite driver in the history of racing?**
It's Michael Schumacher.

**And among those currently racing?**
The same guy.

**Who's been your best team-mate?**
Bernd Schneider the DTM Mercedes-Benz driver.

**If you were a team manager what drivers would you choose?**
I'd choose Michael Schumacher and Christijan Albers.

**What do you love about this profession?**
The sensation you get driving, then transforming a hobby into a profession.

**What don't you like about it?**
The behind-the scenes politicking.

**What's your favourite moment of a Grand Prix?**
The start.

**Do you always get into your car on the same side?**
Yes, I do.

**When you stop racing, what then?**
No, not yet.

**What's your favourite dish?**
Pizza Margherita.

**And the ones you dislike?**
I'm fairly easy in that respect.

**What's your favourite drink ?**
Diet Coke.

**Do you like alcohol?**
I don't drink.

**Have you ever smoked?**
No, I haven't.

**What sports do you do?**
Squash and Jet Ski.

**And your favourite sports?**
Squash matches, Australian football and WRC Rallying.

**Who's your favourite sportsperson?**
Some swimmers.

**What are your hobbies/interests outside racing?**
I love walking.

**What are your favourite films?**
Comedies, above all.

**And your favourite actors?**
I don't really have any. It's their acting that counts.

**What do you watch on TV?**
The series 'Friends.'

**What kind of music do you like?**
The hits you hear on the radio.

**What do you like reading?**
I don't like reading.

**What's your favourite colour?**
I prefer red.

**What's your favourite holiday destination?**
I'm still looking for it.

**And your favourite place for shopping?**
I don't like shopping.

**What do you collect?**
I like watches.

**Have you got any animals?**
No, I haven't.

**Outside motor racing, whom do you admire?**
I've never given it a thought.

**If you were to go to a desert island, what would you bring?**
Water!

**What's your perfect day?**
Relaxing.

**What's been the greatest day of your life so far?**
The day I became an F1 driver.

**What makes you laugh the most?**
I laugh easily.

**If you were not a driver what would you have done?**
It's never crossed my mind.

**What's the most important thing in life for you?**
Achieve your aims.

**What are your best qualities?**
I work hard to succeed.

**And your worst?**
Oh, certainly!

# Magazines

# WHAT CHANGES IN 2005

This year Max Mosley, the FIA President, has set himself two objectives: firstly, limit the performance of F1 cars and secondly, cap the exponential rise in costs. Thus, the legislative body has come up with a new set of regulations that may provoke a few surprises, something sadly lacking on the current F1 front.

## Technical changes

Three parameters in this area have been modified: the engine, the tyres and the aerodynamics.

### Engine

QIn the past teams used to install a special ultra-powerful, short-lifed engine for qualifying to get a good place on the starting grid. This was then replaced by a more reliable, less powerful unit for the race. All this is now a distant memory. In 2004, against all expectations, the FIA imposed a single engine for the weekend and this rule has been up-dated for 2005. The engine now has to last for two grand prix weekends practice included. The following rules apply in case of failure. If this happens on the Friday, the driver drops back ten places on the grid. If the engine blows up after the second qualifying session he goes to the back of the grid. Should a driver retire during the race, he has the right to have a new power unit installed for the following race weekend without incurring a penalty. However, since the BAR-Honda team's exploitation of this rule in Australia, the Stewards now have the right to demand justification if they feel a retirement has been a cosmetic one. This will certainly add a little spice to the proceedings and may lead to a whole new set of strategies. All the teams will go through the range of possibilities with a fine toothcomb to find the best compromise. The FIA has devised a system of seals and plates

that are fixed to the engine after the first race and must remain intact until the next grand prix.
In 2006, new regulations that have caused a fair amount of gnashing and grinding of teeth in the paddock will come into force: the cubic capacity will be reduced from 3000 to 2400 ccs and the number of cylinders will be limited to eight with a 90° angle for the block.

## Tyres

The tyre regs have also evolved. In an attempt to limit cornering speeds tyre changes are out. In 2005, each driver will have only a single set of tyres for qualifying and the grand prix. This

limitation will certainly have an effect on the race. Now, apart from mechanical problems, stops will be for fuel only – unless it starts to rain – and there will probably be fewer of them. Nursing the tyres will become capital for the drivers as will the car's set-up. When the 2005 Ferrari was presented to the press Luca di Montezemolo, the president, stated the problem clearly: *"to win we'll have to be well shod!"* The rule is simplicity itself as the FIA states: *"During the event no driver may use more than four sets of tyres in dry conditions. Two different sets (standard and option –usually*

*softer) will be given to the driver for the first day's practice on Friday. The next day one hour before free practice he must give the specification of the tyre he wants to use for the remainder of the event. Unless damp or extreme weather conditions necessitating a tyre change intervene, one of the two sets of dry rubber that has not been used must be fitted for the two practice sessions and the whole race. Only a damaged or punctured tyre may be replaced during the race itself."*
Tyres have played a vitally important role in Formula 1 over the years and this new rule will certainly liven things up.

## Aerodynamics

The legislator's aim is to reduce ground effect by 30%. The most visible result concerns the wings. The front one has been raised by 10 to 15 cms in relation to the reference plate under the monocoque (except on the 50 cm long central section). Ferrari has developed a 'chin wing' on both the F2004M and the F2005 to try and claw back some grip.
At the rear the wing has been moved forward by 15 cms towards the axis of the rear wheels. The area of the side plates has not been changed.
The height of the side extractors has been reduced by 12.5 cms to diminish ground effect. The final modification concerns the flat bottom. The floor must stop 40 cms from the axis of the rear wheels across a width of 20 cms. The aim of this is to upset the smoothness of the airflow and increase the turbulence provoked by the rotation of the wheels.

## Sporting changes

Last year at Suzuka a typhoon upset F1's usual routine. The circuit was declared unfit for use early on Saturday after torrential rain. Qualifying took place the next morning a few hours before the start of the grand prix. It gave the lawmakers a brilliant idea! Why not hold a second qualifying session on Sunday morning? This year there will be two sessions, one on Saturday and the other on Sunday morning and the grid positions will be decided by the combined times. It is good news for the spectators who have had nothing to watch on raceday morning since the Warm-up was cancelled in 2003. Needless to say the new system has not received unanimous approval and it looks like it will cause problems for TV viewers. The English channel, ITV, has already started that it will not show the Sunday morning session to preserve the interest of the race. In addition, the exploitation of practice in the Sunday papers has been eliminated by this new rule. However, for European spectators there will never be a dull moment on Sunday morning what with qualifying, the GP2 race and the drivers' parade all packed into a few hours.
The single flying lap system stays unchanged. Drivers will take to the track on Sunday morning in

the inverse order to that of the previous day. Let's hope that there will be a large number of giant TV screens and that the commentators will be up to the job of keeping the spectators informed about the evolution of what's happening on the track.
Like last year, the last six teams in the Constructors' Championship will have the right to run a third car in the two Friday practice sessions. McLaren, fifth last year, will receive a real boost thanks to this rule. Kimi Räikkönen made this comment; *"It'll be great for the team especially as the engine now has to last for two races. We can cover as many laps as we like with the third car giving us a lot of precious information. It'll be a big help when it comes to choosing tyres or other things like the set-up."*
Last year BAR took full advantage of the system and made a striking improvement.

The new Grand Prix timetable:
**Friday:** 2 free practice sessions from 11h00 to 12h00 and 14h00 to 15h00
**Saturday:** 2 free practice sessions from 09h00 to 09h45 and from 10h15 to 11h00. / 1st qualifying session from 13h00 to 14h00.
**Sunday:** 2nd qualifying session from 10h00 to 11h00. / Start of the Grand Prix 14h00 (this can vary according to the time zones).

Finally, the last chapter of the regulations concerns private testing. In keeping with the FIA's desire to cut costs all the teams, with the exception of Ferrari, have agreed to limit the number of tests to ten 3-day sessions spread over the whole season. Some of the poorer teams were hoping for an even more drastic reduction in what is a very expensive area. Goodwill seems to have prevailed. It is, however, a great pity that the Scuderia Ferrari has not seen fit to comply with this common agreement.

## Who goes where

### Team
Transfers
- Juan Pablo Montoya from Williams to McLaren.
- David Coulthard from McLaren to Red Bull.
- Ralf Schumacher from Williams to Toyota.
- Mark Webber from Jaguar to Williams.
- Nick Heidfeld from Jordan to à Williams.
- Jarno Trulli from Renault to Toyota (Sept. 2004).
- Giancarlo Fisichella from Sauber to Renault.
- Jacques Villeneuve from Renault to Sauber.
- Tiago Monteiro from Minardi (test driver) to Jordan.
- Marc Gené from Williams to Ferrari (test driver).
- Olivier Panis is now a Toyota test driver.

Out
- Cristiano Da Matta from Toyota to Champ Car (USA).
- Giorgio Pantano from Jordan.
- Timo Glock from Jordan.
- Gianmaria Bruni from Minardi to GP2.

- Zsolt Baumgartner from Minardi.
- Bas Leinders from Minardi (3rd driver).
- Ryan Briscoe from Toyota (test driver) to IRL (USA).
- Bjorn Wirdheim from Jaguar (test driver) to Champ Car (USA).
- Luciano Burti from Ferrari (test driver) to Stock Cars (Brazil).

## Team changes

### Main transfers
- Mark Smith from Renault to Red Bull.
- Pascal Vasselon from Michelin to Toyota.
- Anton Stipinovitch from McLaren to Red Bull.
- Peter Harrisson from Jaguar to Williams.
- Nicolo Petrucci from Jordan to Toyota.
- Loïc Bigois from Minardi to Williams.

## Sponsors

### Main transfers
- Red Bull from Sauber to Red Bull Racing.
- AT&T from Jaguar to McLaren.
- Trust from Minardi to Jordan.

### Main departures
- Fila from Ferrari.
- Brunotti from B.A.R.
- West from McLaren (1st August 2005).
- HSBC from Jaguar.
- Ford from Jaguar.
- Becks from Jaguar.
- Rolex from Jaguar.
- Benson&Hedges from Jordan.
- Wilux from Minardi.

### Main arrivals
- Puma from Ferrari.
- NTN Corporation from B.A.R.
- Seiko from B.A.R.
- Royal Bank of Scotland from Williams.
- Johnny Walker from McLaren.
- Nescafé Expresso from McLaren.

### Technically speaking
- Sauber: Tyre supplier changed from Bridgestone to Michelin.
- Jordan: Engine change from Ford to Toyota.
- Jordan: the team has been bought by the Midland Group hence Midland Jordan.
- Jaguar: the team has been bought by Red Bull hence the name change.

### Main departures
- David Richards from B.A.R. to Prodrive.
- Antonia Terzi from Williams.
- Malcom Oastler from Jaguar.
- Tony Purnell from Jaguar.
- David Pitchforth from Jaguar.
- Ange Pasquali from Toyota.
- Norbert Kreyer from Toyota.
- Tim Edwards from Jordan.
- Sid Watkins, medical delegate.

### In (2005 Rookies)
- Narain Karthikeyan from the Nissan World Series to Jordan.
- Patrick Friesacherfrom F3000 to Minardi.

- Christijan Albers from Mercedes DTM to Minardi.
- Tiago Monteirofrom the Nissan World Series to Jordan.
- Vitantonio Liuzzi from F3000 to Red Bull (3rd driver).

### Newcomers
- Dietrich Mateschitz, owner of the Red Bull team.
- Helmut Marko, Red Bull.
- Christian Horner, Red Bull.
- Günther Steiner, Red Bull.
- Alex Shnaider, owner of the Jordan team.
- Colin Kolles, Jordan.
- Trevor Carlin, Jordan.
- Adrian Burgess, Jordan.
- Christian Geistdorfer, Jordan.

# DID YOU KNOW?
## THE LONGEST, SHORTEST, FASTEST, SLOWEST, ETC.

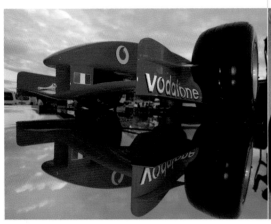

**The shortest circuit used for a grand prix?**
Long Beach in the USA in 1976 (2.220 kms).

**The longest circuit used for a grand prix?**
Pescara in Italy in 1957 (25.838 kms).

**The longest grand prix (distance)?**
The Indianapolis 500 Miles (805 kms) in the 50s.

**The longest grand prix (time)?**
Indianapolis in 1951 (3h57m38s).

**The shortest grand prix (time)?**
Australia (Adelaide) in 1991 (24m34.899s).

**The shortest grand prix (distance)?**
Australia (Adelaide) in 1991 (53 kms).

**The shortest grand prix in 2005 (distance)?**
Monaco (260.520 kms).

**The biggest gap between the first two in a grand prix?**
Two laps in the 1969 Spanish Grand Prix between Jackie Stewart and Bruce McLaren and in the 1995 Australian Grand Prix between Damon Hill and Olivier Panis.

**The smallest gap between the first two in a grand prix?**
Ten thousands of a second between Peter Gethin and Ronnie Peterson in the 1971 Italian Grand Prix at Monza.

**The highest number of starters in an F1 Grand Prix?**
34 in Germany in 1953.

**The lowest number of starters in an F1 Grand Prix?**
10 in Argentina in 1958 (Buenos Aires).

**The highest number of classified finishers in an F1 Grand Prix?**
22 in the 1952 British Grand Prix (Silverstone).

**The smallest number of classified finishers in an F1 Grand Prix?**
4 in Monaco in 1966.

**The circuit that has hosted the most F1 Grands Prix?**
The Italian Grand Prix will be held at Monza for the 56th time in 2005.

**The youngest driver to start a grand prix?**
Australian Mike Thackwell aged 19 years and 182 days (Canada 1980).

**The oldest driver to start a grand prix?**
Louis Chiron aged 55 (Monaco 1955).

**The youngest driver to set pole?**
Fernando Alonso, 21 years and 237 days (Malaysia 2003).

**The oldest driver to set pole?**
Giuseppe Farina aged 47 years and 77 days (Argentina 1954).

**The longest grand prix in 2005 (distance)?**
Malaysia (Sepang 310.408 kms) .

**Fastest-ever pole position?**
Rubens Barrichello at Monza in 2004 average: 260.395 km/h.

**Highest-ever average speed?**
Damon Hill in 1993 (Monza) 249.835 km/h.

**The youngest grand prix winner?**
Fernando Alonso, 22 years and 26 days (Hungary 2003).

**The oldest grand prix winner?**
Luigi Fagioli 53 years (France 1951).

**The youngest F1 World Champion?**
Emerson Fittipaldi was 25 in 1972.

**The oldest F1 World Champion?**
Juan Manuel Fangio was 46 when he won his fifth and last F1 World Championship for Drivers.

**The highest number of F1 World Championship titles?**
7 for Michael Schumacher (1994-95-2000-01-02-03-04).

**The biggest gap between the first and second in the F1 World Championship?**
67 points between Michael Schumacher and Rubens Barrichello in 2002 (144 to 77).

**And the smallest?**
Half-a-point between Niki Lauda and Alain Prost in 1984 (72 – 71.5).

The highest number of consecutive victories?
9: Alberto Ascari (Ferrari) in 1952-53.
**The highest number of kilometres in the lead?**
Michael Schumacher (21954 kms).
**The highest number of laps in the lead?**
Michael Schumacher (4657).
**The highest number of pole positions?**
Ayrton Senna (65).
**The highest number of consecutive pole positions?**
Ayrton Senna, 8 (from Spain 1988 to the USA in 1989).

**The highest number of consecutive victories by a constructor?**
Ferrari, 14 consecutive victories between Switzerland 1952 and Switzerland 1953.
**The highest number of rostrum finishes by a constructor?**
Ferrari with 553.
**The highest number of grands prix per engine?**
Ferrari (704).
**The highest number of victories on a circuit by a constructor?**
Ferrari in Italy at Monza with 16.
**The highest number of victories per engine?**
Ferrari (182).
**The highest number of pole positions per engine?**
Ferrari (178).
**The highest number of victories in a season by an engine?**
Renault in 1995 (16).
**The highest number of pole positions in a season by an engine?**
Renault in 1995 (16).
**The highest number of victories by a tyre manufacturer?**
Goodyear (368 victories).
**Driver having driven for the most teams?**
Andrea De Cesaris drove for ten different teams in 208 grands prix between 1980 and 1994.
**Which driver holds the record for the highest number of consecutive wins in the same grand prix?**
Ayrton Senna in Monaco with 5 victories between 1989 and 1993.

**The driver having raced in the highest number of grands prix?**
Ricardo Patrese (256).
**The highest number of F1 World Championship victories?**
Michael Schumacher (83).
**The highest number of second places in F1 Grands Prix?**
Michael Schumacher (36).
**The highest number of third places in F1 Grands Prix?**
Gerhard Berger (21).
**The highest number of rostrum finishes in F1 Grands Prix?**
Michael Schumacher (137).
**The highest number of rostrum finishes in a season.**
Michael Schumacher in 2004 (15).
**The highest number of points scored in a season?**
Michael Schumacher in 2004 (148).

**The highest number of points scored in F1 grand prix racing?**
Michael Schumacher (1186).
**The highest number of F1 Grands Prix victories in a season?**
Michael Schumacher (15 in 2004).
**The highest number of victories in the same F1 Grand Prix?**
Michael Schumacher, 7 (Canada and France).

**The highest number of pole positions in a season?**
Nigel Mansell with 14 in 1992.
**The highest number of fastest laps?**
Michael Schumacher (66).
**The highest number of fastest laps in a season?**
Michael Schumacher en 2004 (10).
**The highest number of start to finish victories?**
Ayrton Senna (19 times).
**The lowest number of victories by a driver winning the F1 World Championship?**
1: Mike Hawthorn (Ferrari) in 1958 and Keke Rosberg (Williams) in 1982.
**The highest number of F1 Grand Prix victories per nation?**
188 for Great Britain by 17 drivers.
**The highest number of grands prix by a constructor?**
Ferrari (704).
**The highest number of victories by a constructor?**
Ferrari (182).
**The highest number of F1 Drivers' Titles by a constructor?**
Ferrari (14).
**The highest number pole positions by a constructor**
Ferrari (178).
**The highest number of points scored by a constructor?**
Ferrari (3299.5).
**The highest number of doubles in grands prix?**
Ferrari (69).
**The highest number of doubles in a season?**
McLaren in 1998 (10).
**The highest number of pole positions by a constructor?**
Ferrari (178).
**The highest number of consecutive pole positions by a constructor?**
Williams, 24 between France 1992 and Japan 1993.
**The highest number of pole positions by a constructor in a season?**
15: McLaren in 1988 and 89, and Williams in 1992-93.

**Which driver has had the highest number of consecutive finishes in the points?**
Michael Schumacher has scored 24 consecutive points finishes (Hungary 2001 to Malaysia 2003).
**Which driver has had the longest unbroken stint in a team?**
Michael Schumacher who is starting his tenth year at Ferrari.
**Which drivers have raced together for the longest period of time?**
In 2001, David Coulthard and Mika Häkkinen were together at McLaren for the sixth year running.
**Which driver has the highest average per race?**
Michael Schumacher's average score per race is 5.56 points.
**What is the highest speed ever reached by an F1 car?**
367.3 km/h by Michael Schumacher's Ferrari at Monza in 2004.
**What is the biggest pile up in F1 history?**
The 1998 Belgian Grand Prix (12 cars).

# WHERE HAVE THEY GONE? 2005

Since 1990, 118 drivers have raced in at least one Formula 1 Grand Prix and many of them have continued in motor sport after leaving the category. Others have completely reoriented their careers. Here follows an update on what has happened to these drivers. We have tried to make it as accurate as possible, but at this time of the year all the competition programmes have not yet been decided so several are still waiting. Obviously 2005 newcomers do not appear on the list.

Damon Hill

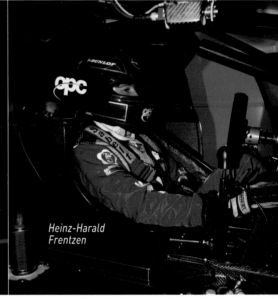

Heinz-Harald Frentzen

## A

| | |
|---|---|
| Adams Philippe (2) | Given up racing |
| Alboreto Michele (194) | Killed testing on 25th April 2001 |
| Alesi Jean (201) | DTM (Mercedes-Benz) |
| Alliot Philippe (109) | In negotiations |
| Alonso Fernando (51) | Formula 1 (Renault) |
| Andretti Michael (13) | Owner of an IRL team |
| Apicella Marco (1) | Japanese Touring Cars (Toyota) |

Jean Alesi

## B

| | |
|---|---|
| Badoer Luca (51) | Formula 1 (Ferrari test driver) |
| Bailey Julian (7) | No motor sporting activity |
| Baumgartner Szolt (20) | In negotiations |
| Barbazza Fabrizio (8) | Businessman |
| Barilla Paolo (8) | Businessman |
| Barrichello Rubens (198) | Formula 1 (Ferrari) |
| Belmondo Paul (7) | Owner of an LMES Team, Paris-Dakar driver (Nissan). |

| | |
|---|---|
| Beretta Olivier (10) | ALMS (America Le Mans Series) with Chevrolet |
| Berger Gerhard (210) | Undecided |
| Bernard Eric (45) | In negotiations |
| Bernoldi Enrique (28) | In negotiations |
| Blundell Mark (61) | TV consultant, driver manager |
| Boullion Jean-Christophe (11) | LMES (Pescarolo Sport) |
| Boutsen Thierry (163) | Businessman (plane hire) |
| Brabham David (163) | Endurance (Saleen) |
| Brundle Martin (158) | TV commentator, driver manager, Andros Trophy (Renault) |
| Bruni Gianmaria (18) | GP2 (Coloni) |
| Burti Luciano (15) | Stock Cars (Brazil) Chevrolet |
| Button Jenson (84) | Formula 1 (B.A.R) |

## C

| | |
|---|---|
| Caffi Alex (56) | Endurance (Porsche 911 GT3) |
| Capelli Ivan (93) | Italian TV consultant |
| Chiesa Andrea (3) | Swiss TV consultant |

Ivan Capelli

| | |
|---|---|
| Comas Erik (59) | GT in Japan (Nissan) plus business |
| Coulthard David (175) | Formula 1 (Red Bull) |

## D

| | |
|---|---|
| Dalmas Yannick (24) | In negotiations |
| Da Matta Cristiano (28) | Champ Car (PKV Racing) Daytona ALMS (Ford-Crawford) |
| Davidson Anthony (2) | Formula 1 (B.A.R test driver) |
| De Cesaris Andrea (208) | Surfing competitions |
| De la Rosa Pedro (63) | Formula 1 (McLaren test driver) |
| Deletraz Jean Denis (3) | Endurance (Ferrari 550) |
| Diniz Pedro (99) | Businessman |
| Donnelly Martin (14) | Businessman |

## E

| | |
|---|---|
| Enge Tomas (3) | IRL (Panther Racing) plus LMES (Aston Martin) |

## F

| | |
|---|---|
| Firman Ralph (14) | Japanese Super GT (Honda) |
| Fisichella Giancarlo (141) | Formula 1 (Renault) |
| Fittipaldi Christian (40) | Grand Am (Doran) Stock Cars (Brazil) |
| Foitek Gregor (7) | Ferrari concessionaire in Zurich (Switzerland) |
| Fontana Norberto (4) | Argentinean Touring Cars |
| Frentzen Heinz-Harald (157) | DTM (Opel) |

## G

| | |
|---|---|
| Gachot Bernard (47) | Businessman |
| Gené Marc (36) | Formula 1 (Ferrari test driver) |
| Giacomelli Bruno (69) | Furniture manufacturer in Brescia (Italy) |

Marc Gené

Ricardo Zonta   Olivier Panis

Schumacher Ralf (127)   Formula 1 (Toyota)
Senna Ayrton (161)   Killed at Imola in 1994
Suzuki Aguri (64)   Owner of a team entered in
F3 and F3000 in Japan and Champ Car

**T**

Takagi Toranosuke (32) Formula Nippon and GT (Japan)
Tarquini Gabriele (38)   WTCC (Alfa Romeo)
Tuero Esteban (16)   Argentinean Touring Cars (VW)
Trulli Jarno (130)   Formula 1 (Toyota)

Morbidelli Gianni (67)   LMES (Ferrari 575GTC)
Moreno Roberto (42)   Grand Am (Crawford-Pontiac)

**N**

Nakajima Satoru (74)   Owner of an F3000 and
F3 team in Japan
Nakano Shinji (33)   No motor sporting activity
Nannini Alessandro (77)   Businessman

**V**

Van de Poele Eric (5)   Formula X Sports Cars
Verstappen Jos (107)   In negotiations
Villeneuve Jacques (134)   Formula 1 (Sauber)

**W**

Warwick Derek (147)   Businessman
Webber Mark (50)   Formula 1 (Williams)
Wendlinger Karl (41)   ALMS (Porsche)

Glock Timo (4)   Champ Car (Rocketsports)
Gounon Jean Marc (9) Team Oreca Audi LMES (Le Mans)
Grouillard Olivier (41)   In negotiations
Gugelmin Maurizio (74)   No more sporting activity

**H**

Häkkinen Mika (162)   DTM (Mercedes-Benz)
Heidfeld Nick (84)   Formula 1 (Williams)
Herbert Johnny (162)   DTM (MG)
Hill Damon (116)   Businessman

**I**

Inoue Taki (18)   No more motor sporting activity
Irvine Eddie (147)   No more motor sporting activity

**J**

Johansson Stefan (79)   Grand Am (Riley & Scott)

**K**

Katayama Ukyo (95)   No more motor sporting activity
Kiesa Nicolas (5)   In negotiations
Klien Christian (18)   Formula 1 (Red Bull)

**L**

Lagorce Franck (2)   Endurance & Andros Trophy (Fiat)
Lammers Jan (23)   Endurance (Dome)
Lamy Pedro (32)   LMES, ALMS (Aston Martin)
FIA-GT (Ferrari)
Larini Nicola (49)   WTCC (Chevrolet)
Lavaggi Giovanni (7)   Owner/driver of an LMES team
Lehto Jyrky (62)   ALMS (Audi)

**M**

McNish Allan (16)   DTM plus Le Mans (Audi)
Mansell Nigel (187)   Golf course owner
Magnussen Jan (24)   Grand Am (Doran) and
Danish Touring Car Championship (Toyota)
Massa Felipe (34)   Formula 1 (Sauber)
Marques Tarso (26)   No motor sporting activity
Martini Pierluigi (119)   Businessman
Mazzacane Gaston (21)   Champ Car (Dale Coyne)
Modena Stefano (70)   Businessman
Montermini Andrea (21)   TV consultant
Montoya Juan Pablo (68)   Formula 1 (McLaren)

Naspetti Emanuele (5)   LMES (Ferrari 575GTC and Panoz)
Noda Hideki (3)   No motor sporting activity

**P**

Panis Olivier (158)   Formula 1 (Toyota test driver)
Pantano Giorgio (14)   GP2 (Super Nova)
Papis Massimo (7)   Grand Am (Riley & Scott Pontiac)
Patrese Ricardo (256)   Businessman
Piquet Nelson (204)   Businessman and looks after
his son Nelsinho's career
Pirro Emanuele (37)   ALMS and Le Mans 24H. (Audi)
Pizzonia Antonio (15)   Formula 1 (Williams test driver)
Prost Alain (199)   Andros Trophy (Toyota) and
GT-FFSA (Viper)

**R**

Räikkönen Kimi (50)   Formula 1 (McLaren)
Ratzenberger Roland (1)   Killed at Imola in 1994
Rosset Ricardo (32)   Businessman in the
textile industry

**S**

Salo Mika (110)   FIA-GT (Maserati)
Sato Takuma (36)   Formula 1 (B.A.R)
Sarrazin Stéphane (1)   Rallies (Subaru Impreza WRC)
and LMES (Aston Martin)
Schiatarella Domenico (6)   In negotiations
Schneider Bernd (9)   DTM (Mercedes-Benz)
Schumacher Michael (213)   Formula 1 (Ferrari)

Alain Prost

Stéphane Sarrazin

Alexander Wurz

Wilson Justin (16)   Champ Car (RuSport)
Wurz Alexander (52)   Formula 1 (3rd driver McLaren)

**Y**

Yoong Alex (16)   A1 Formula

**Z**

Zanardi Alex (41)   ETCC (BMW)
Zonta Ricardo (36)   Formula 1 (3rd driver Toyota)

# HOW MUCH DOES IT COST?

**72 million euros**: Marlboro's yearly contribution to Ferrari.

**85,000 euros**: The cost of an F1 steering wheel, a real on-board computer.

**60 euros**: The price of a pair of driving gloves.

**400,000 euros**: Estimation of the price of renting a 60-metre yacht for the Monaco Grand Prix. This kind of floating 'palace' can welcome around 100 people for cocktails or dinner.

**58 million euros**: Michael Schumacher's annual income (salary and advertising contracts). He is the highest paid sportsman in the world just ahead of Tiger Woods, the American golfer. Football players David Beckham (25 million euros) and Zinedine Zidane (15 million euros) don't punch at the same weight!

**300 million euros**: The cost of the construction of the Shanghai circuit in China.

**1 euro**: The symbolic sum paid by Dietrich Mateschitz, the owner of the Red Bull energy drinks company, for Jaguar. In return he has undertaken to invest some 300 million euros over the next three years, in particular in the Cosworth Engineering Company.

**30 euros**: The price of a 2004 World Championship Michael Schumacher cap.

**800 million euros:** The annual amount earned by the F1 Commercial rights. 23% of this sum (184 million euros) is paid out to the ten teams.

**420 euros**: the highest price for a grandstand seat at the Monaco Grand Prix.

**18,000 euros**: The cost of a truck (cab only). In general, the teams have an agreement with manufacturers like Mercedes-Benz, Renault or Fiat.

**1000 euros**: The cost estimate of one kilometre in private testing.

**18 million euros**: The annual amount spent on travel by the Scuderia Ferrari. Midland-Jordan pays out only 5 million euros.

**84 euros**: The price of a spectator enclosure ticket for 4 days at Indianapolis (F1).

**35 million euros**: The McLaren team's annual research and development budget.

**1000 euros**: The average price of a room in the Hotel de Paris during the Monaco Grand Prix.

**19 million euros**: The price of Michael Schumacher's private Falcon 2000 jet.

**3500 euros**: Average monthly salary of an F1 mechanic. The figure varies from 2000 up to 5000 euros depending on the wealth of the team. In case of victory or points scored the staff can earn bonuses, some of which can be quite substantial.

**400 million euros**: The cost of Paragon, the new McLaren factory.

**10 million euros**: The estimated annual income of Willi Weber, the Schumacher brothers' manager.

**85,000 euros**: The sum fetched by one of the late Ayrton Senna's helmets at an auction.

**12,000 euros**: The cost of an F1 clutch.

**7.5 million euros**: The estimated annual salary of Mike Gascoyne, the former Renault technical

director, seduced by Toyota at the end of 2003. It is a record in this area. Ross Brawn, his equivalent at Ferrari, receives only half this amount.

**15,000 euros**: The cost of a day in a wind tunnel.

**33,000 euros**: The price of a suite in one of the big Monaco Hotels for the Grand Prix weekend.

**41 million euros**: The annual amount of the Scuderia Ferrari staff salaries.

**150 euros**: The price of a pair of Puma driving shoes.

**100,000 euros**: The price of the Richard Mille watch worn by Jean Todt.

**185 million euros**: The annual budget of the BMW engineering department.

**400,000 euros**: The estimated cost of a works engine (Ferrari, BMW, Renault).

**2600 euros**: The price of Jenson Button's Alpinestar brand Sparco driving suit.

**10 euros**: The price of an official Grand Prix programme.

**10 million euros**: The price of an F1 field for a grand prix. The organisers grit their teeth and pay up. The amount depends on the client: the overseas events are much more expensive.

**120 million euros**: Renault's annual investment in Formula 1.

**5 million euros**: Scuderia Ferrari's general manager and competitions director Jean Todt's annual salary.

**130 euros**: The price of an Arai visor on Kimi Raïkkönen's helmet.

**13,000 euros**: The cost price of the Schuberth helmet worn by Michael Schumacher, which took 3000 hours in the wind tunnel to design and make.

**25 euros**: The price of a Renault F1 Tee-shirt.

**2,800 euros**: the cost of a single tyre.

**53 million euros**: Japanese Cigarette company Mild Seven's annual sponsoship of the Renault team.

**125 euros**: the price of a replica Team Renault shirt.

**150 million euros**: The estimated annual income of Bernie Ecclestone.

**3,000 euros**: The average price of a Formula One Paddock club ticket for the whole weekend. This varies from one grand prix to another.

**17,000 euros**: The cost of a trailer transporting an F1 team's cars or equipment.

**50 euros**: The price of a place on the 'Rocher' in Monte Carlo the day of the grand prix.

**20,000 euros** : is the average price of an F1 photographer's equipment consisting of 2 cameras, 4 or 5 lenses, 2 flashes and a laptop for transmission.

**4 million euros**: The estimated annual income of Ross Brawn, the Ferrari technical director.

**630 euros**: The cost of an F1 car's rear-view mirror.

**400,000 euros**: The annual salary of Pierre Dupasquier, the Michelin Competitions director.

**11,000 euros**: The cost of a set of F1 exhaust pipes.

**28,000 euros**: The amount of travel money spent to follow a grand prix season (economy class air tickets, middle range hotel, car rental and food).

**10 million euros**: The estimated annual cost of the McLaren Communications centre at the grands prix. It is the current yardstick in this area in the paddock.

**1600 euros**: The sales price of an Arai helmet like David Coulthard's for example.

**6,000 euros**: The cost of an F1 nose (car that is!).

**130,000 euros**: The cost of an F1 carbon monocoque.

**100 euros**: The price of all Jean Pablo Montoya's Alpine star fireproof underwear.

**1,000,000 euros**: The cost of a conventional motor home.

**4 million euros**: The cost of a hospitality unit made up of two motor homes with the welcome structure stretched between the two units like BAR's or Renault's.

**3000 euros**: The average monthly salary of an F1 journalist.

**1.7 million euros**: The average cost of a two-story transporter like Ferrari's, McLaren's, BAR's.

**40,000 euros**: The cost of a complete bodywork set for an F1 one car.

**190 euros**: The cost of a single Brembo brake pad.

**150 million euros**: Honda's annual investment in B.A.R.

# WILLIAMS
## SOME FIGURES

Paranoia has been an inherent part of Formula 1 for quite some time now. Nonetheless, the BMW-Williams team has been kind enough to provide us with some interesting figures.

BMW assembles some 200 engines each year for the Williams team. Each one is made up of 5,000 parts, 1000 of which are different. It takes 100 hours to put an engine together: it weighs 90 kgs. Its power easily exceeds 900 bhp and maximum revs are limited to 19,000 rpm. The new regulations are supposed to privilege endurance over performance.

A driver burns more than 600 calories and loses an average of 2 kilos during each grand prix. The cockpit temperature is around 50°. His heartbeat can go up to 190 per minute!

A Williams can go from zero to 200 km/h and back to zero in less than 7 seconds! 0 to 100 km/h takes 2.5 seconds.

The race team is made up of 100 people (Williams 70, BMW 20 plus 10 to look after overall management and hospitality). Around 60 people attend test sessions.

Williams F1 transports 25 tons of equipment to each event including 3 chassis. For the European races the equipment is carried in 2 transporters that park in the paddock.

Braking from 200 km/h to a standstill takes 1.9 seconds over a distance of 55 metres. The centrifugal force is around 5 G. This means that a driver who weighs 75 kgs must bear a weight of 375 kgs, five times that of his body.

The temperature of a tyre often goes up to 100 degrees while that of the carbon brake discs exceeds 1000 degrees. Temperatures at the exhaust exit reach 950 degrees C.

BMW provides the team with six engines and transports 6 tons of equipment.

The cars consume around 1200 litres of fuel, 70 litres of oil for the engines and 30 litres for the gearboxes at each grand prix.

At certain races in the summer and also in Malaysia the Williams team and its guests consume 3,300 litres of water and fizzy drinks.

In 2005, in compliance with the rules each car will have 4 sets of tyres per weekend.

250,000 hours' work are necessary to draw up the plans for the chassis and as many again to construct it. It takes 2 days to assemble a Williams FW 27. The cars are dismantled and thoroughly checked between the grands prix.

370 km/h is the highest speed reached during the season (Monza). In Monaco, the highest is around 290 km/h. A driver changes gear some 2,800 times during a normal race as compared with over 3,000 in Monte Carlo.

# RÄIKKÖNEN MONTOYA
## ICE AND FIRE

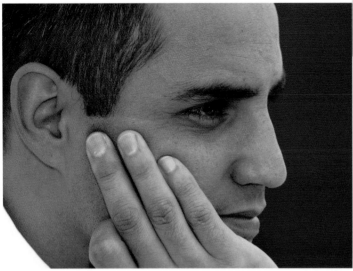

In 1988 and 1989 McLaren had what many journalists christened the 'Dream Team' consisting of the late Ayrton Senna and Alain Prost. Over two years they fought some memorable battles for the title, which have become part of F1 legend. In that era there were no team orders, no commercial or political pressures to cloud the picture and they went at it hammer and tongs dominating their rivals. In 1988, the title went to the Brazilian who scored eight victories and thirteen pole positions. The following year it was Prost's turn even if he won in the courtroom following the infamous collision at Suzuka in the last round of the championship. Senna won six races and again notched up thirteen pole positions. The Frenchman was less brilliant in qualifying with just a couple of poles each year. On the track he scored seven wins in 1988 and four the following season. The man who refereed this family feud was Ron Dennis.

Fifteen years later still at the head of McLaren he has created another Dream Team by persuading Juan Pablo Montoya to join Kimi Räikkönen. It is a mixture of ice and fire. Blue-eyed blond-haired Räikkönen comes from Finland and the stocky dark-haired brown-eyed Montoya from Colombia.

The Finn wears his motto on his helmet, 'Iceman.' He is withdrawn, taciturn almost, and never shows his feelings. His phlegm is legendary. When he won his first grand prix in Malaysia in 2003 he was hardly more demonstrative than usual. His attitude was in striking contrast to that of Michael Schumacher who generally performs his famous victory leap on the rostrum. Kimi is about as easy to interview as the Sphinx. His answers are monosyllabic and banal and trying to extract words from him is like pulling teeth. In addition no flicker of emotion ruffles the calm of his facial expression. He is not a spectator-friendly animal and he does not hang around in the paddock. He lives only for racing, spends his time with his engineers in the truck or motor home when he not at the back of his pit. Racing is his whole world.

His private life and his marriage to Jenny, a model, seem to be in a state of extreme tension at the moment and his recent nocturnal escapades have been spread all over the pages of the gutter press. His temperament changes when he gets into his car's cockpit. The icy exterior is replaced by an Olympian inner calmness. His driving is precision itself: always razor-sharp, consistent and aggressive. Peter Sauber discovered him and he

showed remarkable maturity as soon as he got behind the wheel of an F1 despite limited experience in Formula Renault. Ron Dennis prised him away from the Swiss team to replace Mika Häkkinen who retired at the end of 2001. In 2003, he finished second in the world championship behind Michael Schumacher on whom he exerted intense pressure throughout the season. Not until the last race did the German clinch his sixth title. Given Räikkönen's phenomenal rise to fame he looks like being Schumacher's natural successor.

In 2004, the McLaren team went through a very lean spell and fell almost to the rear of the grid due to a lack of performance and reliability. This, though, did not affect Kimi Rikkönen's motivation and he remained unmoved by the 'slings and arrows of outrageous fortune:' in his case serial retirements! Around mid-season McLaren brought out a heavily revised version of the MP4-19B and it was a whole quicker out of the box. He was in the lead in the German Grand Prix when his rear wing flew off and his car slammed into the barriers at around 250 km/h. It gave him a hell of a fright and when he got out of the smoking wreck, a brief gesture expressed his anger. It was the first time he showed any emotion. His win on the Spa circuit was a fitting reward for his early season bad luck. When he crossed the finishing line, he raised his arms and gestured to the public. He even smiled on the rostrum a few moments later. Soon, though, he was his usual impassive self.

When his car is running properly he never misses an opportunity. On the track he fears no one as testified to by his famous skirmish with Michael Schumacher in the 2003 Australian Grand Prix. The long-trumpeted arrival of Montoya, who is replacing 'Mr Nice Guy' David Coulthard, has not had any effect on him. *"My team-mate's name is of no importance. The real challenge is to beat Michael Schumacher. What Montoya wants won't change my way of working. Each of us will work with our respective engineers and it won't change my position in the team."*

Ron Dennis hopes that Kimi will react positively to the arrival of the bubbly, out-spoken and very quick Colombian. The two drivers met on several occasions last year, often during the drivers' parades. They share a common passion for motor bikes. At Magny-Cours they had a fine old time on mini off-road machines. For the moment they seem to be getting on well together.

Juan Pablo is a very experienced driver. After he won the F3000 Championship in 1998 and did a lot of testing for Williams, he headed off to the United States. There he won the Champ Car title and the Indianapolis 500 Miles. He then came back to Europe and joined the Williams team. He spent four years at Grove and his results were not on a par with his expectations. His arrival at McLaren was announced sixteen months before it became effective, a record! His parting gift to his team was victory in the Brazilian Grand Prix, the last of the 2004 season.

He is a bit of a joker and has a huge zest for life. It takes a big effort for him not to spend all day in the F1 paddock, and instead to bill and coo with his wife Connie or joke with friends! Physical fitness is one of his major preoccupations as his love of hamburgers is not really in keeping with the dietary standards of a modern F1 driver. After his first tests in November he decided it was time to do something about this and he went on a slimming course. In a few weeks he lost six kilos. While Räikkönen is not one to hog the limelight the Colombian likes to be in the public eye; he is not over-enamoured of technical debriefings. He drives by instinct and is capable of getting the best – and even more – out of his car. In that way he reminds one of Nigel Mansell who was very similar in style even if it offended the purists.

His driving is a mixture of opportunism and adrenaline. Ron Dennis is counting on exploiting the talent of his new show-pony. He is hoping to get more out of him that did his old friend, Frank Williams. Montoya never really fitted into the Williams format. Will he do so at McLaren? The intention seems to be there. " I know I'm going to have to work harder and I think I'll become a better driver. Ron has given me an undertaking!" McLaren is noted for its rigour, which provides a striking contrast with Montoya's Latin temperament. For both himself and Ron Dennis it is a big challenge. The latter will not find it easy to manage the two drivers. *"I'm amused by the media's insistence on this subject. I see their rivalry as a very positive element. In fact, I just can't wait! Fair but firm management is what's needed in all circumstances."*
Each driver's main motivation is to dominate his team-mate and in such circumstances neither will give the other the slightest leeway. The McLaren team looks pretty good. After the Piquet-Mansell interlude at Williams and the Senna-Prost years at McLaren, some of the most exciting pages in modern F1 may be written in the coming months. Both drivers, though, have one aim in mind: to knock Michael Schumacher off his pedestal!

# IN THE ALPS
## WITH JARNO

Jarno Trulli is certainly one of the friendliest drivers in Formula 1. At the beginning of January he shared one of his get-fit days with us in his usual pleasant, smiling fashion at St.Moritz in the Swiss Alps.

# CHAMPS ELYSEES MADNESS!

On Sunday 5<sup>th</sup> December 2004 the 'Place Dauphine' was cold and grey. Suddenly the peace and calm of one of the most exclusive quarters in Paris was shattered by the scream of a V10 engine.

And not just any old V10 but the most prestigious of them all, Ferrari. At the wheel of the car was Michael Schumacher, 7-times world champion. The man behind it all was Jean Todt who, together with a few friends like film producer and director, Luc Besson, decided to put on a parade to lend their support to the Health Ministry's 'ICM.' This is an institute dedicated to the study of the human brain and the spinal cord, in which they have all invested a lot of energy along with Professor Saillant.

The world champion was a victim of his fans massed at the top of the Champs Elysées. The Ferrari's engine was unable to cope with the snail's pace of the parade on the way up the Avenue Foch. The V10 gave up the ghost just as the procession solemnly marched its way under the 'Arc de Triomphe' on the 'Place de l'Etoile,' and the F2004 started to freewheel down the Champs Elysées! Suddenly it disappeared under a mass of humanity and for a moment it looked like the worst was about to happen. The police were completely overwhelmed by the Parisians' enthusiasm as they surged forward to touch the helmet of their idol or failing that, the bodywork of the car. The absence of barriers facilitated their task and Michael found himself eye

to eye with his fans, literally. He coped with it all with his usual Olympian calm. The Ferrari then continued on its way to the 'Place de la Concorde' pushed by its mechanics. Police protection was reinforced and a slightly shaken Michael Schumacher finished his journey in a Ferrari 360 Modena spyder in the hands of former Scuderia works driver, René Arnoux. The Paris Police headquarters reckoned that around 300,000 people attended the parade.

Michael managed to fan the flames of public enthusiasm like Johnny Halliday during his concerts in the 'Stade de France.' Indeed, the previous day he had also brought the crowd to its feet in the aforementioned stadium during the Race of Champions. Overall, it was a striking demonstration of both the German's and F1's popularity. The parade itself was an excellent way of setting the record straight. Motor racing's top division is not as ailing as all that! It may be true that the TV audience is falling but it is the same thing for sport as a whole.

The undisputed popularity of F1 among town dwellers is not new and is helped certainly by the fact that it is free. More and more events of this kind are being held and the spectators flock to them in ever-increasing numbers. Early last summer around Regent Street and Picadilly circus in the heart of London a display by eight F1 cars – one of which driven by Nigel Mansell – attracted over 400,000 people. The success of this event led to promoters putting forward several proposals for a grand prix passing in front of Buckingham Palace, the home of Queen Elizabeth II. Paris did not want to be left out and the idea of a grand prix under Jacques Chirac's windows has also been mooted. Michael Schumacher could be said to have laid the foundation of this race!

A new orientation is on the move. Formula 1 has now come to cities to do its own promotion and further its renown by touching a wider audience than the spectators who go to grands prix paying sometimes-exorbitant prices. Renault understood this very quickly and its exhibitions in Moscow, Madrid and Lyon have attracted huge crowds. Should the circuits eventually price themselves out of the market events organised in the heart of cities like London, New York and Paris could save Formula 1.

# GP2 SERIES, FUTURE F1 'STARS' STOMPING GROUND

Among the entries are several famous names like Piquet, Rosberg and Lauda. This year the sons of three former F1 World Champions will race against each other in the GP2 Series. It has replaced F3000 and looks like it has a rosy future ahead of it. The Dallaras are powered by a 4-litre V8 Renault engine putting out some 600 bhp and the grooved tyres are supplied by Bridgestone. The races are part of the European F1 Grand Prix programmes and will be run in two heats, one on race morning. Among the other leading contenders are Heikki Kovalainen, hero of the Race of Champions, Frenchmen Pla, Premat and Lapierre, Viso from Venezuela, Bruni from Italy and the very promising American Speed Scott. GP2 has all the necessary ingredients to provide a passionately exciting and hard-fought championship.

Gianmaria Bruni (I), Coloni Motorsport.
Giorgio Pantano (I), Super Nova.

Scott Speed (USA), iSport International.

Borja Garcia (E), Racing Engineering.

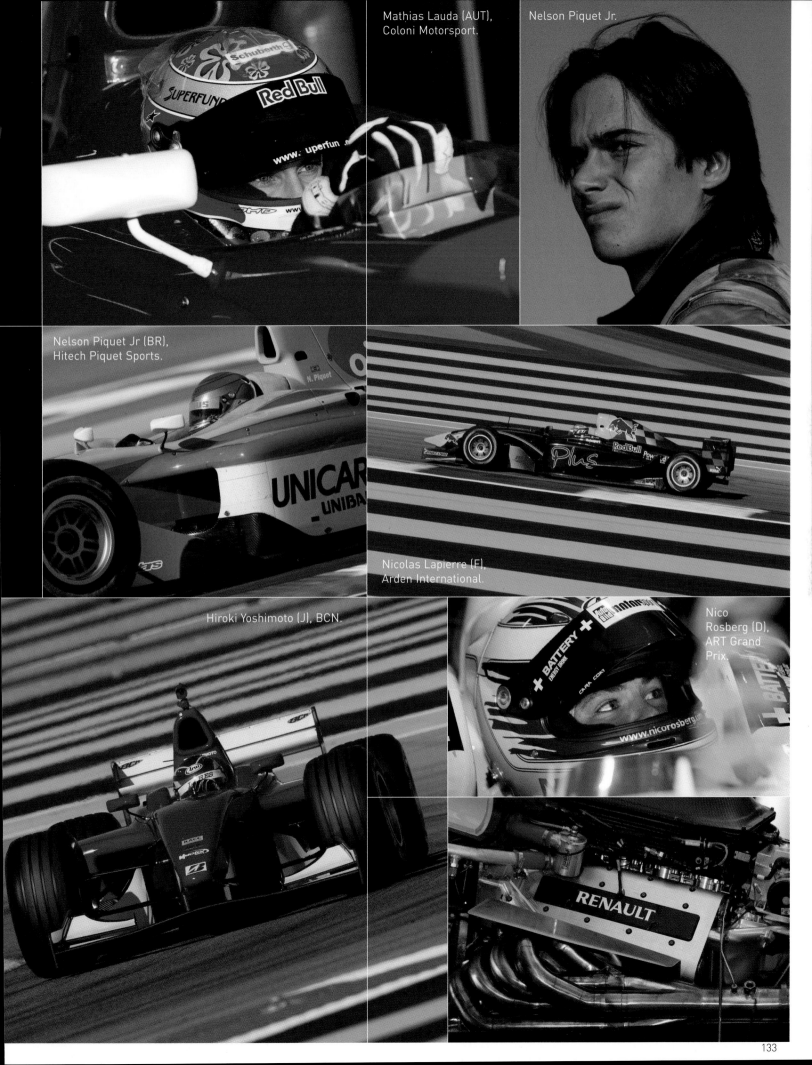

Mathias Lauda (AUT),
Coloni Motorsport.

Nelson Piquet Jr.

Nelson Piquet Jr (BR),
Hitech Piquet Sports.

Nicolas Lapierre (F),
Arden International.

Hiroki Yoshimoto (J), BCN.

Nico Rosberg (D),
ART Grand Prix.

# F1GIRLS

# The 2005 Calendar

## 19 Grands Prix

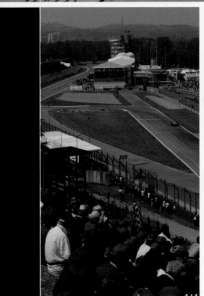

**Sunday 6th March 2005**

**Start** 14h00 local time,
(04h00 in Europe).

**Distance** 58 laps of the 5.303 km
circuit: 307.574 km.

**Crowed in 2004** 360,000 spectators
over the 3 days with 120,000 on
race day.

# 1

# AUSTRALIA
## MELBOURNE ALBERT PARK

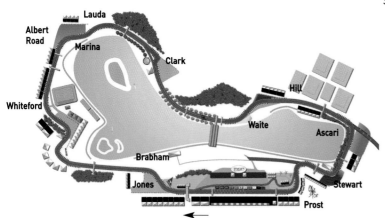

Since 1996, the grand prix season has begun in Australia. Melbourne is about 20 hours by plane from Europe and the ten-hour time difference causes more than a little disorientation! The neatly laid out paddock behind the pits is conducive to a certain conviviality even in the suspicious world of modern F1. New faces, new ideas, fresh hopes for the coming season are all part of the Melbourne ambience: until the flag drops and reality cuts in as it is only on the track that pre-season hopes are confirmed or dashed. Although it does take a few grands prix for the strengths and weaknesses of the different cars to appear, the dusty surface of the Australian circuit - used only once a year – usually gives a pointer as to who is on the right track and who isn't.

The Aussies love the race and the resurgence in interest in their home grand prix has been helped by the presence of two of their own, Paul Stoddart, and Mark Webber who at last is in a car, the Williams, that will show whether or not he has got what it takes to make it to the very top.

A few days before battle begins the grand prix organiser has scheduled a parade in the town centre to give maximum exposure to his grand prix and Mark will be the centre of attraction.

The circuit, situated in a park dotted with eucalyptus trees, winds its way around a lake inhabited by a large number of swans, which have long since become accustomed to this once-yearly din.

The ocean is nearby; only some hundreds of metres from the circuit with hot sand, blue water and beautiful girls. Unfortunately, the F1circus has little time to take advantage of these pleasures!

**The records to beat**

**Pole position**
M. Schumacher (Ferrari) in 2004, 1:24.408 (226.172 km/h)

**Average race speed**
M. Schumacher (Ferrari) in 2004, 1:24:15.757 (219.010 km/h)

**Lap records**
M. Schumacher (Ferrari) in 2004, 1:24.125 (226.933 km/h)

## 2004 statistics

**Pole position**
M. Schumacher (Ferrari), 1:24.408 (226.172 km/h)

**GP results**

| | |
|---|---|
| 1. M. Schumacher (Ferrari) | 1:24:15.757 |
| | (58 laps, 219.010 km/h) |
| 2. Barrichello (Ferrari) | + 13.605 |
| 3. Alonso (Renault) | + 34.673 |
| 4. R. Schumacher (Williams-BMW) | + 1:00.423 |
| 5. Montoya (Williams-BMW) | + 1:08.536 |
| 6. Button (B.A.R-Honda) | + 1:10.598 |
| 7. Trulli (Renault) | 1 lap |
| 8. Coulthard (McLaren-Mercedes) | 1 lap |

**Fastest lap**
M. Schumacher (Ferrari), 1:24.125 (226.933 km/h)

**Address**
Australian Grand Prix Corporation
Grand Prix House
220, Albert Road, P.O. Box 577,
South Melbourne, Victoria 3205
Australia
Tel.: (+61) 3 92 58 71 00
Fax: (+61) 3 96 99 37 27
Internet: www.grandprix.com.au

**Location**
The circuit is located to the south of Melbourne, less than 10 kilometres from the city centre. The international airport, Melbourne-Tullamarine is 20 kilometres north of the city.

**Previous winners**
2004: M. Schumacher (Ferrari)
2003: D. Coulthard (McLaren-Mercedes)
2002: M. Schumacher (Ferrari)
2001: M. Schumacher (Ferrari)
2000: M. Schumacher (Ferrari)
1999: E. Irvine (Ferrari)
1998: M. Häkkinen ( McLaren-Mercedes)
1997: D. Coulthard (McLaren-Mercedes)
1996: D. Hill (Williams-Renault)
1995: D. Hill (Williams-Renault)
1994: N. Mansell (Williams-Renault)
1993: A. Senna (McLaren-Ford)
1992: R. Patrese (Williams-Renault)
1991: A. Senna (McLaren-Honda)
1990: N. Piquet (Benetton-Ford)
...

Michael Schumacher has won the Australian Grand Prix four times (2000-01-02-04).
Alain Prost (1985-86), Ayrton Senna (1991-93) and Damon Hill (1995-96) have all scored doubles.

The first winner of an Australian Grand Prix counting for the F1 World Championship was Keke Rosberg who saw the chequered flag in his Williams in Adelaide on 3rd November 1985.

The 2005 event will be the 21st Australian Grand Prix.
- Adelaide: 1985-1995 (11 times)
- Melbourne: 1996 - 2005 (10 times)

Sunday 20th March 2005

**Start** 15h00 local time,
(08h00 in Europe).

**Distance** 56 laps of the 5.543 km
circuit: 310.408 km.

**Crowed in 2004**
92,000 spectators on race day.

2

# MALAYSIA
## KUALA LUMPUR SEPANG

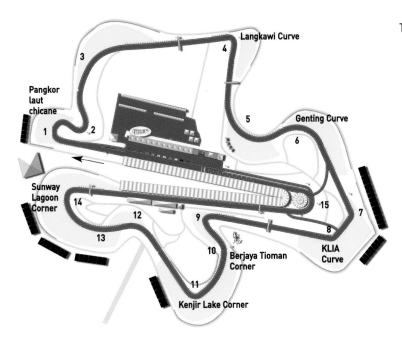

## The records to beat

**Pole position**

M. Schumacher (Ferrari) in 2004, 1:33.074 (214.397 km/h)

**Average race speed**

M. Schumacher (Ferrari) in 2004, 1:31:07.490 (204.384 km/h)

**Lap record**

Montoya (Williams-BMW) in 2004, 1:34.223 (211.782 km/h)

## 2004 statistics

**Pole position**

M. Schumacher (Ferrari), 1:33.074 (214.397 km/h)

**GP results**

| | |
|---|---|
| 1. M. Schumacher (Ferrari) | 1:31:07.490 |
| | (56 laps, 204.384 km/h) |
| 2. Montoya (Williams-BMW) | + 5.022 |
| 3. Button (B.A.R-Honda) | + 11.568 |
| 4. Barrichello (Ferrari) | + 13.616 |
| 5. Trulli (Renault) | + 37.360 |
| 6. Coulthard (McLaren-Mercedes) | + 53.098 |
| 7. Alonso (Renault) | + 1:07.877 |
| 8. Massa (Sauber-Petronas) | 1 lap |

**Fastest lap**

Montoya (Williams-BMW), 1:34.223 (211.782 km/h)

The Malaysian race is the hottest grand prix of the year with the thermometer hovering around the 50° C mark. Add to this a humidity level of 90% and everybody turns into a kind of walking sponge! Indeed, the organisers use this to spearhead their promotion campaign. Despite their best efforts the grand prix has still not really caught on. The ticket prices are prohibitive for the majority of the population and it is the spectators from abroad who form the bulk of the crowd. Petronas, the national petrol company, proudly flies its country's colours in F1 thanks to its links with the Sauber team.

This round has now become part of the F1 trail. The people are charming, always smiling and very welcoming. The Malaysians look after the organisation whose quality is irreproachable and the infrastructure is about as modern as you can get.

It is a very tough grand prix for the drivers obliged to undergo special physical preparation, as it gets incredibly hot in the cockpit due to the ambient temperatures.

Finally, the period between the Australian and Malaysian Grands Prix is an excellent opportunity to spend a few days' holiday lounging on the beach under the palm trees.

**Address**

Sepang International Circuit Sdn Bhd
(457 149-T)
Pusat Pentadbiran Litar
Jalan Pekeliling
64000 Klia, Selangor Darul Ehsan,
Malaysia
Tel.: (+60 3) 85 26 20 00
Fax: (+60 3) 85 26 10 00
Internet: www.malaysiangp.com.my

**Location**

The Sepang circuit is located in the south of the Malaysian peninsula 60 kilometres to the south of the capital Kuala Lumpur. The international airport is only 5 kilometres from this ultra modern facility.

**Previous winners**

2004: M. Schumacher (Ferrari)
2003: K. Räikkönen (McLaren-Mercedes)
2002: M. Schumacher (Ferrari)
2001: M. Schumacher (Ferrari)
2000: M. Schumacher (Ferrari)
1999: E. Irvine (Ferrari)

2005 will be the seventh Malaysian Grand Prix all held on the Sepang circuit. Michael Schumacher has dominated the event winning three out of the six races held up to the present (2000-01-04). Eddie Irvine in his Ferrari won the first Malaysian Grand Prix on 17th October 1999.

**Sunday 3rd April 2005**

**Start** 14h30 local time,
(12h30 in Europe).

**Distance** 57 laps of the 5.412 km
circuit: 308.238 km*
(*start line offset: 0.246 km).

**Crowed in 2004**
45,000 spectators

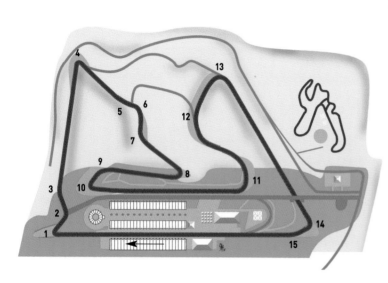

The Bahrain archipelago has been **independent since 1971. Its surface** covers 710 square kilometres. It is situated in the Persian Gulf between the east coast of Saudi Arabia linked to the main island by a 25-kilometre bridge and the peninsula made up of around thirty islands including Qatar. It is a very small country whose principal assets are its immense oil reserves. It has also begun to develop tourism and investment as a means of enlarging its economy. Bernie Ecclestone wanted to gain a foothold in the region and after various contacts he reached an agreement with the Bahrain organisers who snatched the grand prix from under their neighbour Dubai's nose. The latter was somewhat miffed about this and to make a point built a circuit in the desert for international events.

In 2004, the arrival of Philippe Gurdjian in Bahrain proved crucial as the construction work had fallen way behind. The inspiration for the circuit, designed by Hermann Tilke, comes from local architecture and the paddock and pits bear a close resemblance to an oasis with palm trees and lawns.
The first grand prix in the Middle East was impeccably organised and it received the FOM (Formula One Management) award for the best organisation of a grand prix counting towards the F1 World Championship. The circuit is located on the edge of the desert and for the visitor it is in a complete change of scenery. On raceday last year there was a slight wind that brought a few drops of rain and grains of sand to the track. The F1 circus received a warm welcome from the population and overall the grand prix went down well with everybody.

**Address**
Bahrain International Circuit
Gate 255
Gulf of Bahrain Avenue
Umm Jidar 1062
Kingdom of Bahrain
Tel.: + 973 40 64 44
Fax: + 973 40 65 55
Internet: www.bahraingp.com

**Previous winners**
2004: M. Schumacher (Ferrari)

## The records to beat
### Pole position
M. Schumacher (Ferrari) in 2004, 1:30.139 (216.345 km/h)
### Average race speed
M. Schumacher (Ferrari) in 2004, 1:28:34.875 (208.976 km/h)
### Lap records
M. Schumacher (Ferrari) in 2004, 1:30.252 (216.074 km/h)

## 2004 statistics
### Pole position
M. Schumacher (Ferrari), 1:30.139 (216.345 km/h)
### GP results

| | | |
|---|---|---|
| 1. M. Schumacher (Ferrari) | 1:28:34.875 | |
| | (57 laps, 208.976 km/h) | |
| 2. Barrichello (Ferrari) | + 1.367 | |
| 3. Button (B.A.R-Honda) | + 26.687 | |
| 4. Trulli (Renault) | + 32.214 | |
| 5. Sato (B.A.R-Honda) | + 52.460 | |
| 6. Alonso (Renault) | + 53.156 | |
| 7. R. Schumacher (Williams-BMW) | + 58.155 | |
| 8. Webber (Jaguar) | 1 lap | |

### Fastest lap
M. Schumacher (Ferrari), 1:30.252 (216.074 km/h)

**Sunday 24th April 2005**

**Start** 14h00 local time.

**Distance** 62 laps of the 4.933 km circuit: 305.609 km* (*start line offset: 0.237 km).

**Crowed in 2004** 80,000 spectators on race day.

4

## SAN MARINO
IMOLA  AUTODROMO ENZO & DINO FERRARI

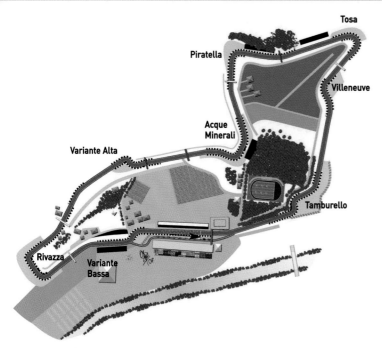

## The records to beat

### Pole position
Button (B.A.R-Honda) in 2004, 1:19.753 (222.672 km/h)

### Average race speed
M. Schumacher (Ferrari) in 2004, 1:26:19.670 (212.405 km/h)

### Lap records
M. Schumacher (Ferrari) in 2004, 1:20.411 (220.850 km/h)

## 2004 statistics

### Pole position
Button (B.A.R-Honda), 1:19.753 (222.672 km/h)

### GP results

| | |
|---|---|
| 1. M. Schumacher (Ferrari) | 1:26:19.670 |
| | (62 laps, 212.405 km/h) |
| 2. Button (B.A.R-Honda) | + 9.702 |
| 3. Montoya (Williams-BMW) | + 21.617 |
| 4. Alonso (Renault) | + 23.654 |
| 5. Trulli (Renault) | + 36.216 |
| 6. Barrichello (Ferrari) | + 36.683 |
| 7. R. Schumacher (Williams-BMW) | + 55.730 |
| 8. Räikkönen (McLaren-Mercedes) | 1 lap |

### Fastest lap
M. Schumacher (Ferrari), 1:20.411 (220.850 km/h)

Once again the San Marino Grand Prix nearly disappeared from the calendar. Over the last few years its existence has been under quasi-permanent threat but it has somehow managed to survive. Bernie Ecclestone stated that the 2005 race would be the last; then at the end of the year it was announced that the mayor of Imola had signed a new contract until 2009. Thus, the opening round of the European F1 season will take place on the borders of the Tuscany region. The Enzo and Dino Ferrari circuit needs a serious facelift and the infrastructure is from another age.

The communications systems are completely outdated and bear no relation to the current needs of journalists. The main building housing the teams, the pressroom and a few hospitality units is no longer appropriate for today's Formula 1. The paddock, squashed by the proximity of the River Santerno, is far too cramped to welcome the fleet of modern trucks.

By what miracle has Imola been saved? Ferrari's power certainly has something to do with it. However, this event has lost a lot of its glamour. The Tifosi's enthusiasm seems to have waned and they do not have the same fervour as at Monza.

It is a pity as the region is very attractive and Bologna, noted for its cuisine, is only a short drive down the motorway.

### Address
Autodromo Internazionale Enzo e Dino Ferrari
Sagis Spa, Via Fratelli Rosselli 2,
40 026 Imola (Bo),
Italy
Tel.: (+39) 05 42 63 45 11
Fax: (+39) 05 42 30 420
Internet: www.autodromoimola.com

### Location
The Dino and Enzo Ferrari circuit is 35 kilometres southeast of Bologna and a short walk from the little town of Imola. The nearest airports are Bologna and Forli.

### Previous winners
2004: M. Schumacher (Ferrari)
2003: M. Schumacher (Ferrari)
2002: M. Schumacher (Ferrari)
2001: R. Schumacher (Williams-BMW)
2000: M. Schumacher (Ferrari)
1999: M. Schumacher (Ferrari)
1998: D. Coulthard (McLaren-Mercedes)
1997: H.-H. Frentzen (Williams-Renault)
1996: D. Hill (Williams-Renault)
1995: D. Hill (Williams-Renault)
1994: M. Schumacher (Benetton-Ford)
1993: A. Prost (Williams-Renault)
1992: N. Mansell (Williams-Renault)
1991: A. Senna (McLaren-Honda)
1990: R. Patrese (Williams-Renault)
...

Michael Schumacher holds the record for the number of victories with a total of six (1994-99-2000-02-03-04) ahead of Ayrton Senna (1988-89-91) and Alain Prost (1984-86-93) who have both won the race three times.

The first San Marino F1 Grand Prix was won by Nelson Piquet in a Brabham on 3rd May 1981 on the Imola circuit.

In 2005, the San Marino Grand Prix will be held for the 25th time.

**Sunday 8th May 2005**

**Start** 14h00 local time.

**Distance** 66 laps of the 4.627 km circuit: 305.256 km* (*start line offset: 0.126 km).

**Crowed in 2004**
109,000 spectators on race day.

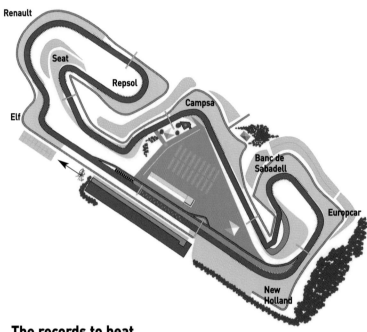

The Barcelona circuit is used a lot during the winter months for testing. It is a technical layout, which provides valuable information to help iron out problems with new cars. It is F1's favourite test track because of its relatively mild climate. Spain is where the winter action is as the teams also go to Valencia and Jerez. **Barcelona has become one of the places where new cars are launched after which engineers get down to the job of testing the efficacy of their latest innovations.**

Fernando Alonso's F1 success has led to a big increase in the number of F1 fans in Spain (on raceday last year the crowd exceeded 100,000) and thanks to the fact that the circuit is well-served by motor ways, the traffic jams that are so much a part of F1 tend to dissipate quickly.

Every year the King of Spain, Juan Carlos, attends the event hoping no doubt that one day he well present the winner's cup to his young fellow-countryman. In addition, the promoters of the race do their best to improve the quality of their infrastructure: they have renewed their contract for the organisation of the race until 2011. The only fly in the ointment in the longer term is the law concerning tobacco advertising.

**Address**
Circuit de Catalunya
Mas La Moreneta,
08160 Montmelo (Barcelona),
Apartat de Correus 27
Spain
Tel.: (+34) 93 57 19 700
Fax: (+34) 93 57 22 772
Internet: www.circuitcat.com

**Location**
The circuit is located 20 kilometres northeast of Barcelona. The closest airports are Barcelona to the south and Gerona to the north. The motorway linking Barcelona to France passes within a kilometre of the circuit.

**Previous winners**
2004: M. Schumacher (Ferrari)
2003: M. Schumacher (Ferrari)
2002: M. Schumacher (Ferrari)
2001: M. Schumacher (Ferrari)
2000: M. Häkkinen (McLaren-Mercedes)
1999: M. Häkkinen (McLaren-Mercedes)
1998: M. Häkkinen (McLaren-Mercedes)
1997: J. Villeneuve (Williams-Renault)
1996: M. Schumacher (Ferrari)
1995: M. Schumacher (Benetton-Renault)
1994: D. Hill (Williams-Renault)
1993: A. Prost (Williams-Renault)
1992: N. Mansell (Williams-Renault)
1991: N. Mansell (Williams-Renault)
1990: A. Prost (Ferrari)
...

Michael Schumacher has won the Spanish Grand Prix six times (1995-96-2001-02-03-04. Behind him come Mika Häkkinen (1998-99-2000), Alan Prost 1988-90-93) and Jackie Stewart (1969-70-73) all three-time winners.

Juan Manuel Fangio in his Alfa Romeo won the first F1 Spanish Grand Prix on the Pedralbes circuit on 28th October 1951.

2005 will be the 35th Spanish Grand Prix.
- 2 times at Pedralbes (Barcelona) 1951-54.
- 9 times on the Jarama circuit (Madrid) 1968-70-72-74, from 1976 to 1979 and then in 1981.
- 4 times on the Montjuich Park circuit (Barcelona) in 1969-71-73-75.
- 5 times on the Jerez de la Frontera circuit from 1986 to 1990.
- 14 times on the Catalunya circuit (Barcelona) from 1991 to 2004.

## The records to beat
**Pole position**
M. Schumacher (Ferrari) in 2004, 1:15.022 (222.030 km/h)

**Average race speed**
M. Schumacher (Ferrari) in 2004, 1:27:32.841 (209.205 km/h)

**Lap records**
M. Schumacher (Ferrari) in 2004, 1:17.450 (215.070 km/h)

## 2004 statistics
**Pole position**
M. Schumacher (Ferrari), 1:15.022 (222.030 km/h)

**GP results**

| | | |
|---|---|---|
| 1. M. Schumacher (Ferrari) | | 1:27:32.841 |
| | | (66 laps, 209.205 km/h) |
| 2. Barrichello (Ferrari) | | + 13.290 |
| 3. Trulli (Renault) | | + 32.294 |
| 4. Alonso (Renault) | | + 32.952 |
| 5. Sato (B.A.R-Honda) | | + 42.327 |
| 6. R. Schumacher (Williams-BMW) | | + 1:13.804 |
| 7. Fisichella (Sauber-Petronas) | | + 1:17.108 |
| 8. Button (B.A.R-Honda) | | 1 lap |

**Fastest lap**
M. Schumacher (Ferrari), 1:17.450 (215.070 km/h)

Sunday 22nd May 2005

Start 14h00 local time

Distance 78 laps of the 3.340 km circuit: 260.520 km

Crowed in 2004
90,000 spectators, 40,000 of which in the grandstands

6

# MONACO
# MONTE-CARLO

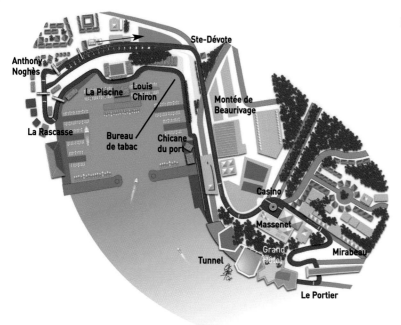

## The records to beat
### Pole position
Trulli (Renault) in 2004, 1:13.985 (162.519 km/h)
### Average race speed
Montoya (Williams-BMW) in 2003, 1:42:19.010 (152.772 km/h)
### Lap records
M. Schumacher (Ferrari) in 2004, 1:14.439 (161.528 km/h)

## 2004 statistics
### Pole position
Trulli (Renault), 1:13.985 (162.519 km/h)
### GP results

| | |
|---|---|
| 1. Trulli (Renault) | 1:45:46.601 |
| | (77 laps, 145.880 km/h) |
| 2. Button (B.A.R-Honda) | + 0.497 |
| 3. Barrichello (Ferrari) | + 1:15.766 |
| 4. Montoya (Williams-BMW) | 1 lap |
| 5. Massa (Sauber-Petronas) | 1 lap |
| 6. Da Matta (Toyota) | 1 lap |
| 7. Heidfeld (Jordan-Ford) | 2 laps |
| 8. Panis (Toyota) | 3 laps |

### Fastest lap
M. Schumacher (Ferrari), 1:14.439 (161,528 km/h)

Monaco is in a state of upheaval. The Principality on the Mediterranean used to represent the picture-postcard side of Formula 1; this is now becoming less and less relevant. The days when a car was prepared with just a monkey wrench and a few nuts and bolts are long gone. Now telemetry and tons of equipment are necessary to set up the high-technology vehicles that today's F1s have become. The era when the mechanics had to trudge back and forth between the paddock and the pit lane is finished as well. The Monaco Automobile Club did not have a choice and realised that the event had to evolve to survive. In this respect it is all over for nostalgia buffs. The famous Monaco pit lane now belongs to the past. Like everywhere else the cars are hidden from the stroller's eye.

A huge public works programme over several years is planned to bring this mythic circuit up to the draconian safety standards that now prevail in F1. The pit lane faces the sea and the organisers have begun to look after their public. The enormous port grandstand is a marvellous viewing spot that overlooks both the pits and the track. However, the rest of the circuit has not been modified and retains its atmosphere and incomparable character. The Monaco Grand Prix is unique.

### Address
Automobile Club de Monaco
23, Bd Albert-1er, BP 464,
98 012 Monaco Cedex
Tel.: (+377) 93 15 26 00
Fax: (+377) 93 25 80 08
Internet: www.acm.mc

### Location
The circuit is located 18 kilometres to the east of Nice and the race is held in the streets of the Principality. Nice is the nearest airport and Monte Carlo can be reached by car, train, boat and helicopter.

### Previous winners
2004: J. Trulli (Renault)
2003: J.P. Montoya (Williams-BMW)
2002: D. Coulthard (McLaren-Mercedes)
2001: M. Schumacher (Ferrari)
2000: D. Coulthard (McLaren-Mercedes)
1999: M. Schumacher (Ferrari)
1998: M. Häkkinen (McLaren-Mercedes)
1997: M. Schumacher (Ferrari)
1996: O. Panis (Ligier-Mugen Honda)
1995: M. Schumacher (Benetton-Renault)
1994: M. Schumacher (Benetton-Ford)
1993: A. Senna (McLaren-Ford)
1992: A. Senna (McLaren-Honda)
1991: A. Senna (McLaren-Honda)
1990: A. Senna (McLaren-Honda)
...

The late Ayrton Senna holds the record for Monaco victories with six (1987 and then 1989 to 1993). Then come Graham Hill and Michael Schumacher who have both won the event five times: 1963 to 1965 and 1968-69 for the Englishman and 1994-95-97-99 and 2001 for the German. Alain Prost has triumphed four times in the Principality: 1984-86 and 1988.

In 1950, Juan Manuel Fangio in his Alfa Romeo won the first Monaco Grand Prix counting for the F1 World Championship on 21st May.

2005 will be the 63rd event.

Sunday 29th May 2005

**Start** 14h00 local time.

**Distance** 60 laps of the 5.148 km circuit: 308.863 km* (*start line offset: 0.017 km).

**Crowed in 2004** 120,000 spectators on race day.

7

EUROPE
NÜRBURG   NÜRBURGRING

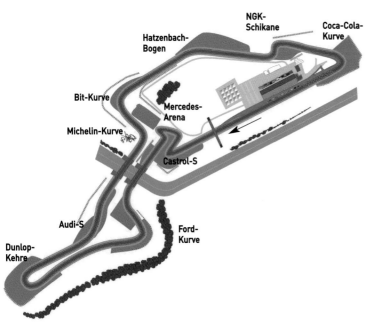

## The records to beat

**Pole position**
M. Schumacher (Ferrari) in 2004, 1:28.351 (209.763 km/h)

**Average race speed**
M. Schumacher (Ferrari) in 2004, 1:32:35.101 (200.159 km/h)

**Lap records**
M. Schumacher (Ferrari) in 2004, 1:29.468 (207.144 km/h)

## 2004 statistics

**Pole position**
M. Schumacher (Ferrari), 1:28.351 (209.763 km/h)

**GP results**

| | |
|---|---|
| 1. M. Schumacher (Ferrari) | 1:32:35.101 |
| | (60 laps, 200.159 km/h) |
| 2. Barrichello (Ferrari) | + 17.989 |
| 3. Button (B.A.R-Honda) | + 22.533 |
| 4. Trulli (Renault) | + 53.673 |
| 5. Alonso (Renault) | + 1:00.987 |
| 6. Fisichella (Sauber-Petronas) | + 1:13.448 |
| 7. Webber (Jaguar) | + 1:16.206 |
| 8. Montoya (Williams-BMW) | 1 lap |

**Fastest lap**
M. Schumacher (Ferrari), 1:29.468 (207.144 km/h)

Michael Schumacher's presence on the grid is a guarantee of success for the organisers. Last year over one hundred thousand fans filled the grandstands to cheer on their hero. Michael's accumulation of titles and victories only serve to enhance the phenomenon. His brother, Ralf, does not have the same charisma and as in the cinema has to make do with the second role.

The presence on the calendar of what is in fact a second German Grand Prix is down to the involvement of the national manufacturers, Mercedes-Benz and BMW, in F1. For the moment they are totally dominated by their fellow-countryman in his Ferrari.

The Nürburgring is one of the mythic circuits in the history of motor racing. Today, the former Nordschliefe has become a tourist attraction for nostalgia lovers. A trip around its 22 kilometres will convince even the most hardened cynic that it is no longer capable of welcoming the modern grand prix car. Thus, the present 'Ring uses only a few hundred metres of the old track. Dominating it is the spooky old Nürburg castle and this modern layout is similar to Hockenheim in that it is a kind of arena where the spectators have a panoramic view of the goings-on on the track. Which, alas, is completely lacking in character. In addition, the end of May is no guarantee of good weather and it cannot be said that the 'Ring is one of the best-loved stops on the F1 trail.

**Address**
Nürburgring Gmbh
53520 Nürburg/Eifel,
Germany
Tel.: (+49) 26 91 30 20
Fax: (+49) 26 91 30 21 55
Internet: www.nuerburgring.de

**Location**
The Nürburgring is located 90 kilometres southeast of Cologne and 60 kilometres northwest of Koblenz. The main airports are Cologne and Dusseldorf (120 kms away). The region has an excellent motorway network but reaching them on Sunday evening can prove difficult because of traffic jams outside the circuit.

**Previous winners**
2004: M. Schumacher (Ferrari)
2003: R. Schumacher (Williams-BMW)
2002: R. Barrichello (Ferrari)
2001: M. Schumacher (Ferrari)
2000: M. Schumacher (Ferrari)
1999: J. Herbert (Stewart-Ford)
1998: M. Häkkinen (McLaren-Mercedes)
1997: J. Villeneuve (Williams-Renault)
1996: J. Villeneuve (Williams-Renault)
1995: M. Schumacher (Benetton-Renault)
1994: M. Schumacher (Benetton-Ford)
1993: A. Senna (McLaren-Ford)
1985: N. Mansell (Williams-Honda)
1984: A. Prost (McLaren-TAG Porsche)

Michael Schumacher is the record-holder for the number of victories with five (1994-95, 2000-01-04).

The race will be held for the 15th time in 2005.

Giuseppe Farina won the first European Grand Prix – also the first round of the new F1 World Championship – on the Silverstone circuit on 13th May 1950. It was an honorary title attributed to the British GP.

**Sunday 12th June 2005**

**Start:** 13h00 local time
(19h00 in Europe)

**Distance:** 70 laps of the 4.361 km
circuit (305.270 km)

**Crowd in 2004:**
320,000 spectators over the 3 days,
121,000 on race day.

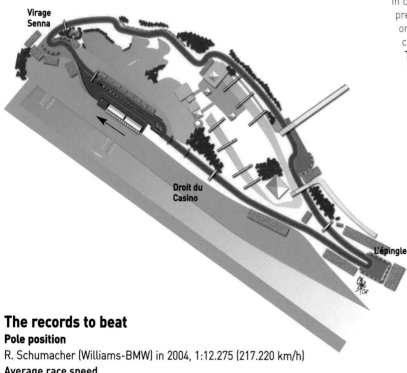

Virage
Senna

Droit du
Casino

L'épingle

## The records to beat
### Pole position
R. Schumacher (Williams-BMW) in 2004, 1:12.275 (217.220 km/h)
### Average race speed
M. Schumacher (Ferrari) in 2004, 1:28:24.803 (207.165 km/h)
### Lap records
Barrichello (Ferrari) in 2004, 1:13.622 (213.246 km/h)

## 2004 statistics
### Pole position
R. Schumacher (Williams-BMW), 1:12.275 (217.220 km/h)
### GP results

| | | |
|---|---|---|
| 1. M. Schumacher (Ferrari) | 1:28:24.803 | |
| | (70 laps, 207.165 km/h) | |
| 2. Barrichello (Ferrari) | + 5.108 | |
| 3. Button (B.A.R-Honda) | + 20.409 | |
| 4. Fisichella (Sauber-Petronas) | 1 lap | |
| 5. Räikkönen (McLaren-Mercedes) | 1 lap | |
| 6. Coulthard (McLaren-Mercedes) | 1 lap | |
| 7. Glock (Jordan-Ford) | 2 laps | |
| 8. Heidfeld (Jordan-Ford) | 2 laps | |

### Fastest lap
Barrichello (Ferrari), 1:13.622 (213.246 km/h)

In contrast to the grand prix preceding it the Montreal event is one of the most popular on the calendar with the F1 fraternity. **The Canadians provide a warm welcome and the return of Jacques Villeneuve to a track that bears his father's name will certainly add extra interest to the race.**

**The Canadian circuit is often the scene of exciting grands prix with frequent upsets.** The first corner after the start has been the graveyard of many a driver's hopes. The fact that the green light is given at 13h00 local time generally means a large number of TV viewers in Europe as it corresponds to 19h00 on early Sunday evening.

Montreal is only a few hours flight from the 'Old' continent and is a marvellous change of scenery. The town goes grand prix crazy during race week. Sainte Catherine, one of the main thoroughfares, is black with people and all the shops decorate their windows in motor racing paraphernalia. A festive air invades the city and every street corner has its own entertainment.

As the following weekend sees the running of the USA Grand Prix, the intervening period provides an excellent opportunity for a few days' holiday in Quebec, a province that is well worth the visit.

### Address
Grand Prix F1 du Canada Inc.
413 rue St Jacques, Suite 630
H2Y 1N9 Montreal,
Canada.
Tel.: (+1) 514 350 47 31
Fax: (+1) 514 350 00 07
Internet: www.grandprix.ca

### Location
The Ile de Notre Dame circuit is located a few kilometres from the town centre. This island hosted the International Exhibition and some of the events in the 1976 Olympics. The Dorval International airport is quite near the centre of Montréal. The best way to get to the circuit is by underground.

### Previous winners
2004: M. Schumacher (Ferrari)
2003: M. Schumacher (Ferrari)
2002: M. Schumacher (Ferrari)
2001: R. Schumacher (Williams-BMW)
2000: M. Schumacher (Ferrari)
1999: M. Häkkinen (McLaren-Mercedes)
1998: M. Schumacher (Ferrari)
1997: M. Schumacher (Ferrari)
1996: D. Hill (Williams-Renault)
1995: J. Alesi (Ferrari)
1994: M. Schumacher (Benetton-Ford)
1993: A. Prost (Williams-Renault)
1992: G. Berger (McLaren-Honda)
1991: N. Piquet (Benetton-Ford)
1990: A. Senna (McLaren-Honda)
...

Again Michael Schumacher dominates his rivals head and shoulders in terms of wins in this event with a total of seven (1994-97-98, 2000-02-03-04).
Nelson Piquet won the event three times (1982-84-91).
The first Canadian Grand Prix was held on the Mosport circuit on 27th August 1967 and victory went to Jack Brabham in his Repco-Brabham.

2005 will be the 37th Canadian Grand Prix.
- Mosport, 8 times (1967-69-71-72-73-74-76-77)
- Mont Tremblant, twice (1968-1970)
- Montreal, 26 times (from 1978 to 1986 and from 1998 to 2004).

Sunday 19th June 2005

**Start** 13h00 local time
(20h00 in Europe).

**Distance** 73 laps of the 4.192 km
circuit: 306.016 km.

**Crowed in 2004**
110,000 spectators on race day.

9

# UNITED STATES
## INDIANAPOLIS

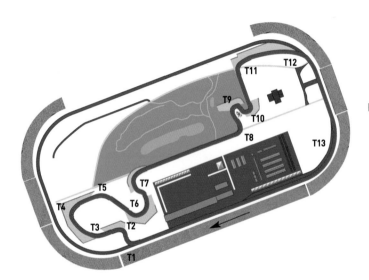

### Address
International Motor Speedway
4790 West 16th Street
Indianapolis, IN 46222
United States
Tel.: (+1) 317 492 67 80
Fax: (+1) 317 492 64 82
Internet: www.usgpindy.com

Filling the grandstands only three weeks after the mythic Indianapolis 500-Mile race attended by over 300,000 spectators is one big challenge for the American organiser. The FIA decided to group the two events on the North American continent for budgetary reasons as it cuts down travel costs. This was also the case in the mid-eighties when the Detroit and Canadian GPs were held within a week of each other. Nonetheless, the grandstands opposite the pits are usually crowded, especially with the fans of Juan Pablo Montoya and Michael Schumacher who rival each other in terms of noise and colour in what is one of the most hallowed sanctuaries of motor racing.

The race itself is usually an incident-packed one and slowly but surely Formula 1 is gaining a foothold in the USA. The grand prix is vital to the credibility of the sport's world championship image given the importance of the North America market for car manufacturers and suppliers. Red Bull, which recently bought the Jaguar team, is an example as it has declared that it wants to have an American in one of its cars in the near future. Danny Sullivan, the ex-Tyrrell driver in the 1983 F1 World Championship with the late Michele Alboreto, looks after fledgling talents in different US and European Championships in the hope that one of them will make into F1. If this were to be the case it would generate greater interest in F1 among the US public.

### Location
Location: Indianapolis is the capital of the state of Indiana in the Midwest south of the great lakes. The famous oval, part of which is used for the F1 grand prix, is about 10 kilometres from the town centre in the western suburb. The city has a population of 700,000 and is 300 kilometres southwest of Chicago and 400 kilometres northeast of Saint Louis. The Indianapolis airport does not have direct links with the main European centres. Delays on Sunday evening may lead to problems catching connecting flights.

### Previous winners
2004: M. Schumacher (Ferrari)
2003: M. Schumacher (Ferrari)
2002: R. Barrichello (Ferrari)
2001: M. Häkkinen (McLaren-Mercedes)
2000: M. Schumacher (Ferrari)
1991: A. Senna (McLaren-Honda)
1990: A. Senna (McLaren-Honda)
1989: A. Prost (Ferrari)
1988: A. Senna (McLaren-Honda)
1987: A. Senna (Lotus-Honda)
1986: A. Senna (Lotus-Renault)
1985: K. Rosberg (Williams-Honda)
1984: N. Piquet (Brabham-BMW)
1984: K. Rosberg (Williams-Honda)
1983: J. Watson (McLaren-Ford)
1983: M. Alboreto (Tyrrell-Ford)
...

Ayrton Senna, the king of city circuits, won the US Grand Prix on 5 occasions (1986-87-89-90-91).

Bruce McLaren in his Cooper-Climax won the first USA F1 Grand Prix held at Sebring on 12th December 1959.

The US Grand Prix came back onto the F1 calendar in the year 2000 after a long break. Before that it had been held on various circuits like Watkins Glen, Detroit, Phoenix etc.

Between 1950 and 1960 the Indy 500 Miles counted for the F1 World Championship.

## The records to beat
### Pole position
M. Schumacher (Ferrari) in 2004, 1:10.223 (214.903 km/h)
### Average race speed
Barrichello (Ferrari) in 2002, 1:31:07.934 (201.475 km/h)
### Lap records
Barrichello (Ferrari) in 2004, 1:10.399 (214.366 km/h)

## 2004 statistics
### Pole position
M. Schumacher (Ferrari), 1:10.223 (214.903 km/h)
### GP results

| | | |
|---|---|---|
| 1. M. Schumacher (Ferrari) | 1:40:29.914 | |
| | (73 laps, 182.698 km/h) | |
| 2. Barrichello (Ferrari) | + 2.950 | |
| 3. Sato (B.A.R-Honda) | + 22.036 | |
| 4. Trulli (Renault) | + 34.544 | |
| 5. Panis (Toyota) | + 37.534 | |
| 6. Räikkönen (McLaren-Mercedes) | 1 lap | |
| 7. Coulthard (McLaren-Mercedes) | 1 lap | |
| 8. Baumgartner (Minardi-Cosworth) | 3 laps | |

### Fastest lap
Barrichello (Ferrari), 1:10.399 (214.366 km/h)

| | |
|---|---|
| - Watkins Glen | 20 times (from 1961 to 1980) |
| - Long Beach | 8 times (1976-1983) |
| - Las Vegas | twice (1981-82) |
| - Detroit | 7 times (1982-1988) |
| - Dallas | once (1984) |
| - Phoenix | 3 times (1989-1991) |
| - Indianapolis | 4 times since the year 2000. |

2005 will be the 49th US Grand Prix:
| | |
|---|---|
| - Sebring | once (1959) |
| - Riverside | once (1960) |

←←

**Sunday 3rd July 2005**

**Start** 14h00 local time.

**Distance** 70 laps of the 4.411 km circuit: 308.586 km*
(*start line offset: 0.184 km).

**Crowed in 2004**
70,000 spectators on race day.

Jacques Régis, the President of the F.F.S.A. (French Motor Sporting Federation) does not lack drive. The French Grand Prix was in a very precarious situation and has finally been saved. It appears that a contract has been signed up to the year 2009. New grands prix on the calendar like Bahrain, China and Turkey have made things very problematic for events in financial difficulties. There was talk that Magny-Cours would be the European season opener but finally it was allocated its usual slot in early July, a much better solution from a weather point of view!

The circuit itself does not meet with unanimous approval: it is in the middle of the country and its hotel capacity is limited. The locals whose sole aim is to take their guests for a ride do not help this situation! Nonetheless, a bucolic ambience reigns and the region is peppered with excellent and not too expense restaurants.

The French Grand Prix is one of the oldest events on the motor racing calendar. It was held for the first time in 1906 on a circuit near Le Mans. It measured 103 kms and had to be covered twelve times a total distance of 1236 kms against which the 300 odd kms of today's GPs pale into insignificance! The event lasted two days and the winners were the Hungarian Ferenc Szisz and Frenchman Georges Moreau in their red 90 hp Renault.

**Address**
Circuit de Nevers-Magny-Cours
Technopole, 58470 Magny-Cours
France.
Tel.: (+33) (0)3 86 21 80 00
Fax: (+33) (0)3 86 21 80 80
Internet: www.magnyf1.com

**Location**
The Nevers-Magny-Cours circuit is 12 kilometres south of Nevers, 250 kilometres south of Paris and 220 kilometres north of Lyon.

**Previous winners**
2004: M. Schumacher (Ferrari)
2003: R. Schumacher (Williams-BMW)
2002: M. Schumacher (Ferrari)
2001: M. Schumacher (Ferrari)
2000: D. Coulthard (McLaren-Mercedes)
1999: H.H. Frentzen (Jordan-Mugen Honda)
1998: M. Schumacher (Ferrari)
1997: M. Schumacher (Ferrari)
1996: D. Hill (Williams-Renault)
1995: M. Schumacher (Benetton-Renault)
1994: M. Schumacher (Benetton-Ford)
1993: A. Prost (Williams-Renault)
1992: N. Mansell (Williams-Renault)
1991: N. Mansell (Williams-Renault)
1990: A. Prost (Ferrari)
...

Michael Schumacher has also won this grand prix a record 7 times (1994-95-97-98-2001-02-04). Close behind him comes Alain Prost who has triumphed in his home GP on 6 occasions (1981-83-88-89-90-93).

Juan Manuel Fangio in his Alfa Romeo won the first French Grand Prix counting for the F1 World Championship on the Reims circuit on 2nd July 1950.

2005 will be the 55th F1 France Grand Prix:
- Reims: 11 times (1950-51-53-54-56-58-59-60-61-63-66)
- Rouen: 5 times (1952-57-62-64-68)
- Clermont-Ferrand: 4 times (1965-69-70-72)
- Le Mans: Once (1967)
- Le Castellet: 14 times (1971-73-75-76-78-80-82-83-85-86-87-88-89-90)
- Dijon Prenois: 5 times (1974-77-79-81-84)
- Magny-Cours: 14 times (1991-2004).

## The records to beat

**Pole position**
Alonso (Renault) in 2004, 1:13.698 (215.468 km/h)

**Average race speed**
M. Schumacher (Ferrari) in 2004, 1:30:18.133 (205.035 km/h)

**Lap records**
M. Schumacher (Ferrari) in 2004, 1:15.377 (210.669 km/h)

## 2004 statistics

**Pole position**
Alonso (Renault), 1:13.698 (215.468 km/h)

**GP results**

| | | |
|---|---|---|
| 1. M. Schumacher (Ferrari) | 1:30:18.133 | |
| | (70 laps, 205.035 km/h) | |
| 2. Alonso (Renault) | + 8.329 | |
| 3. Barrichello (Ferrari) | + 31.622 | |
| 4. Trulli (Renault) | + 32.082 | |
| 5. Button (B.A.R-Honda) | + 32.484 | |
| 6. Coulthard (McLaren-Mercedes) | + 35.520 | |
| 7. Räikkönen (McLaren-Mercedes) | + 36.230 | |
| 8. Montoya (Williams-BMW) | + 43.419 | |

**Fastest lap**
M. Schumacher (Ferrari), 1:15.377 (210.669 km/h)

GREAT BRITAIN
SILVERSTONE

11

**Sunday 10th July 2005**

**Start** 13h00 local time
(14h00 in Europe).

**Distance** 60 laps of the 5.141 km
circuit: 308.355 km*
(*start line offset: 0.105 km).

**Crowed in 2004**
100,000 spectators on race day.

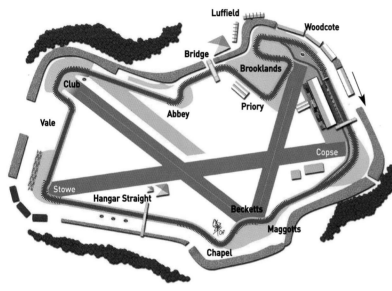

## The records to beat

**Pole position**
Räikkönen (McLaren-Mercedes) in 2004, 1:18.233 (236.570 km/h)

**Average race speed**
M. Schumacher (Ferrari) in 2004, 1:24:42.700 (218.403 km/h)

**Lap records**
M. Schumacher (Ferrari) in 2004, 1:18.739 (235.049 km/h)

## 2004 statistics

**Pole position**
Räikkönen (McLaren-Mercedes), 1:18.233 (236.570 km/h)

**GP results**

1. M. Schumacher (Ferrari)                    1:24:42.700
                                       (60 laps, 218.403 km/h)
2. Räikkönen (McLaren-Mercedes)               + 2.130
3. Barrichello (Ferrari)                      + 3.114
4. Button (B.A.R-Honda)                       + 10.683
5. Montoya (Williams-BMW)                     + 12.173
6. Fisichella (Sauber-Petronas)               + 12.888
7. Coulthard (McLaren-Mercedes)               + 19.668
8. Webber (Jaguar)                            + 23.701

**Fastest lap**
M. Schumacher (Ferrari), 1:18.739 (235.049 km/h)

There is no love lost between Bernie Ecclestone and Silverstone. *"It's like a run-down estate that you patch up from time to time by adding a new access route here, a new car park there. It has to be completely rebuilt but the owners don't want to do it."* To twist the knife in the wound he added, "Silverstone is a country fair that takes itself for an international event!"

The British Racing Drivers Club, the famous BRDC, a very exclusive club for former drivers finally found an agreement with the F1 entrepreneur on the eve of the FIA World Council. The British Grand Prix was saved once again and the teams have all agreed to take part. Last September Ecclestone said that Silverstone was *"one of the worst circuits in the world."* However, he did not want to be held responsible for the disappearance of what is a national institution. The intervention of the British Government obviously weighed heavily in the balance. A 5-year contract appears to have been signed on condition that certain works are carried out. More than just a face-lift is necessary to prevent the event from being taken off the calendar. The track has to be slightly modified without compromising its speed. A new motorway exit, a few gates welcoming the visitors and big flowerpots do little to hide the dilapidation. The circuit is laid out on an old Royal Air Force base and the weather is often capricious despite the race being held in mid-July. It is an integral part of F1 history as in May 1950 it hosted the first round of the newly created F1 World Championship.

**Address**
Silverstone Circuits Ltd
Northamptonshire, NN 12 8TN
Great Britain
Tel.: (+44) (0)1327 85 72 71
Fax: (+44) (0)1327 85 76 63
Internet: www.silverstone-circuit.co.uk

**Location**
Silverstone is situated 110 kilometres northeast of London. 25 kilometres southeast of Northampton and 45 kilometres from Oxford. The nearest airports are Birmingham (50 kms) Luton and London Heathrow.

**Previous winners**
2004: M. Schumacher (Ferrari)
2003: R. Barrichello (Ferrari)
2002: M. Schumacher (Ferrari)
2001: M. Häkkinen (McLaren-Mercedes)
2000: D. Coulthard (McLaren-Mercedes)
1999: D. Coulthard (McLaren-Mercedes)
1998: M. Schumacher (Ferrari)
1997: J. Villeneuve (Williams-Renault)
1996: J. Villeneuve (Williams-Renault)
1995: J. Herbert (Benetton-Renault)
1994: D. Hill (Williams-Renault)
1993: A. Prost (Williams-Renault)
1992: N. Mansell (Williams-Renault)
1991: N. Mansell (Williams-Renault)
1990: A. Prost (Ferrari)
...

Five-time winners of the event are Alain Prost and Jim Clark: the Frenchman in 1983-85-89-90-93 and the Scot in 1962-63-64-65-67.

Nino Farina in his Alfa Romeo won the first F1 British Grand Prix on 13th May 1950 on the Silverstone circuit.

2005 will be the 57th British Grand Prix:
- Silverstone: 40 times (1950-1958, 1960-63-65-67-69-71-73-75-77-79-81-83-85 and from 1987 to the present.
- Brands Hatch: 11 times (1964-66-68-70-72-74-76-80-82-84-86)
- Aintree: 5 times (1955-57-59-61-62).

**Sunday 24th July 2005**

**Start** 14h00 local time.

**Distance** 67 laps of the 4.574 km circuit: 306.458 km.

**Crowed in 2004**
120,000 spectators on race day.

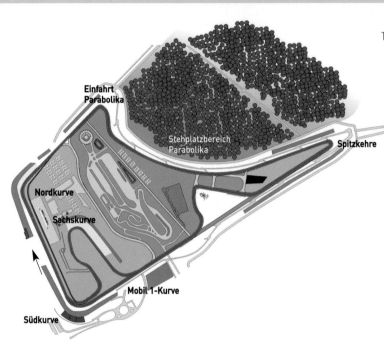

## The records to beat

**Pole position**
M. Schumacher (Ferrari) in 2004, 1:13.306 (224.625 km/h)

**Average race speed**
M. Schumacher (Ferrari) in 2004, 1:23:54.848 (215.852 km/h)

**Lap records**
Räikkönen (McLaren-Mercedes) in 2004, 1:13.780 (223.182 km/h)

## 2004 statistics

**Pole position**
M. Schumacher (Ferrari), 1:13.306 (224.625 km/h)

**GP results**

| | |
|---|---|
| 1. M. Schumacher (Ferrari) | 1:23:54.848 |
| | (66 laps, 215.852 km/h) |
| 2. Button (B.A.R-Honda) | + 8.388 |
| 3. Alonso (Renault) | + 16.351 |
| 4. Coulthard (McLaren-Mercedes) | + 19.231 |
| 5. Montoya (Williams-BMW) | + 23.055 |
| 6. Webber (Jaguar) | + 41.108 |
| 7. Pizzonia (Williams-BMW) | + 41.956 |
| 8. Sato (B.A.R-Honda) | + 46.842 |

**Fastest lap**
Räikkönen (McLaren-Mercedes), 1:13.780 (223.182 km/h)

Traditionally the German Grand Prix was held on the Nürburgring until Niki Lauda's serious accident there in 1976 following which it was declared too dangerous for F1 cars. Thus, the German authorities moved the event **to the Hockenheim circuit where it has taken place ever since apart from a brief return to the new** Nürburging in 1985.

The original circuit built by the town of Hockenheim saw the light of day in 1939 and consisted of a couple of long straights joined by a fast curve and a hairpin. It was used after WWII and then a new version opened in 1966 with a twisty infield section linked by two long straights that ran through the pine forest to a very fast curve. Following Jim Clark's fatal accident there in 1968 a couple of chicanes were added in an attempt to reduce speed. In 2002, the layout was again redesigned between the first and third chicanes to eliminate the long straights through the forest, which held little interest. The new portion enabled huge grandstands to be built and this has helped to make the grand prix more profitable. It is a colourful event especially whenever Michael Schumacher's Ferrari screams through the infield section as the spectators rise to their feet to cheer on their hero brandishing Ferrari flags and setting off rockets! This is an excellent antidote to the sleepiness induced by the long nights in the camping sites necking litres upon litres of beer hence the walls of bottles and cans proudly displayed outside certain tents!

**Address**
Hockenheim-Ring Gmbh,
Postfach 1106, D-68766 Hockenheim,
Germany
Tel.: (+49) (0)62 05 95 00
Fax: (+49) (0)62 05 95 02 99
Internet: www.hockenheimring.de

**Location**
The circuit is around 90 kilometres south of Frankfort, 110 kilometres northeast of Stuttgart and 20 kilometres from the historic town of Heidelberg. It is easily accessible thanks to the motorway network.

**Previous winners**
2004: M. Schumacher (Ferrari)
2003: J.P. Montoya (Williams-BMW)
2002: M. Schumacher (Ferrari)
2001: R. Schumacher (Williams-BMW)
2000: R. Barrichello (Ferrari)
1999: E. Irvine (Ferrari)
1998: M. Häkkinen (McLaren-Mercedes)
1997: G. Berger (Benetton-Renault)
1996: D. Hill (Williams-Renault)
1995: M. Schumacher (Benetton-Renault)
1994: G. Berger (Ferrari)
1993: A. Prost (Williams-Renault)
1992: N. Mansell (Williams-Renault)
1991: N. Mansell (Williams-Renault)
1990: A. Senna (McLaren-Honda)
...

Four drivers have won this race three times: Juan Manuel Fangio in 1954-56-57, Nelson Piquet in 1981-86-87, Ayrton Senna in 1988-89-90 and Michael Schumacher in 1995-2002-2004. In 2001, Ralf Schumacher also saw the chequered flag the first time in the history of Formula 1 that two brothers have won their home grand prix.

Alberto Ascari in his Ferrari saw the chequered flag in the first German F1 Grand Prix on 29th July 1951 on the Nürburgring.

2005 will be the 53rd German F1 World Championship Grand Prix:
- The Nürburgring, 23 times (1951-54, 1956-58, 1961-69, 1971-76 and in 1985.
- Avus (Berlin), Once in 1959
- Hockenheim, 28 times (1970, from 1977-1984 and 1986-2005).

Sunday 31st July 2005

**Start** 14h00 local time.

**Distance** 70 laps of the 4.381 km circuit: 306.663 km* (*start line offset: 0.007 km).

**Crowed in 2004**
54,000 spectators on race day.

13

# HUNGARY
## BUDAPEST HUNGARORING

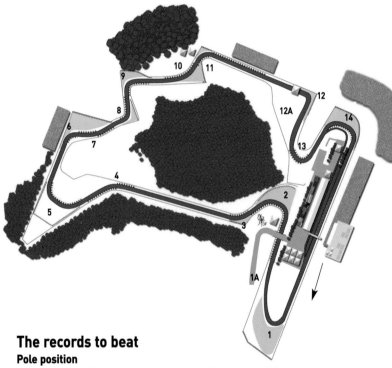

The Hungarian Grand Prix is the main sporting event in the country. In 2004, the presence of local driver Zsolt Baumgartner in his Minardi did not provoke a rush to buy tickets and the grandstands and spectator enclosures were not exactly packed to the gills. The price of seats in relation to people's income certainly did not help and the rumour that Baumgartner had received government aid acted as a turn-off for many. The various Russian GP projects have all ended up in the waste paper basket so the Hungarian Grand Prix is still safe. Its most likely rival could be Rumania as the Arad region near the Hungarian Border has a grand prix project on the cards, and it seems that the government is ready to invest the 100 million euros that it will cost.

The grand prix was held for the first time in 1986 and this year it will celebrate its 20th anniversary. It was the first F1 World Championship event in what was the Soviet Block. Much has changed since then: for example, the Trabant the people's car constructed in East Germany has become a museum piece and today the vehicles seen in Hungary are no different from those found in a modern capitalist country. Budapest is one of the most beautiful cities in Europe thanks to its architecture and history. For those whose idea of a holiday is not the crowded beaches of the Mediterranean it is an ideal destination.

**Address**
Hungaroring Sport Rt.
2146 Mogyorod Pf. 10,
Hungary
Tel.: (+36) 28 444 444
Fax: (+36) 28 441 860
Internet: www.hungaroring.hu

**Location**
The Hungaroring is 20 kilometres northeast of Budapest and Ferihegy, the international airport. A motor way runs past the circuit. On Sunday evening slot in behind a police escort to avoid the traffic jams!

**Previous winners**
2004: M. Schumacher (Ferrari)
2003: F. Alonso (Renault)
2002: R. Barrichello (Ferrari)
2001: M. Schumacher (Ferrari)
2000: M. Häkkinen (McLaren-Mercedes)
1999: M. Häkkinen (McLaren-Mercedes)
1998: M. Schumacher (Ferrari)
1997: J. Villeneuve (Williams-Renault)
1996: J. Villeneuve (Williams-Renault)
1995: D. Hill (Williams-Renault)
1994: M. Schumacher (Benetton-Ford)
1993: D. Hill (Williams-Renault)
1992: A. Senna (McLaren-Honda)
1991: A. Senna (McLaren-Honda)
1990: T. Boutsen (Williams-Renault)
...

Michael Schumacher is the record holder of the number of victories in this race with 4 (1994-98-2001-2004). Ayrton Senna won it 3 times (1988-91-92). Damon Hill (1993-95) and Jacques Villeneuve (1996-97) have both scored doubles.

Nelson Piquet in his Williams won the first Hungarian Grand Prix on 10th August 1986.

2005 will be the 20th Hungarian Grand Prix all held on the Budapest Hungaroring.

## The records to beat
**Pole position**
M. Schumacher (Ferrari) in 2004, 1:19.146 (199.272 km/h)
**Average race speed**
M. Schumacher (Ferrari) in 2004, 1:35:26.131 (192.798 km/h)
**Lap records**
M. Schumacher (Ferrari) in 2004, 1:19.071 (199.461 km/h)

## 2004 statistics
**Pole position**
M. Schumacher (Ferrari), 1:19.146 (199.272 km/h)
**GP results**

| | | |
|---|---|---|
| 1. M. Schumacher (Ferrari) | 1:35:26.131 | |
| | (70 laps, 192.798 km/h) | |
| 2. Barrichello (Ferrari) | + 4.696 | |
| 3. Alonso (Renault) | + 44.599 | |
| 4. Montoya (Williams-BMW) | + 1:02.613 | |
| 5. Button (B.A.R-Honda) | + 1:07.439 | |
| 6. Sato (B.A.R-Honda) | 1 lap | |
| 7. Pizzonia (Williams-BMW) | 1 lap | |
| 8. Fisichella (Sauber-Petronas) | 1 lap | |

**Fastest lap**
M. Schumacher (Ferrari), 1:19.071 (199.461 km/h)

Sunday 21st August 2005

**Start** 15h00 local time
(14h00 in Europe).

**Distance** 58 laps of the 5.340 km
circuit: 309.720 km.

14

TURKEY
ISTANBUL ISTANBUL OTODROMO

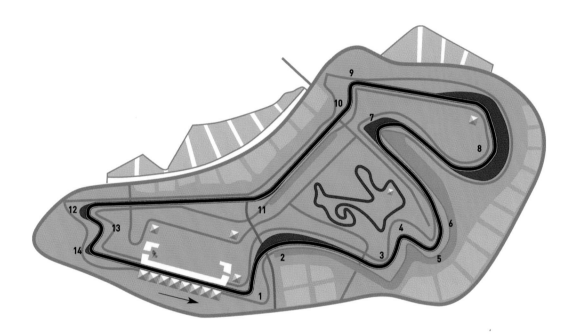

**Address**
Istanbul Kurtkoy International
Circuit Turkey
Karaaliler Place,
1935 Parcel, 9-10-11 Plots,
Tepeoren Road, Akfirat County,
Tuzla, Istanbul
Turkey
Tel.: (+90) 211 25 22 41 55
Fax: (+90) 211 25 22 42 39

**Location**
The Istanbul Otodrom is located in
Kurtkoy, some 80 kilometres east of
Istanbul on the Asian side of the
motorway leading to Ankara. The
nearest airport is Istanbul-Ataturk.
Four access roads should prevent traffic
jams.

**New event,
new circuit.**

The Turkish population numbers some 70 million and the country's best-known city is Istanbul with around 13 million inhabitants. In 1923, Ataturk decided that Ankara would be the new capital despite which Istanbul remains the cultural, intellectual, economic and social centre. The city has been the theatre of two great empires (the Byzantine and Ottoman) and this has given it an incredible architectural richness. Its strategic importance should not be underestimated in this day and age of 'intelligent' weaponry as it overlooks the Bosphorus straits that join the Black and Marmara seas. For centuries it has been a vital commercial link between Central Europe, the Middle East and Asia and has absorbed multiple influences from the different peoples that have passed through it.

The Muslim religion predominates in a country with a booming economy and Turkey wants to join the European Economic Community. This has caused a fair amount of waffling and blathering among certain members of the afore-mentioned organisation. However, the decision to hold the F1 grand prix must be seen as a step towards the West even if the Istanbul Chamber of Commerce – overseeing the operation – looks on it as an opportunity to make a handsome profit.

The Turkish Prime Minister, Recep Tayyip Erdogan, has stated that he would like to see the F1 grand prix boost the local economy. *"We expect F1 to bring in a lot of money and we've invested 27 million euros in the project,"* he said. "Even if only two people out of the millions of TV viewers who watch the race decide to come and holiday in out country, that'll add up to three million tourists."

A 7-year contract has been signed and the first stone was laid in September 2003 in the presence of Bernie Ecclestone. The winter in the region of Kurtkoy is hard with heavy snowfalls. Last summer almost 1500 hundred labourers worked night and day to respect the deadlines in the contract.

This new circuit will be finished in March 2005 and will measure 5.340 kms. It includes 13 corners and can welcome up to 150,000 spectators with grandstand seating for 90,000. It is located in a hilly region and the designer is Herman Tilke, F1's favourite architect.

In contrast to the recent mega-circuits of Sepang, Bahrain and Shanghai Kurtkoy is more conventional and has cost a lot less to build. Rumour has it that the price was in the region of 60 million euros. Turkey's main interest is to make a statement about its intentions and its economic and strategic importance.

Sunday 4th September 2005

**Start** 14h00 local time

**Distance** 53 laps of the 5.793 km
circuit: 306.720 km*
(*start line offset: 0.309 km).

**Crowed in 2004**
100,000 spectators on race day.

15

ITALY
MONZA   AUTODROMO NAZIONALE DI MONZA

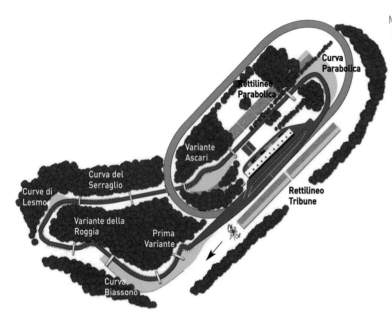

Monza, situated in a beautiful park, is one of last remaining historic F1 circuits. The first race was held there in 1922 and it has hosted the Italian Grand Prix every year since the creation of the F1 World Championship in 1950 with the exception of 1980 when this honour was given to Imola. The remains of the oval moulder among the trees in the park and whether or not this relic from a bygone age will be preserved is a moot point as it is under threat of demolition. Just a few metres from the first chicane the **striking contrast between the two types of circuit is at its most obvious. 'Grand Prix' made by the late John Frankenheimer is one of the best films about motor racing to come out of Hollywood, and the way he used the two layouts has remained firmly engraved in the memory of all** enthusiasts.

The fever that grips Monza during the grand prix weekend is unique and has to be lived to be believed. The appearance of a Ferrari on the track during practice is greeted with loud cheers. This, though, is nothing to the screams of the commentator and fans should one of the red cars claim pole. It is reminiscent of the Brazilian football commentators whenever Pele scored a goal during the 1970 Football World Cup.

Balmy weather usually envelops the Monza park during September and non-Italian spectators cannot fail to be moved by the almost mystical sense of communion that exists between the Tifosi and the red cars. There is nowhere else in the world that generates the ambience reigning on the Sunday afternoon of the race. Many of the modern circuits on which millions of dollars have been spent are soulless places. This is not the case with Monza where it vibrates in harmony with the spectators who are there to see one thing: a Ferrari victory. When this happens they all pour onto the circuit after the race and rush towards the rostrum under which they gather like pilgrims participating in a religious ritual. And long may it last!

## The records to beat

**Pole position**
Barrichello (Ferrari) in 2004, 1:20.089 (260.395 km/h)

**Average race speed**
M. Schumacher (Ferrari) in 2003, 1:14:19.838 (247.585 km/h)

**Lap records**
Barrichello (Ferrari) in 2004, 1:21.046 (257.320 km/h)

## 2004 statistics

**Pole position**
Barrichello (Ferrari), 1:20.089 (260.395 km/h)

**GP results**

| | |
|---|---|
| 1. Barrichello (Ferrari) | 1:15:18.448 |
| | (53 laps, 244.374 km/h) |
| 2. M. Schumacher (Ferrari) | + 1.347 |
| 3. Button (B.A.R-Honda) | + 10.197 |
| 4. Sato (B.A.R-Honda) | + 15.370 |
| 5. Montoya (Williams-BMW) | + 32.352 |
| 6. Coulthard (McLaren-Mercedes) | + 33.439 |
| 7. Pizzonia (Williams-BMW) | + 33.752 |
| 8. Fisichella (Sauber-Petronas) | + 35.431 |

**Fastest lap**
Barrichello (Ferrari), 1:21.046 (257.320 km/h)

**Address**
Autodromo Nazionale di Monza
Via Vedano 5. Parco di Monza
20052 Monza
Italy
Tel.: (+39) 03 92 48 21
Fax: (+39) 03 932 03 24
Internet: www.monzanet.it

**Location**
Monza is located in the royal park of the eponymous town some 15 kilometres northeast of Milan. It is well served by a motorway network. The two nearest international airports are Linate and Malpensa. Beware of massive traffic jams on Sunday evening!

**Previous winners**
2004: R. Barrichello (Ferrari)
2003: M. Schumacher (Ferrari)
2002: R. Barrichello (Ferrari)
2001: J.-P. Montoya (Williams-BMW)
2000: M. Schumacher (Ferrari)
1999: H.-H. Frentzen (Jordan-Mugen Honda)
1998: M. Schumacher (Ferrari)
1997: D. Coulthard (McLaren-Mercedes)
1996: M. Schumacher (Ferrari)
1995: J. Herbert (Benetton-Renault)
1994: D. Hill (Williams-Renault)
1993: D. Hill (Williams-Renault)
1992: A. Senna (McLaren-Honda)
1991: N. Mansell (Williams-Renault)
1990: A. Senna (McLaren-Honda)
...

Both Michael Schumacher (1996-98-2000-03) and Nelson Piquet (1980-83-86-87) have won this grand prix four times.

Juan Manuel Fangio (1953-54-55) Stirling Moss (1956-57-59) Ronnie Peterson (1973-74-76) and Alain Prost (1981-85-89) have all seen the chequered flag on three occasions.

Guiseppe Farina in his Alfa Romeo won the first Italian Grand Prix counting towards the F1 World Championship on 3rd September 1950 at Monza.

2005 will be the 56th Italian Grand Prix and the 55th on the Monza autodrome. Imola hosted the event in 1980.

**Sunday 11ˢᵗ September 2005**

**Start** 14h00 local time.

**Distance** 44 laps of the 6.976 km circuit: 306.944 km.

**Crowed in 2004**
58,000 spectators.

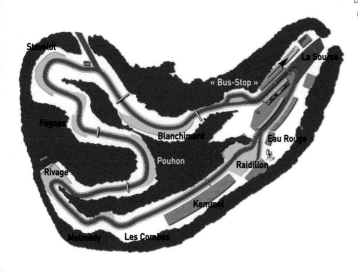

This year no threat hangs over the Belgian Grand Prix, which was taken off the calendar in 2003 because of tobacco advertising problems. An artful manipulation of the law overcame this hurdle. Had the Belgian round vanished many drivers would have been very unhappy and although it has been watered down a little to improve safety, it is still one of the most challenging circuits on the calendar. It requires precision, speed and a fair dose of courage as its combination of very fast, medium-fast and slow corners laid out in the Ardennes puts a premium on set-up, driving skills and expertise without forgetting the fickle climate. Last year the Saturday morning sessions were cut short because of fog and light rain, and the spectators huddled under their umbrellas saw only about 15-minutes action. The event was one of the most exciting of the 2004 season and was the scene of a break in Ferrari domination thanks to Raïkkönen's victory in his McLaren.

On what he calls his home circuit Michael Schumacher was crowned for the seventh time. It was here that he made his F1 debut in 1991, all six hundred metres of it as his clutch went almost immediately after the start. The following year he scored his first grand prix victory at Spa and he has won the race a further five times.

One of the black spots of the 2004 weekend was the totally unacceptable behaviour of the local police force. They threw photographers out of an enclosure specially provided for their use just under a minute before the start. In another case a journalist was threatened at gunpoint, as he did not obey orders quickly enough at a roundabout. This kind of heavy-handed behaviour does nothing for the prestige of the event. It is one of the few remaining myths of F1. Let's protect it!

**Address**
55, route du circuit
4790 Francorchamps,
Belgium
Tel.: +32 (0) 87 27 51 46
Fax: +32 (0) 87 27 55 51
Internet: www.spa-francorchamps.be

**Location**
The circuit is in the east of Belgium in the Walloon region halfway between Luxemburg and Brussels. It is 50 kilometres southeast of Liège and the same distance from Aix la Chapelle in Germany. Brussels is 100 kilometres away. A good motorway network makes access easy but watch out for radars!

**Previous winners**
2004: K. Räikkönen (McLaren-Mercedes)
2002: M. Schumacher (Ferrari)
2001: M. Schumacher (Ferrari)
2000: M. Häkkinen (McLaren-Mercedes)
1999: D. Coulthard (McLaren-Mercedes)
1998: D.Hill (Jordan-Mugen Honda)
1997: M. Schumacher (Ferrari)
1996: M. Schumacher (Ferrari)
1995: M. Schumacher (Benetton-Renault)
1994: D. Hill (Williams-Renault)
1993: D. Hill (Williams-Renault)
1992: M. Schumacher (Benetton-Ford)
1991: A. Senna (McLaren-Honda)
1990: A. Senna (McLaren-Honda)
...

Michael Schumacher has won at Spa six times (1992-95-96-97-2001-02). Behind him comes the late Ayrton Senna with five victories (1985-88-89-90-91). Neither, however, has equalled Jim Clark's record of 4 wins on the trot between 1962 and 1965 on the old full-length circuit.

2005 will be the 51ˢᵗ Belgian Grand Prix: 38 times at Spa-Francorchamps (1950 to 1956, 1958, 1960 to 1968, 1970 and 1983 and without interruption from 1985 to 2002 and then in 2004).
Nivelles twice (1972-74).
Zolder 10 times (1973, 1975 to 1982 and 1984).

## The records to beat
**Pole position**
Trulli (Renault) in 2004, 1:56.232 (216.064 km/h)
**Average race speed**
Räikkönen (McLaren-Mercedes) in 2004, 1:32:35.274 (198.898 km/h)
**Lap records**
Räikkönen (McLaren-Mercedes) in 2004, 1:45.108 (238.931 km/h)

## 2004 statistics
**Pole position**
Trulli (Renault), 1:56.232 (216.064 km/h)
**GP results**

| | |
|---|---|
| 1. Räikkönen (McLaren-Mercedes) | 1:32:35.274 |
| | (44 laps, 198.898 km/h) |
| 2. M. Schumacher (Ferrari) | + 3.132 |
| 3. Barrichello (Ferrari) | + 4.371 |
| 4. Massa (Sauber-Petronas) | + 12.504 |
| 5. Fisichella (Sauber-Petronas) | + 14.104 |
| 6. Klien (Jaguar) | + 14.614 |
| 7. Coulthard (McLaren-Mercedes) | + 17.970 |
| 8. Panis (Toyota) | + 18.693 |

**Fastest lap**
Räikkönen (McLaren-Mercedes), 1:45.108 (238.931 km/h)

Sunday 25ᵗʰ September 2005

**Start** 14h00 local time
(20h00 in Europe).

**Distance** 71 laps of the 4.309 km
circuit: 305.909 km*
(*start line offset: 0.030 km).

**Crowed in 2004**
70,000 spectators on race day.

17

# BRAZIL
## SÃO PAULO INTERLAGOS

A cold, wet Brazil without sunshine does not correspond to the usual image of this exotic country. And yet this was the situation in 2004 when it began to rain just before the start. It was the final round of the season and Williams **saved its bacon thanks to Juan-Pablo Montoya who scored a well-deserved victory for the BMW-powered team before heading off to McLaren.**

**Local lad, Rubens Barrichello, did not fulfil his dream of winning in** front of his home crowd despite being on pole. He came home third. The race is run in an anti-clockwise direction and is very demanding on both man and machine. It is generally a hotly disputed event and its favourable time slot guarantees it a good TV audience beyond Brazilian frontiers.

São Paolo is not your ideal picture postcard city and does not ooze the charm synonymous with Brazil. The shantytowns are a striking contrast to the affluence on show in the paddock and this can lead to a sentiment of unease. From time to time a return to exotic Rio de Janeiro is rumoured but in vain for the moment. In addition, the Jacarepagua complex is undergoing considerable modifications.

**Address**
Autodromo Jose Carlos Pace
Avenida Senador Teotonio Vilelia
261 São Paolo,
Brazil
Tel.: (+55) 11 56 66 78 13
Fax: (+55) 11 56 66 88 22
Internet: www.gpbrasil.com.br

**Location**
Interlagos is around fifteen kilometres south of the city centre of São Paolo. The São Paolo-Guarulhous airport is 50 kilometres to the north on the other side of the city.

**Previous winners**
2004: J.P. Montoya (Williams-BMW)
2003: G. Fisichella (Jordan-Ford)
2002: M. Schumacher (Ferrari)
2001: D. Coulthard (McLaren-Mercedes)
2000: M. Schumacher (Ferrari)
1999: M. Häkkinen (McLaren-Mercedes)
1998: M. Häkkinen (McLaren-Mercedes)
1997: J. Villeneuve (Williams-Renault)
1996: D. Hill (Williams-Renault)
1995: M. Schumacher (Benetton-Renault)
1994: M. Schumacher (Benetton-Ford)
1993: A. Senna (McLaren-Ford)
1992: N. Mansell (Williams-Renault)
1991: A. Senna (McLaren-Honda)
1990: A. Prost (Ferrari)
...

All-time winner of the Brazilian Grand Prix is Alain Prost with six successes (1982-84-85-87-88-90). Michael Schumacher has seen the topmost step of the rostrum 4 times (1994-95-2000-02).

On the Interlagos circuit Emerson Fittipaldi in his Lotus 72 won the first Brazilian Grand Prix counting for the F1 World Championship on 11th February 1973.

2005 will be the 33ʳᵈ Brazilian Grand Prix

São Paolo (1973 to 1978, then 1980 and without interruption from 1990 to 2005). Jacarepagua (Rio de Janeiro) 10 times (1978 and then 1981 to 1989).

## The records to beat
**Pole position**
Barrichello (Ferrari) in 2004, 1:10.646 (219.579 km/h)
**Average race speed**
Montoya (Williams-BMW) in 2004, 1:28:01.451 (208.516 km/h)
**Lap records**
Montoya (Williams-BMW) in 2004, 1:11.473 (217.038 km/h)

## 2004 statistics
**Pole position**
Barrichello (Ferrari), 1:10.646 (219.579 km/h)
**GP results**

| | | |
|---|---|---|
| 1. Montoya (Williams-BMW) | 1:28:01.451 | |
| | (71 laps, 208.516 km/h) | |
| 2. Räikkönen (McLaren-Mercedes) | + 1.022 | |
| 3. Barrichello (Ferrari) | + 24.099 | |
| 4. Alonso (Renault) | + 48.908 | |
| 5. R. Schumacher (Williams-BMW) | + 49.740 | |
| 6. Sato (B.A.R-Honda) | + 50.248 | |
| 7. M. Schumacher (Ferrari) | + 50.626 | |
| 8. Massa (Sauber-Petronas) | + 1:02.310 | |

**Fastest lap**
Montoya (Williams-BMW), 1:11.473 (217,038 km/h)

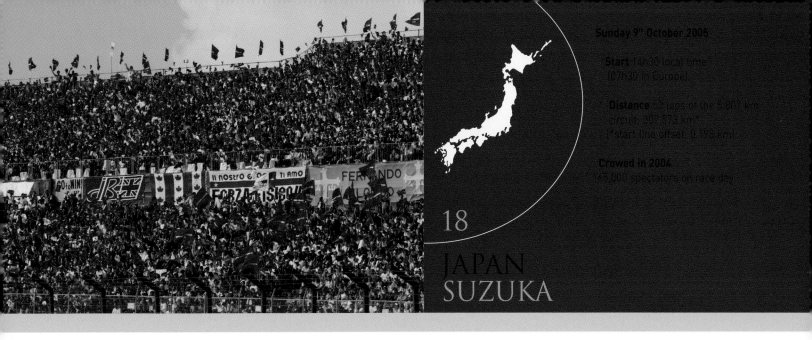

Sunday 9th October 2005

Start 14h30 local time
(07h30 in Europe)

Distance 53 laps of the 5.807 km
circuit 307.573 km*
(*start line offset: 0.173 km)

Crowded in 2004
155,000 spectators on race day

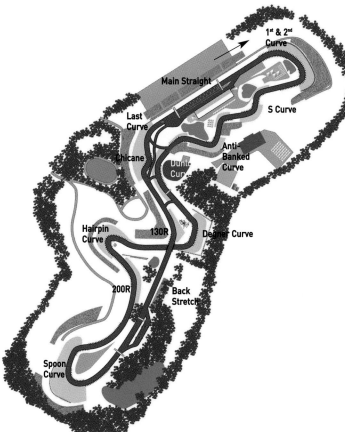

Many storms have rocked the little world of F1 but last year was the first time it was faced by a typhoon! As things turned out the storm veered away from Suzuka at the last moment though not before the whole of Saturday's activities had been cancelled as **a precautionary measure. Qualifying took place on Sunday morning and the race** was held in glorious sunshine!

A huge crowd turned up even though the championship had long since been decided, and one of the main reasons for this was the draw of Japanese driver, Takuma Sato, who had been having a brilliant season. In addition, the circuit is located in an amusement park for Honda factory personnel and Sato's car was evolving into what is a Honda works entry. Every time he sped past a grandstand it erupted in a multitude of small white flags like spring apple blossom, carrying his name.

Because of the dire weather forecast the circuit was closed on Saturday and when it reopened the spectators packed into the enclosures to grab the best places, many of them spending the night in the open air. The Japanese and Chinese Grand Prix are separated by one week for convenience sake. In Japan the organisation is excellent and the teams always receive a warm welcome in keeping with oriental hospitality.

Toyota, which owns Mount Fuji, has unveiled plans to organise a grand prix on this circuit where the first two Japanese F1 Grands Prix were held in 1976-77.

## 2004 statistics

### Pole position
M. Schumacher (Ferrari), 1:33.542 (223.484 km/h)

### GP results

| | | |
|---|---|---|
| 1. M. Schumacher (Ferrari) | 1:24:26.985 | |
| | (53 laps, 218.524 km/h) | |
| 2. R. Schumacher (Williams-BMW) | + 14.098 | |
| 3. Button (B.A.R-Honda) | + 19.662 | |
| 4. Sato (B.A.R-Honda) | + 31.781 | |
| 5. Alonso (Renault) | + 37.767 | |
| 6. Räikkönen (McLaren-Mercedes) | + 39.362 | |
| 7. Montoya (Williams-BMW) | + 55.347 | |
| 8. Fisichella (Sauber-Petronas) | + 56.276 | |

### Fastest lap
Barrichello (Ferrari), 1:32.730 (225.441 km/h)

## The records to beat

### Pole position
Barrichello (Ferrari) in 2003, 1:31.713 (227.941 km/h)

### Average race speed
M. Schumacher (Ferrari) in 2004, 1:24:26.985 (218.524 km/h)

### Lap records
Barrichello (Ferrari) in 2004, 1:32.730 (225.441 km/h)

### Address
Suzuka International Racing Course
7992 Ino-Cho, Suzuka-City,
Mie-ken 510-0295,
Japan
Tel.: (+81) 593 70 14 78
Fax: (+81) 593 78 11 65
Internet: www.suzukacircuit.co.jp

### Location
The Suzuka circuit is 500 kilometres southeast of Tokyo, 150 kilometres east of Osaka and 70 from Nagoya. Japan is a whole different world. The circuit hotel is reserved for drivers and team principals. Mechanics, team personnel and journalists find accommodation in the small towns in the surrounding area.

### Previous winners
2004: M. Schumacher (Ferrari)
2003: R. Barrichello (Ferrari)
2002: M. Schumacher (Ferrari)
2001: M. Schumacher (Ferrari)
2000: M. Schumacher (Ferrari)
1999: M. Häkkinen (McLaren-Mercedes)
1998: M. Häkkinen (McLaren-Mercedes)
1997: M. Schumacher (Ferrari)
1996: D. Hill (Williams-Renault)
1995: M. Schumacher (Ferrari)
1994: D. Hill (Williams-Renault)
1993: A. Senna (McLaren-Ford)
1992: N. Mansell (Williams-Renault)
1991: G. Berger (McLaren-Honda)
1990: N. Piquet (Benetton-Ford)
...

Michael Schumacher loves this circuit on which he has scored 6 victories (1995-97-2000-01-02-04). Then there is a big gap to Mika Häkkinen (1998-99), Damon Hill (1994-96) and Gerhard Berger (1987-91) all of whom have won the race twice.

Mario Andretti in his Lotus 78 won the first Japanese Grand Prix on the Mount Fuji circuit on 24th October 1976.

2005 will be the 21st Japanese Grand Prix:
- Mount Fuji twice (1976-77)
- Suzuka 19 times (from 1987 to 2005

Sunday 16ᵗʰ October 2005

**Start** 14h00 local time
(06h00 in Europe).

**Distance** 56 laps of the 5.451 km
circuit: 305.066 km*
(*start line offset: 0.190 km).

**Crowed in 2004**
163,000 spectators on race day.

19

# CHINA
# SHANGHAI

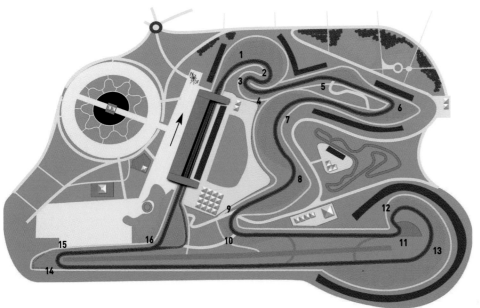

**Address**
Shanghai International Circuit Co ltd
1558 Dingxi Road
200010 Shanghai,
Popular Chinese Republic
Tel: +86 216 252 00 00
Fax :+86 216 252 37 34
Internet: www.f1china.com.cn

**Previous winners**
2004: R. Barrichello (Ferrari)

## The records to beat
**Pole position**
Barrichello (Ferrari) in 2004, 1:34.012 (208.735 km/h)
**Average race speed**
Barrichello (Ferrari) in 2004, 1:29:12.420 (205.185 km/h)
**Lap records**
M. Schumacher (Ferrari) in 2004, 1:32.238 (212.749 km/h)

## 2004 statistics
**Pole position**
Barrichello (Ferrari), 1:34.012 (208.735 km/h)
**GP results**

| | |
|---|---|
| 1. Barrichello (Ferrari) | 1:29:12.420 |
| | (56 laps, 205.185 km/h) |
| 2. Button (B.A.R-Honda) | + 1.035 |
| 3. Räikkönen (McLaren-Mercedes) | + 1.469 |
| 4. Alonso (Renault) | + 32.510 |
| 5. Montoya (Williams-BMW) | + 45.193 |
| 6. Sato (B.A.R-Honda) | + 54.791 |
| 7. Fisichella (Sauber-Petronas) | + 1:05.464 |
| 8. Massa (Sauber-Petronas) | + 1:20.080 |

**Fastest lap**
M. Schumacher (Ferrari), 1:32.238 (212.749 km/h)

In 2008, Peking will host the Olympic Games as a symbol of its arrival in the modern era. Shanghai, on the other hand, has chosen Formula 1 to impact the western mind and attract the investors who are swarming to China.
The economic dynamism of the region is breathtaking and business is thriving. Nothing is too extravagant or expensive to boost this phenomenal growth. Already Shanghai is reaping the benefits of the three hundred million plus dollars invested in the construction of a new-generation circuit that sets the standards by which those currently on the calendar will be judged - and in many cases found lacking. The track is built on a marsh and to consolidate the foundations a huge concrete slab had to be cast on which the circuit and its infrastructure have been constructed. Last year, over 160,000 spectators crowded the grandstands and spectator enclosures on raceday and the proposed additional seating will only serve to reinforce the success of the operation.
From a propaganda point of view it has been a triumph. In contrast to the Olympic Games the Chinese promoter is assured of making a profit on his investment over a minimum 5-year period. In addition, there is a project to construct a huge commercial and industrial centre dedicated to the motor car, and this will favour the long-term implantation of the grand prix in the region. The Chinese market is a kind of 21st century El Dorado for car manufacturers and all the makes involved in F1 to a greater or lesser degree are delighted with the presence of this event on the calendar in a market that is vital for their future.
While the heart of Shanghai and the Pudong financial centre bear a close resemblance to those of Wall Street, London or Hong Kong, the visitor finds himself in another world once he leaves the main thoroughfares. It is impossible to rent a car without a driver and the journey to the circuit, some 30 kilometres from the city centre, is an adventure in itself. Traffic is very dense and the local drivers' conduct is erratic to say the least! Trying to get there by bus or taxi is not exactly a picnic!
However, the organiser has promised to do something about the problem by building a metro line to the circuit. In China, things move very fast.

# 1950-2004

## STATISTICS

The statistics given hereafter are calculated up to 31st December 2004.

The increase in the number of grands prix tends to distort certain figures, as today the possibility of accumulating results quickly is much greater than in the past.
This, though, in no way detracts from the value of contemporary drivers.

In addition, the points system has changed several times since 1950:
- From 1950 to 1959 the system was as follows: 8 points for a win, 6 points for 2nd, 4 points for 3rd, 3 points for 4th, 2 points for 5th and 1 point for the lap record.
- In 1960, the point for the lap record was cancelled and 1 point was awarded for 6th place.
- In 1961, an extra point was awarded to the winner (9 points).
- Since 1991, another point was awarded to the winner (10) to encourage panache!
- In 2003, points were awarded to the first eight: 10 for a win, 8 for 2nd, 6 for 3rd, 5 for 4th, 4 for 5th, 3 for 6th, 2 for 7th and 1 for 8th.

### FINAL CLASSIFICATION OF THE 2004 DRIVERS' WORLD CHAMPIONSHIP

| | Nat. | Team | Points | Poles | Wins | Fastest race laps | Podiums |
|---|---|---|---|---|---|---|---|
| 1. Michael Schumacher | GER | (Ferrari) | 148 | 8 | 13 | 10 | 15 |
| 2. Rubens Barrichello | BRA | (Ferrari) | 114 | 4 | 2 | 4 | 14 |
| 3. Jenson Button | GB | (B.A.R-Honda) | 85 | 1 | - | - | 10 |
| 4. Fernando Alonso | ESP | (Renault) | 59 | 1 | - | - | 4 |
| 5. Juan Pablo Montoya | COL | (Williams-BMW) | 58 | - | 1 | 2 | 3 |
| 6. Jarno Trulli | ITA | (Renault / Toyota) | 46 | 2 | 1 | - | 2 |
| 7. Kimi Räikkönen | FIN | (McLaren-Mercedes) | 45 | 1 | 1 | 2 | 4 |
| 8. Takuma Sato | JAP | (B.A.R-Honda) | 34 | - | - | - | 1 |
| 9. Ralf Schumacher | GER | (Williams-BMW) | 24 | 1 | - | - | 1 |
| 10. David Coulthard | GB | (McLaren-Mercedes) | 24 | - | - | - | - |
| 11. Giancarlo Fisichella | ITA | (Sauber-Petronas) | 22 | - | - | - | - |
| 12. Felipe Massa | BRA | (Sauber-Petronas) | 12 | - | - | - | - |
| 13. Mark Webber | AUS | (Jaguar) | 7 | - | - | - | - |
| 14. Olivier Panis | FRA | (Toyota) | 6 | - | - | - | - |
| 15. Antonio Pizzonia | BRA | (Williams-BMW) | 6 | - | - | - | - |
| 16. Christian Klien | AUT | (Jaguar) | 3 | - | - | - | - |
| 17. Cristiano Da Matta | BRA | (Toyota) | 3 | - | - | - | - |
| 18. Nick Heidfeld | GER | (Jordan-Ford) | 3 | - | - | - | - |
| 19. Timo Glock | GER | (Jordan-Ford) | 2 | - | - | - | - |
| 20. Zsolt Baumgartner | HUN | (Minardi-Cosworth) | 1 | - | - | - | - |
| 21. Jacques Villeneuve | CDN | (Renault) | 0 | - | - | - | - |
| 22. Ricardo Zonta | BRA | (Toyota) | 0 | - | - | - | - |
| 23. Marc Gené | ESP | (Williams-BMW) | 0 | - | - | - | - |
| 24. Giorgio Pantano | ITA | (Jordan-Ford) | 0 | - | - | - | - |
| 25. Gianmaria Bruni | ITA | (Minardi-Cosworth) | 0 | - | - | - | - |

### FINAL CLASSIFICATION OF THE 2004 CONSTRUCTORS' WORLD CHAMPIONSHIP

| | Nat. | Points | Poles | Wins | Fastest race laps | Podiums |
|---|---|---|---|---|---|---|
| 1. Ferrari | ITA | 262 | 12 | 15 | 14 | 29 |
| 2. B.A.R-Honda | GB | 119 | 1 | - | - | 11 |
| 3. Renault | FRA | 105 | 3 | 1 | - | 6 |
| 4. Williams-BMW | GB | 88 | 1 | 1 | 2 | 4 |
| 5. McLaren-Mercedes | GB | 69 | 1 | 1 | 2 | 4 |
| 6. Sauber-Petronas | CH | 34 | - | - | - | - |
| 7. Jaguar | USA | 10 | - | - | - | - |
| 8. Toyota | JPN | 9 | - | - | - | - |
| 9. Jordan-Ford | GB | 5 | - | - | - | - |
| 10. Minardi-Cosworth | ITA | 1 | - | - | - | - |

### DRIVERS - THE WORLD CHAMPIONS

| | | | |
|---|---|---|---|
| 1950 | Giuseppe Farina | ITA | Alfa Roméo |
| 1951 | Juan Manuel Fangio | ARG | Alfa Roméo |
| 1952 | Alberto Ascari | ITA | Ferrari |
| 1953 | Alberto Ascari | ITA | Ferrari |
| 1954 | Juan Manuel Fangio | ARG | Mercedes/Maserati |
| 1955 | Juan Manuel Fangio | ARG | Mercedes |
| 1956 | Juan Manuel Fangio | ARG | Lancia/Ferrari |
| 1957 | Juan Manuel Fangio | ARG | Maserati |
| 1958 | Mike Hawthorn | GB | Ferrari |
| 1959 | Jack Brabham | AUS | Cooper Climax |
| 1960 | Jack Brabham | AUS | Cooper Climax |
| 1961 | Phil Hill | USA | Ferrari |
| 1962 | Graham Hill | GB | BRM |
| 1963 | Jim Clark | GB | Lotus Climax |
| 1964 | John Surtees | GB | Ferrari |
| 1965 | Jim Clark | GB | Lotus Climax |
| 1966 | Jack Brabham | AUS | Brabham Repco |
| 1967 | Denny Hulme | NZ | Brabham Repco |
| 1968 | Graham Hill | GB | Lotus Ford |
| 1969 | Jackie Stewart | GB | Matra Ford |
| 1970 | Jochen Rindt | AUT | Lotus Ford |
| 1971 | Jackie Stewart | GB | Tyrrell Ford |
| 1972 | Emerson Fittipaldi | BRA | Lotus Ford |
| 1973 | Jackie Stewart | GB | Tyrrell Ford |
| 1974 | Emerson Fittipaldi | BRA | McLaren Ford |
| 1975 | Niki Lauda | AUT | Ferrari |
| 1976 | James Hunt | GB | McLaren Ford |
| 1977 | Niki Lauda | AUT | Ferrari |
| 1978 | Mario Andretti | USA | Lotus Ford |
| 1979 | Jody Scheckter | SA | Ferrari |
| 1980 | Alan Jones | AUS | Williams Ford |
| 1981 | Nelson Piquet | BRA | Brabham Ford |
| 1982 | Keke Rosberg | FIN | Williams Ford |
| 1983 | Nelson Piquet | BRA | Brabham BMW Turbo |
| 1984 | Niki Lauda | AUT | McLaren TAG Porsche Turbo |
| 1985 | Alain Prost | FRA | McLaren TAG Porsche Turbo |
| 1986 | Alain Prost | FRA | McLaren TAG Porsche Turbo |
| 1987 | Nelson Piquet | BRA | Williams Honda Turbo |
| 1988 | Ayrton Senna | BRA | McLaren Honda Turbo |
| 1989 | Alain Prost | FRA | McLaren Honda |
| 1990 | Ayrton Senna | BRA | McLaren Honda |
| 1991 | Ayrton Senna | BRA | McLaren Honda |
| 1992 | Nigel Mansell | GB | Williams Renault |
| 1993 | Alain Prost | FRA | Williams Renault |
| 1994 | Michael Schumacher | GER | Benetton Ford |
| 1995 | Michael Schumacher | GER | Benetton Renault |
| 1996 | Damon Hill | GB | Williams Renault |
| 1997 | Jacques Villeneuve | CDN | Williams Renault |
| 1998 | Mika Häkkinen | FIN | McLaren Mercedes |
| 1999 | Mika Häkkinen | FIN | McLaren Mercedes |
| 2000 | Michael Schumacher | GER | Ferrari |
| 2001 | Michael Schumacher | GER | Ferrari |
| 2002 | Michael Schumacher | GER | Ferrari |
| 2003 | Michael Schumacher | GER | Ferrari |
| 2004 | Michael Schumacher | GER | Ferrari |

### NUMBER OF WORLD CHAMPIONSHIPS PER DRIVER

| | | |
|---|---|---|
| 7 titles: | Michael Schumacher (GER) | 1994, 1995, 2000, 2001, 2002, 2003 et 2004 |
| 5 titles: | Juan Manuel Fangio ( Argentina) | 1951, 1954, 1955, 1956 et 1957 |
| 4 titles: | Alain Prost (France) | 1985, 1986, 1989 et 1993 |
| 3 titles: | Jack Brabham (Australia) | 1959, 1960 et 1966 |
| | Niki Lauda (Austria) | 1975, 1977 et 1984 |
| | Nelson Piquet (Brazil) | 1981, 1983 et 1987 |
| | Ayrton Senna (Brazil) | 1988, 1990 et 1991 |
| | Jackie Stewart (Great Britain) | 1969, 1971 et 1973 |
| 2 titles: | Alberto Ascari (Italy) | 1952 et 1953 |
| | Jim Clark (Great Britain) | 1963 et 1965 |
| | Emerson Fittipaldi (Brazil) | 1972 et 1974 |
| | Mika Häkkinen (Finland) | 1998 et 1999 |
| | Graham Hill (Great Britain) | 1962 et 1968 |
| 1 title: | Mario Andretti (United States) | 1978 |
| | Giuseppe Farina (Italy) | 1950 |
| | Mike Hawthorn (Great Britain) | 1958 |
| | Damon Hill (Great Britain) | 1996 |
| | Phil Hill (United States) | 1961 |
| | Dennis Hulme (New Zealand) | 1967 |
| | Alan Jones (Australia) | 1980 |
| | Nigel Mansell (Great Britain) | 1992 |
| | Jochen Rindt ( Austria) | 1970 |
| | Keke Rosberg (Finland) | 1982 |
| | Jody Scheckter (South Africa) | 1979 |
| | John Surtees (Great Britain) | 1964 |
| | Jacques Villeneuve (Canada) | 1997 |

### NUMBER OF WINS PER DRIVER

| | | | | | |
|---|---|---|---|---|---|
| **M. Schumacher** | **83** | J. Rindt | 6 | J. Alesi | 1 |
| A. Prost | 51 | **R. Schumacher** | **6** | **F. Alonso** | **1** |
| A. Senna | 41 | J. Surtees | 6 | G. Baghetti | 1 |
| N. Mansell | 31 | G. Villeneuve | 6 | L. Bandini | 1 |
| J. Stewart | 27 | M. Alboreto | 5 | J-P. Beltoise | 1 |
| J. Clark | 25 | G. Farina | 5 | J. Bonnier | 1 |
| N. Lauda | 25 | C. Regazzoni | 5 | V. Brambilla | 1 |
| J.M. Fangio | 24 | K. Rosberg | 5 | J. Bryan | 1 |
| N. Piquet | 23 | J. Watson | 5 | F. Cevert | 1 |
| D. Hill | 22 | D. Gurney | 4 | L. Fagioli | 1 |
| M. Häkkinen | 20 | E. Irvine | 4 | **G. Fisichella** | **1** |
| S. Moss | 16 | B. McLaren | 4 | P. Flaherty | 1 |
| J. Brabham | 14 | **J.P. Montoya** | **4** | P. Gethin | 1 |
| E. Fittipaldi | 14 | T. Boutsen | 3 | R. Ginther | 1 |
| G. Hill | 14 | P. Collins | 3 | S. Hanks | 1 |
| A. Ascari | 13 | H-H. Frentzen | 3 | I. Ireland | 1 |
| **D. Coulthard** | **13** | J. Herbert | 3 | J. Mass | 1 |
| Ma. Andretti | 12 | P. Hill | 3 | L. Musso | 1 |
| A. Jones | 12 | M. Hawthorn | 3 | A. Nannini | 1 |
| C. Reutemann | 12 | D. Pironi | 3 | G. Nilson | 1 |
| **J. Villeneuve** | **11** | E. De Angelis | 2 | C. Pace | 1 |
| G. Berger | 10 | P. Depailler | 2 | O. Panis | 1 |
| J. Hunt | 10 | J-F Gonzales | 2 | J. Parsons | 1 |
| R. Peterson | 10 | J-P. Jabouille | 2 | L. Scarfiotti | 1 |
| J. Scheckter | 10 | **K. Räikkönen** | **2** | B. Sweikert | 1 |
| **R. Barrichello** | **9** | P. Revson | 2 | J. Rathman | 1 |
| D. Hulme | 8 | P. Rodriguez | 2 | T. Ruttman | 1 |
| J. Ickx | 8 | J. Siffert | 2 | P. Taruffi | 1 |
| R. Arnoux | 7 | P. Tambay | 2 | J. Trulli | 1 |
| T. Brooks | 6 | M. Trintignant | 2 | L. Wallard | 1 |
| J. Laffite | 6 | W. Von Trips | 2 | R. Ward | 1 |
| R. Patrese | 6 | B. Vukovich | 2 | | |

### NUMBER OF POLE POSITIONS PER DRIVER

| | | | | | |
|---|---|---|---|---|---|
| A. Senna | 65 | G. Hill | 13 | **R. Schumacher** | **5** |
| **M. Schumacher** | **63** | J. Ickx | 13 | P. Tambay | 5 |
| J. Clark | 33 | **J. Villeneuve** | **13** | M. Hawthorn | 4 |
| A. Prost | 33 | G. Berger | 12 | D. Pironi | 4 |
| N. Mansell | 32 | **D. Coulthard** | **12** | F. Alonso | 3 |
| J.M. Fangio | 29 | **J.P. Montoya** | **11** | T. Brooks | 3 |
| M. Häkkinen | 26 | J. Rindt | 10 | E. De Angelis | 3 |
| N. Lauda | 24 | J. Surtees | 8 | T. Fabi | 3 |
| N. Piquet | 24 | R. Patrese | 8 | J-F. Gonzales | 3 |
| D. Hill | 20 | J. Laffite | 7 | D. Gurney | 3 |
| Ma. Andretti | 18 | E. Fittipaldi | 6 | J-P. Jarier | 3 |
| R. Arnoux | 18 | P. Hill | 6 | **K. Räikkönen** | **3** |
| J. Stewart | 17 | J.P. Jabouille | 6 | J. Scheckter | 3 |
| S. Moss | 16 | A. Jones | 6 | ... | |
| A. Ascari | 14 | C. Reutemann | 6 | | |
| J. Hunt | 14 | C. Amon | 5 | Then: | |
| R. Peterson | 14 | G. Farina | 5 | **J. Trulli** | **2** |
| **R. Barrichello** | **13** | C. Regazzoni | 5 | **J. Button** | **1** |
| J. Brabham | 13 | K. Rosberg | 5 | **G. Fisichella** | **1** |

### NUMBER OF GRANDS PRIX CONTESTED PER DRIVER

| | |
|---|---|
| Riccardo Patrese | 256 |
| **Michael Schumacher** | **211** |
| Gerhard Berger | 210 |
| Andrea de Cesaris | 208 |
| Nelson Piquet | 204 |
| Jean Alesi | 201 |
| Alain Prost | 199 |
| **Rubens Barrichello** | **195** |
| Michele Alboreto | 194 |
| Nigel Mansell | 187 |
| Graham Hill | 176 |
| Jacques Laffite | 176 |
| **David Coulthard** | **175** |
| Niki Lauda | 171 |
| Thierry Boutsen | 163 |
| Ayrton Senna | 161 |
| Mika Häkkinen | 161 |
| Johnny Herbert | 160 |
| Martin Brundle | 158 |
| Olivier Panis | 157 |
| Heinz-Harald Frentzen | 156 |
| John Watson | 152 |
| René Arnoux | 149 |
| Carlos Reutemann | 146 |
| Derek Warwick | 146 |
| Eddie Irvine | 146 |
| Emerson Fittipaldi | 144 |
| **Giancarlo Fisichella** | **141** |
| Jean Pierre Jarier | 134 |
| **Jacques Villeneuve** | **133** |
| Clay Regazzoni | 132 |
| Eddie Cheever | 132 |
| Mario Andretti | 128 |
| **Jarno Trulli** | **128** |
| **Ralf Schumacher** | **127** |
| Jack Brabham | 126 |
| Ronnie Peterson | 123 |
| Pierluigi Martini | 119 |
| Alan Jones | 116 |
| Damon Hill | 115 |
| Jacky Ickx | 114 |
| Keke Rosberg | 114 |
| Patrick Tambay | 114 |
| Denny Hulme | 112 |
| John Surtees | 111 |
| Jody Scheckter | 111 |
| Philippe Alliot | 109 |
| Mika Salo | 109 |
| Elio de Angelis | 108 |
| Jos Verstappen | 106 |
| Jo Bonnier | 104 |
| Jochen Mass | 104 |
| Bruce McLaren | 100 |
| Jackie Stewart | 99 |
| Pedro Diniz | 98 |
| Jo Siffert | 96 |
| Chris Amon | 96 |
| Patrick Depailler | 95 |
| Ukyo Katayama | 94 |
| Ivan Capelli | 93 |
| James Hunt | 92 |
| Dan Gurney | 86 |
| Jean Pierre Beltoise | 84 |
| **Jenson Button** | **84** |
| **Nick Heidfeld** | **84** |
| Maurice Trintignant | 82 |
| Marc Surer | 82 |
| Jonathan Palmer | 82 |
| Stefan Johansson | 79 |
| Alessandro Nannini | 76 |
| Hans Joachim Stuck | 74 |
| Vittorio Brambilla | 74 |
| Piercarlo Ghinzani | 74 |
| Satoru Nakajima | 74 |
| Mauricio Gugelmin | 74 |
| Jim Clark | 72 |
| Carlos Pace | 71 |
| Didier Pironi | 70 |
| Stefano Modena | 70 |
| Bruno Giacomelli | 69 |
| **Juan Pablo Montoya** | **68** |
| Gilles Villeneuve | 67 |
| Gianni Morbidelli | 67 |
| **Kimi Räikkönen** | **67** |
| Stirling Moss | 66 |
| Teo Fabi | 64 |
| Aguri Suzuki | 64 |
| J J Lehto | 62 |
| Pedro de la Rosa | 62 |
| Mark Blundell | 61 |
| Jochen Rindt | 60 |
| Erik Comas | 59 |
| Arturo Merzario | 57 |
| Harry Schell | 56 |
| Henri Pescarolo | 56 |
| Alex Caffi | 56 |
| Pedro Rodriguez | 54 |

| | |
|---|---|
| Rolf Stommelen | 53 |
| Philippe Streiff | 53 |
| Jean Behra | 52 |
| Richie Ginther | 52 |
| Alexander Wurz | 52 |
| Juan Manuel Fangio | 51 |
| **Fernando Alonso** | **50** |
| Innes Ireland | 50 |
| **Mark Webber** | **50** |
| Mike Hailwood | 49 |
| Jean Pierre Jabouille | 49 |
| Derek Daly | 49 |
| Nicola Larini | 49 |
| Phil Hill | 48 |
| Jackie Oliver | 48 |
| Luca Badoer | 48 |
| Roy Salvadori | 47 |
| Manfred Winkelhock | 47 |
| Bertrand Gachot | 47 |
| François Cevert | 46 |
| Mike Hawthorn | 45 |
| Eric Bernard | 45 |
| Lorenzo Bandini | 42 |
| Tom Pryce | 42 |
| Hector Rebaque | 41 |
| Olivier Grouillard | 41 |
| Roberto Moreno | 41 |
| Karl Wendlinger | 41 |
| Alessandro Zanardi | 41 |
| Christian Fittipaldi | 40 |
| Louis Rosier | 38 |
| Tony Brooks | 38 |
| Masten Gregory | 38 |
| Gabriele Tarquini | 38 |
| Emanuele Pirro | 37 |
| Mike Spence | 36 |
| Mauro Baldi | 36 |
| Marc Gené | 36 |
| **Takuma Sato** | **36** |
| Ricardo Zonta | 36 |
| Howden Ganley | 35 |
| Wilson Fittipaldi | 35 |
| Christian Danner | 35 |
| Tim Schenken | 34 |
| Brett Lunger | 34 |
| **Felipe Massa** | **34** |
| Nino Farina | 33 |
| Shinji Nakano | 33 |
| Alberto Ascari | 32 |
| Peter Collins | 32 |
| Pedro Lamy | 32 |
| Toranosuke Takagi | 32 |
| Luigi Villoresi | 31 |
| Gunnar Nilsson | 31 |
| Peter Revson | 30 |
| Peter Gethin | 30 |
| Andrea de Adamich | 29 |
| Robert Manzon | 28 |
| Carel Godin de Beaufort | 28 |
| Mike Beuttler | 28 |
| Enrique Bernoldi | 28 |
| Cristiano da Matta | 28 |
| Wolfgang von Trips | 27 |
| Trevor Taylor | 27 |
| Piers Courage | 27 |
| Jose Froilan Gonzalez | 26 |
| Luis Perez-Sala | 26 |
| Ricardo Rosset | 26 |
| Tony Maggs | 25 |
| Bob Anderson | 25 |
| Rupert Keegan | 25 |
| Huub Rothengatter | 25 |
| Jan Magnussen | 25 |
| Luigi Musso | 24 |
| Eliseo Salazar | 24 |
| Yannick Dalmas | 24 |
| David Brabham | 24 |
| Tarso Marques | 24 |
| Johnny Claes | 23 |
| Raul Boesel | 23 |
| Jan Lammers | 23 |
| Toulo de Graffenried | 22 |
| Reine Wisell | 22 |
| Giancarlo Baghetti | 21 |
| Roberto Guerrero | 21 |
| Gaston Mazzacane | 21 |
| Stefan Bellof | 20 |
| Zsolt Baumgartner | 20 |
| ... | |
| | |
| Then: | |
| **Christian Klien** | **18** |

### NUMBER OF FASTEST LAPS PER DRIVER

| | | | |
|---|---|---|---|
| **M. Schumacher** | **66** | **J. Villeneuve** | **9** |
| A. Prost | 41 | J. Hunt | 8 |
| N. Mansell | 30 | G. Villeneuve | 8 |
| J. Clark | 28 | **R. Schumacher** | **7** |
| M. Häkkinen | 25 | E. Fittipaldi | 6 |
| N. Lauda | 24 | H-H. Frentzen | 6 |
| J.M. Fangio | 23 | J-F. Gonzalez | 6 |
| N. Piquet | 23 | D. Gurney | 6 |
| G. Berger | 21 | M. Hawthorn | 6 |
| D. Hill | 19 | P. Hill | 6 |
| S. Moss | 19 | J. Laffite | 6 |
| A. Senna | 19 | **K. Räikkönen** | **6** |
| **D. Coulthard** | **18** | C. Reutemann | 6 |
| **R. Barrichello** | **15** | M. Alboreto | 5 |
| C. Regazzoni | 15 | G. Farina | 5 |
| J. Stewart | 15 | C. Pace | 5 |
| J. Ickx | 14 | D. Pironi | 5 |
| A. Jones | 13 | J. Scheckter | 5 |
| R. Patrese | 13 | J. Watson | 5 |
| R. Arnoux | 12 | J. Alesi | 4 |
| J. Brabham | 12 | J.P. Beltoise | 4 |
| A. Ascari | 11 | P. Depailler | 4 |
| **J.P. Montoya** | **11** | J. Siffert | 4 |
| Ma. Andretti | 10 | ... | |
| G. Hill | 10 | | |
| J. Surtees | 10 | Then: | |
| D. Hulme | 9 | **F. Alonso** | **1** |
| R. Peterson | 9 | **G. Fisichella** | **1** |

### TOTAL POINTS SCORED PER DRIVER

| | | | |
|---|---|---|---|
| **M. Schumacher** | **1186** | N. Farina | 127.3 |
| A. Prost | 798.5 | E. De Angelis | 122 |
| A. Senna | 614 | **J. Trulli** | **117** |
| N. Piquet | 485.5 | **G. Fisichella** | **116** |
| N. Mansell | 482 | **F. Alonso** | **114** |
| **D. Coulthard** | **475** | J. Rindt | 109 |
| **R. Barrichello** | **451** | R. Ginther | 107 |
| N. Lauda | 420.5 | G. Villeneuve | 107 |
| M. Häkkinen | 420 | P. Tambay | 103 |
| G. Berger | 385 | D. Pironi | 101 |
| J. Stewart | 360 | M. Brundle | 98 |
| D. Hill | 360 | J. Herbert | 98 |
| C. Reutemann | 310 | P. Hill | 98 |
| G. Hill | 289 | F. Cevert | 89 |
| E. Fittipaldi | 281 | S. Johanson | 88 |
| R. Patrese | 281 | C. Amon | 83 |
| J.M. Fangio | 277.5 | J-F Gonzales | 77.64 |
| J. Clark | 274 | J-P. Beltoise | 77 |
| J. Brabham | 261 | O. Panis | 76 |
| **R. Schumacher** | **259** | T. Brooks | 75 |
| J. Scheckter | 255 | M. Trintignant | 72.33 |
| D. Hulme | 248 | P. Rodriguez | 71 |
| J. Alesi | 241 | J. Mass | 71 |
| J. Laffite | 228 | D. Warwick | 71 |
| **J.P. Montoya** | **221** | E. Cheever | 70 |
| **J. Villeneuve** | **219** | J. Siffert | 68 |
| C. Regazzoni | 212 | A. Nannini | 65 |
| A. Jones | 206 | P. Revson | 61 |
| R. Peterson | 206 | A. De Cesaris | 59 |
| B. McLaren | 196.5 | L. Bandini | 58 |
| E. Irvine | 191 | C. Pace | 58 |
| M. Alboreto | 186.6 | W. Von Trips | 56 |
| S. Moss | 186.5 | J. Behra | 51.14 |
| R. Arnoux | 181 | L. Villoresi | 49 |
| J. Ickx | 181 | P. Collins | 47 |
| Ma. Andretti | 180 | I. Ireland | 47 |
| J. Surtees | 180 | L. Musso | 44 |
| J. Hunt | 179 | P. Taruffi | 41 |
| H-H. Frentzen | 174 | J. Bonnier | 39 |
| **K. Räikkönen** | **169** | **T. Sato** | **39** |
| J. Watson | 169 | M. Salo | 33 |
| K. Rosberg | 159.5 | ... | |
| P. Depailler | 141 | | |
| A. Ascari | 140 | Then: | |
| D. Gurney | 133 | **N. Heidfeld** | **28** |
| T. Boutsen | 132 | **M. Webber** | **26** |
| **J. Button** | **130** | **F. Massa** | **16** |
| M. Hawthorn | 127.5 | **C. Klien** | **3** |

## THE PODIUM REGULARS

| | | | |
|---|---|---|---|
| M. Schumacher | 137 | R. Arnoux | 22 |
| A. Prost | 106 | G. Farina | 20 |
| A. Senna | 80 | J. Watson | 20 |
| D. Coulthard | 60 | Ma. Andretti | 19 |
| N. Piquet | 60 | P. Depailler | 19 |
| N. Mansell | 59 | D. Gurney | 19 |
| R. Barrichello | 57 | M. Hawthorn | 18 |
| N. Lauda | 54 | K. Räikkönen | 18 |
| M. Häkkinen | 51 | A. Ascari | 17 |
| G. Berger | 48 | H.-H. Frentzen | 17 |
| C. Reutemann | 45 | K. Rosberg | 17 |
| J. Stewart | 43 | P. Hill | 16 |
| D. Hill | 42 | T. Boutsen | 15 |
| R. Patrese | 37 | F. Gonzales | 15 |
| G. Hill | 36 | R. Ginther | 14 |
| J.-M. Fangio | 35 | J.-P. Beltoise | 13 |
| E. Fittipaldi | 35 | F. Cevert | 13 |
| D. Hulme | 33 | D. Pironi | 13 |
| J. Scheckter | 33 | J. Rindt | 13 |
| J. Clark | 32 | G. Villeneuve | 13 |
| J. Laffite | 32 | C. Amon | 11 |
| J. Alesi | 31 | S. Johansson | 12 |
| J. Brabham | 31 | C. Amon | 11 |
| C. Regazzoni | 28 | P. Tambay | 11 |
| B. McLaren | 27 | J. Button | 10 |
| E. Irvine | 26 | G. Fisichella | 10 |
| R. Peterson | 26 | M. Trintignant | 10 |
| J. Ickx | 25 | T. Brooks | 10 |
| A. Jones | 24 | ... | |
| S. Moss | 24 | | |
| R. Schumacher | 24 | Then: | |
| J. Surtees | 24 | F. Alonso | 8 |
| M. Alboreto | 23 | J. Trulli | 4 |
| J. Hunt | 23 | N. Heidfeld | 1 |
| J.P. Montoya | 23 | T. Sato | 1 |
| J. Villeneuve | 23 | | |

## NUMBER OF LAPS IN THE LEAD PER DRIVER

| | | | |
|---|---|---|---|
| M. Schumacher | 4'657 | B. Vukovich | 485 |
| A. Senna | 2'986 | E. Fittipaldi | 478 |
| A. Prost | 2'684 | D. Hulme | 449 |
| N. Mansell | 2'089 | J. Rindt | 387 |
| J. Clark | 1'943 | R. Schumacher | 387 |
| J. Stewart | 1'921 | J.P. Montoya | 382 |
| N. Piquet | 1'600 | C. Regazzoni | 360 |
| N. Lauda | 1'592 | N. Farina | 338 |
| M. Häkkinen | 1'488 | J. Surtees | 312 |
| D. Hill | 1'358 | D. Pironi | 295 |
| J.M. Fangio | 1'348 | J. Laffite | 283 |
| S. Moss | 1'181 | J. Watson | 282 |
| G. Hill | 1'102 | J-F. Gonzalez | 272 |
| A. Ascari | 926 | J. Alesi | 265 |
| D. Coulthard | 894 | M. Hawthorn | 225 |
| J. Brabham | 825 | M. Alboreto | 218 |
| Ma. Andretti | 798 | J. Bryan | 216 |
| R. Peterson | 707 | K. Räikkönen | 209 |
| R. Barrichello | 699 | D. Gurney | 200 |
| G. Berger | 692 | P. Tambay | 195 |
| J. Scheckter | 675 | ... | |
| J. Hunt | 666 | | |
| C. Reutemann | 649 | Then: | |
| J. Villeneuve | 633 | F. Alonso | 157 |
| A. Jones | 589 | J. Trulli | 141 |
| R. Patrese | 567 | G. Fisichella | 36 |
| G. Villeneuve | 534 | J. Button | 70 |
| J. Ickx | 529 | F. Massa | 2 |
| K. Rosberg | 517 | T. Sato | 2 |
| R. Arnoux | 506 | M. Webber | 2 |

## TOTAL KILOMETRES IN THE LEAD PER DRIVER

| | | | |
|---|---|---|---|
| M. Schumacher | 21'954 | K. Rosberg | 2'165 |
| A. Senna | 13'672 | J. Surtees | 2'117 |
| A. Prost | 12'481 | D. Hulme | 1'971 |
| J. Clark | 10'125 | J. Rindt | 1'898 |
| N. Mansell | 9'642 | R. Schumacher | 1'858 |
| J.M. Fangio | 9'322 | C. Regazzoni | 1'851 |
| J. Stewart | 9'191 | J.P. Montoya | 1'792 |
| N. Piquet | 7'611 | M. Hawthorn | 1'635 |
| M. Häkkinen | 7'189 | D. Gurney | 1'612 |
| N. Lauda | 7'064 | P. Hill | 1'528 |
| S. Moss | 6'372 | J.F. Gonzalez | 1'525 |
| D. Hill | 6'309 | J. Laffite | 1'519 |
| G. Hill | 4'767 | J. Alesi | 1'285 |
| J. Brabham | 4'540 | T. Brooks | 1'268 |
| D. Coulthard | 4'195 | D. Pironi | 1'240 |
| G. Berger | 3'718 | J. Watson | 1'218 |
| Ma. Andretti | 3'577 | K. Räikkönen | 1'071 |
| R. Barrichello | 3'389 | P. Tambay | 962 |
| J. Hunt | 3'363 | J.P. Jabouille | 948 |
| R. Peterson | 3'262 | P. Collins | 946 |
| C. Reutemann | 3'255 | ... | |
| J. Ickx | 3'119 | | |
| J. Villeneuve | 2'965 | Then: | |
| J. Scheckter | 2'851 | F. Alonso | 718 |
| A. Jones | 2'847 | J. Trulli | 574 |
| G. Farina | 2'651 | J. Button | 358 |
| R. Arnoux | 2'571 | G. Fisichella | 176 |
| R. Patrese | 2'553 | T. Sato | 10 |
| G. Villeneuve | 2'251 | F. Massa | 9 |
| E. Fittipaldi | 2'235 | M. Webber | 8 |

## DRIVER CONSISTENCY

This is the ability of a driver to finish the greatest number of Grands Prix in the course of a season.
This statistic does not include the Indianapolis 500 Miles race, which was included in the Formula 1 World Championship from 1951 to 1960.

| | | | | |
|---|---|---|---|---|
| 1. | M. Schumacher | 2002 | Ferrari | 17/17 |
| 2. | J. Clark | 1963 | Lotus | 10/10 |
| 3. | R. Ginther | 1964 | BRM | 10/10 |
| 4. | G. Hill | 1962 | BRM | 9/9 |
| 5. | M. Hawthorn | 1953 | Ferrari | 8/8 |
| 6. | J. M. Fangio | 1954 | Maserati & Mercedes | 8/8 |
| 7. | D. Gurney | 1961 | Porsche | 8/8 |
| 8. | M. Schumacher | 2004 | Ferrari | 17/18 |
| 9. | R. Barrichello | 2004 | Ferrari | 17/18 |
| 10. | J. Alesi | 2001 | Prost & Jordan | 16/17 |
| 11. | A. Senna | 1991 | McLaren | 15/16 |
| 12. | A. Prost | 1993 | Williams | 15/16 |
| 13. | E. Irvine | 1999 | Ferrari | 15/16 |
| 14. | M. Schumacher | 2003 | Ferrari | 15/16 |
| 15. | D. Hulme | 1973 | McLaren | 14/15 |
| 16. | M. Schumacher | 2001 | Ferrari | 15/17 |
| 17. | J. Laffite | 1978 | Ligier | 14/16 |
| 18. | A. Senna | 1988 | McLaren | 14/16 |
| 19. | A. Prost | 1988 | McLaren | 14/16 |
| 20. | M. Alboreto | 1992 | Footwork | 14/16 |
| Etc. | | | | |

As an anecdote to illustrate this statistic, consistency was not the greatest strength of Italian driver Andrea de Cesaris. From the 1985 French Grand Prix to the 1988 race in Mexico, he only saw the chequered flag 3 times from 41 starts...
He holds a famous record: 19 consecutive retirements and non-qualifications from the 1985 French Grand Prix to the 1986 Mexican Grand Prix.

## CONSTRUCTORS - THE WORLD CHAMPIONS

In 1958, a Formula 1 constructors' cup is established.
In 1982, it becomes the Constructors' World Championship

| | | | | | | | |
|---|---|---|---|---|---|---|---|
| 1958 | Vanwall | 1970 | Lotus | 1982 | Ferrari | 1994 | Williams |
| 1959 | Cooper | 1971 | Tyrrell | 1983 | Ferrari | 1995 | Benetton |
| 1960 | Cooper | 1972 | Lotus | 1984 | McLaren | 1996 | Williams |
| 1961 | Ferrari | 1973 | Lotus | 1985 | McLaren | 1997 | Williams |
| 1962 | BRM | 1974 | McLaren | 1986 | Williams | 1998 | Mclaren |
| 1963 | Lotus | 1975 | Ferrari | 1987 | Williams | 1999 | Ferrari |
| 1964 | Ferrari | 1976 | Ferrari | 1988 | McLaren | 2000 | Ferrari |
| 1965 | Lotus | 1977 | Ferrari | 1989 | McLaren | 2001 | Ferrari |
| 1966 | Brabham | 1978 | Lotus | 1990 | McLaren | 2002 | Ferrari |
| 1967 | Brabham | 1979 | Ferrari | 1991 | McLaren | 2003 | Ferrari |
| 1968 | Lotus | 1980 | Williams | 1992 | Williams | 2004 | Ferrari |
| 1969 | Matra | 1981 | Williams | 1993 | Williams | | |

## NUMBER OF WORLD CHAMPIONSHIP TITLES PER COUNTRY

**12 titles**
GREAT BRITAIN: Hawthorn (1), G. Hill (2), Clark (2), Surtees (1), Stewart (3), Hunt (1), Mansell (1) et D. Hill (1)

**8 titles**
BRAZIL: E. Fittipaldi (2), Piquet (3) et Senna (3)

**7 titles**
GERMANY: M. Schumacher (7)

**5 titles**
ARGENTINA: Fangio (5)

**4 titles**
AUSTRALIA: Brabham (3) et Jones (1)
AUSTRIA: Rindt (1) et Lauda (3)
FRANCE: Prost (4)

**3 titles**
ITALY: Farina (1) et Ascari (2)
FINLAND: Rosberg (1) et Häkkinen (2)

**2 titles**
UNITED STATES: P. Hill (1) et Ma. Andretti (1)

**1 title**
NEW ZEALAND: Hulme (1)
SOUTH AFRICA: Scheckter (1)
CANADA: J. Villeneuve (1)

## CONSTRUCTORS' WORLD CHAMPIONSHIP: NUMBER OF WINS

| | | | | | | | |
|---|---|---|---|---|---|---|---|
| Ferrari | 182 | BRM | 17 | Kurtis Kraft | 5 | Porsche | 1 |
| McLaren | 138 | Cooper | 16 | Jordan | 4 | Eagle | 1 |
| Williams | 113 | Alfa Roméo | 10 | March | 3 | Hesketh | 1 |
| Lotus | 79 | Ligier | 9 | Watson | 3 | Penske | 1 |
| Brabham | 35 | Maserati | 9 | Wolf | 3 | Shadow | 1 |
| Benetton | 26 | Matra | 9 | Honda | 2 | Stewart | 1 |
| Tyrrell | 23 | Mercedes | 9 | Salih | 2 | | |
| Renault | 17 | Vanwall | 9 | Kuzma | 1 | | |

## CONSTRUCTORS' WORLD CHAMPIONSHIP: NUMBER OF POLE POSITIONS

| | | | | | | | |
|---|---|---|---|---|---|---|---|
| Ferrari | 178 | Cooper | 11 | Shadow | 3 | Honda | 1 |
| Williams | 124 | BRM | 11 | Lancia | 2 | Wolf | 1 |
| McLaren | 115 | Maserati | 10 | Watson | 2 | Arrows | 1 |
| Lotus | 107 | Ligier | 9 | Jordan | 2 | Toleman | 1 |
| Brabham | 39 | Mercedes | 8 | Stevens | 1 | Stewart | 1 |
| Renault | 36 | Vanwall | 7 | Lesovsky | 1 | B.A.R | 1 |
| Benetton | 15 | Kurtis Kraft | 6 | Ewing | 1 | | |
| Tyrrell | 14 | March | 5 | Lola | 1 | | |
| Alfa Romeo | 12 | Matra | 4 | Porsche | 1 | | |

## CONSTRUCTORS' WORLD CHAMPIONSHIP: NUMBER OF FASTEST LAPS

| | | | | | | | | |
|---|---|---|---|---|---|---|---|---|
| **Ferrari** | 181 | BRM | 15 | Surtees | 3 | Lancia | 1 |
| **Williams** | 127 | Cooper | 14 | Epperly | 2 | Lesovsky | 1 |
| **McLaren** | 114 | Alfa Romeo | 14 | Eagle | 2 | Watson | 1 |
| Lotus | 71 | Matra | 12 | Honda | 2 | Hesketh | 1 |
| Brabham | 41 | Mercedes | 9 | Shadow | 2 | Parnelli | 1 |
| Benetton | 36 | Ligier | 9 | Wolf | 2 | Kojima | 1 |
| Tyrrell | 20 | Kurtis Kraft | 7 | Toleman | 2 | Ensign | 1 |
| **Renault** | 19 | March | 7 | **Jordan** | **2** | | |
| Maserati | 15 | Vanwall | 6 | Gordini | 1 | | |

## CONSTRUCTORS' WORLD CHAMPIONSHIP: NUMBER OF GRANDS PRIX CONTESTED

| | | | | | | | | |
|---|---|---|---|---|---|---|---|---|
| **Ferrari** | 704 | Benetton | 260 | Surtees | 118 | Prost | 83 |
| **McLaren** | 577 | **Jordan** | **231** | Alfa Romeo | 110 | Dallara | 78 |
| **Williams** | 496 | BRM | 197 | Shadow | 104 | Maserati | 70 |
| Lotus | 491 | March | 197 | Fittipaldi | 103 | Matra | 60 |
| Tyrrell | 430 | **Sauber** | **197** | **B.A.R** | **101** | Toleman | 57 |
| Brabham | 394 | **Renault** | **174** | Ensign | 99 | Zakspeed | 53 |
| Ligier | 326 | Lola | 149 | Footwork | 91 | Hesketh | 52 |
| **Minardi** | **321** | Osella | 132 | ATS | 89 | **Toyota** | **51** |
| Arrows | 291 | Cooper | 129 | **Jaguar** | **85** | ... | |

## CONSTRUCTORS' WORLD CHAMPIONSHIP: NUMBER OF POINTS SCORED

| | | | | | | | | |
|---|---|---|---|---|---|---|---|---|
| **Ferrari** | 3299,5 | Tyrrell | 621 | **B.A.R** | **189** | Shadow | 67,5 |
| **McLaren** | 2856,5 | **Renault** | **528** | **Sauber** | **175** | ... | |
| **Williams** | 2429,5 | BRM | 433 | March | 173,5 | | |
| Lotus | 1370 | Ligier | 388 | Arrows | 167 | **Jaguar** | **49** |
| Brabham | 865 | Cooper | 342 | Matra | 163 | **Minardi** | **31** |
| Benetton | 851,5 | **Jordan** | **279** | Wolf | 79 | **Toyota** | **27** |

## CONSTRUCTORS' WORLD CHAMPIONSHIP: NUMBER OF TITLES

**14 titles:**
FERRARI: 1961, 1964, 1975, 1976, 1977, 1979, 1982, 1983, 1999, 2000, 2001, 2002, 2003 et 2004.
**9 titles:**
WILLIAMS: 1980, 1981, 1986, 1987, 1992, 1993, 1994, 1996 et 1997.
**8 titles:**
McLAREN: 1974, 1984, 1985, 1988, 1989, 1990, 1991 et 1998
**7 titles:**
LOTUS: 1963, 1965, 1968, 1970, 1972, 1973 et 1978
**2 titles:**
COOPER: 1959 et 1960
BRABHAM: 1966 et 1967
**1 title:**
VANWALL: 1958,
BRM: 1962,
MATRA: 1969,
TYRRELL: 1971
BENETTON: 1995

## RECORD FOR NUMBER OF POINTS SCORED BY A CONSTRUCTOR IN A SINGLE SEASON

| | | | | |
|---|---|---|---|---|
| Ferrari: 262 points in 2004 | Ferrari: 179 points in 2001 | Williams: 168 points in 1993 | McLaren: 156 points in 1998 | McLaren: 141 points in 1989 |
| Ferrari: 221 points in 2002 | Williams: 175 points in 1986 | Ferrari: 158 points in 2003 | McLaren: 152 points in 2000 | Williams: 141 points in 1986. |
| McLaren: 199 points in 1988 | Ferrari: 170 points in 2000 | Williams: 164 points in 1992 | McLaren: 143,5 in 1984 | Etc. |

## NUMBER OF CONSTRUCTOR TITLES PER ENGINE MANUFACTURER

**14 titles:**
FERRARI: 1961, 1964, 1975, 1976, 1977, 1979, 1982, 1983, 1999, 2000, 2001, 2002, 2003 et 2004.
**10 titles:**
FORD: 1968, 1969, 1970, 1971, 1972, 1973, 1974, 1978, 1980 et 1981.
**6 titles:**
HONDA: 1986, 1987, 1988, 1989, 1990 et 1991.
RENAULT: 1992, 1993, 1994, 1995, 1996 et 1997.
**4 titles:**
CLIMAX: 1959, 1960, 1963 et 1965.
**2 titles:**
REPCO: 1966 et 1967.
TAG PORSCHE: 1984 et 1985.
**1 title:**
BRM: 1962.
MERCEDES: 1998.
VANWALL: 1958.

## NUMBER OF DRIVER WORLD CHAMPIONSHIP TITLES PER ENGINE MANUFACTURER

**14 titles:**
FERRARI: 1952, 1953, 1956, 1958, 1961, 1964, 1975, 1977, 1979, 2000, 2001, 2002, 2003 et 2004.
**13 titles:**
FORD: 1968, 1969, 1970, 1971, 1972, 1973, 1974, 1976, 1978, 1980, 1981, 1982 et 1994.
**5 titles:**
HONDA: 1987, 1988, 1989, 1990 et 1991.
RENAULT: 1992, 1993, 1995, 1996 et 1997.
**4 titles:**
CLIMAX: 1959, 1960, 1963 et 1965.
MERCEDES: 1954, 1955, 1998 et 1999.
**3 titles:**
TAG PORSCHE: 1984, 1985 et 1986.
**2 titles:**
ALFA ROMEO: 1950 et 1951.
MASERATI: 1954 et 1957.
REPCO: 1966 et 1967.
**1 title:**
BRM: 1962.
BMW: 1983.

## NUMBER OF POLE POSITIONS PER ENGINE MANUFACTURER

| | | | | | |
|---|---|---|---|---|---|
| **Ferrari** | 178 | Alfa Romeo | 15 | Hart | 2 |
| **Renault** | 141 | BRM | 11 | Lancia | 2 |
| **Ford** | 137 | Maserati | 11 | Mecachrome | 1 |
| **Honda** | 75 | Repco | 7 | Mugen Honda | 1 |
| Climax | 44 | TAG Porsche | 7 | Porsche | 1 |
| **Mercedes** | 44 | Vanwall | 7 | | |
| **BMW** | 31 | Matra | 4 | | |

## NUMBER OF GRANDS PRIX CONTESTED PER ENGINE MANUFACTURER

| | | | | | |
|---|---|---|---|---|---|
| **Ferrari** | 704 | Mercedes | 204 | Toyota | 51 |
| **Ford** | 568 | BRM | 197 | Supertec | 49 |
| **Renault** | 354 | **BMW** | **176** | Mugen Honda | 47 |
| **Honda** | 287 | Petronas | 134 | Asiatech | 33 |
| Alfa Romeo | 212 | Peugeot | 132 | ... | |

## NUMBER OF WINS PER ENGINE MANUFACTURER

| | | | | | |
|---|---|---|---|---|---|
| **Ferrari** | 182 | TAG Porsche | 25 | Repco | 8 |
| **Ford** | 175 | **BMW** | **19** | Mugen Honda | 4 |
| **Renault** | 97 | BRM | 18 | Matra | 3 |
| **Honda** | 72 | Alfa Romeo | 12 | Porsche | 1 |
| **Mercedes** | 43 | Maserati | 11 | Weslake | 1 |
| Climax | 40 | Vanwall | 9 | | |

## NUMBER OF WINS PER TYRE MANUFACTURER

| | | | | |
|---|---|---|---|---|
| GoodYear | 368 | Firestone | 49 |
| **Bridgestone** | **94** | Pirelli | 45 |
| Dunlop | 83 | Continental | 10 |
| **Michelin** | **75** | | |